Writing Ethnographic Fieldnotes

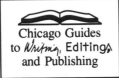

Chicago Guides
to *Writing*, Editing,
and Publishing

Robert M. Emerson
Rachel I. Fretz
Linda L. Shaw

Writing Ethnographic Fieldnotes

The University of Chicago Press
Chicago & London

The University of Chicago Press, Chicago 60637
The University of Chicago Press, Ltd., London
© 1995 by The University of Chicago
All rights reserved. Published 1995
Printed in the United States of America
09 08 07 06 05 04 03 02 01 00   5 6 7 8 9

ISBN (paper): 0-226-20681-5

Library of Congress Cataloging-in-Publication Data

Emerson, Robert M.
    Writing ethnographic fieldnotes / Robert M. Emerson, Rachel
  I. Fretz, Linda L. Shaw.
      p.   cm. — (Chicago guides to writing, editing, and
  publishing)
    Includes bibliographical references (p.   ) and index.
    ISBN 0-226-20680-7 (cloth). — ISBN 0-226-20681-5 (pbk.)
    1. Ethnology—Authorship. 2. Ethnology—Field work.
  3. Ethnology—Research. I. Fretz, Rachel I. II. Shaw, Linda L.
  III. Title.   IV. Series.
  GN307.7.E44   1995
  305.8′00723—dc20   94-7093
                                                                CIP

Contents

Preface

In recent years many ethnographers have emphasized the central place of *writing* in their craft. Geertz's (1973) characterization of "inscription" as the core of ethnographic "thick description" and Gusfield's (1976) dissection of the rhetorical underpinnings of science provided seminal statements in the 1970s. Subsequently, Clifford and Marcus's edited collection, *Writing Culture: The Poetics and Politics of Ethnography* (1986), Van Maanen's *Tales of the Field* (1988), and Atkinson's *The Ethnographic Imagination* (1990) have advanced consideration of ethnographic writing.

Yet examinations of ethnographic writing remain partial in scope: all begin with *already written* fieldnotes and move on to examine matters such as the rhetorical character of these fieldnotes or the more general structure of the whole, finished ethnographies built up from them. In so doing they neglect a primal occasion of ethnographic writing—*writing fieldnotes*. Thus they ignore a key issue in the making of ethnographies—understanding how an observer/researcher sits down and turns a piece of her lived experience into a bit of written text in the first place.

Indeed, most analyses of the "poetics of ethnography" (Clifford and Marcus 1986) take as their subject matter the polished accounts of social life provided in published monographs. But such finished texts incorporate and are built up out of these smaller, less coherent bits and pieces of writings—out of fieldnotes, many composed long before any comprehensive ethnographic overview has been developed. Moreover, fieldnotes in finished ethnographies are reordered and rewritten, selected and molded to some analytic purpose. They thus appear in very different forms and carry very different implications than the original corpus of fieldnotes that the ethnographer produced in the field. In these respects, writing fieldnotes, not writing polished ethnographies, lies at the core of constructing ethnographic texts.

On the practical methodological level, field researchers have similarly neglected issues of how to write fieldnotes. "How to do it" manuals of field work provide reams of advice on how to manage access and relations with unknown others in different cultures and settings. But they offer only occasional, ad hoc commentary on how to take fieldnotes, what to take notes on, and so on.[1] Field researchers in general have not given close, systematic attention to how fieldnotes are written in particular projects. Nor have they considered how to effectively train field work novices to write more sensitive, useful, and stimulating fieldnotes. Instead, field-work manuals direct practical advice toward how to work with existing fieldnotes in order to organize and write finished ethnographies. For example, Strauss (1987) and his co-workers (Strauss and Corbin 1990) provide detailed treatments of how to code notes and how to work with codings to produce finished ethnographies. But this focus on coding assumes that the ethnographer has completed writing a set of fieldnotes and now faces the task of analyzing, organizing, and making sense of them. These guides say nothing about how ethnographers wrote these fieldnotes in the first place or about how they might have written notes differently. Similarly, three practical guides to field research—Fetterman (1989), Richardson (1990), and Wolcott (1990)—devote primary attention to developing and writing finished ethnographic analyses in ways that presuppose the existence of a set of fieldnotes.

In the past few years, however, some ethnographers have begun to redress this problem, giving serious attention to the nature and uses of fieldnotes. In 1990 Sanjek's edited volume, *Fieldnotes: The Making of Anthropology,* brought together a collection of papers written in response to a symposium call "to examine what anthropologists do with fieldnotes, how they live with them, and how attitudes toward the construction and use of fieldnotes may change through individual professional careers" (Sanjek 1990b:xii). The collection includes an extended history of "fieldnote practice" in Western anthropology (Sanjek 1990d), as well as analyses of the research and personal uses and meanings of fieldnotes to anthropologists (Jackson 1990b; Sanjek 1990c; Ottenberg 1990), of field-notes as means of describing and representing cultures (Clifford 1990;

Lederman 1990), and of reading and using others' fieldnotes (Lutkehaus 1990).

At the same time, Atkinson's *The Ethnographic Imagination* (1990) began to examine the textual properties of classic and contemporary sociological ethnography. Although he focuses on the rhetorical structure of completed ethnographies, Atkinson does call attention to the importance of analyzing fieldnotes. Emphasizing that at the moment "field notes remain private documents" unavailable for analysis, he urges the future importance of close study of "the stylistic features of field notes from particular authors or sociological schools" (1990:57) and takes an initial step in this direction by analyzing two fieldnote extracts originally published in Junker's *Field Work: An Introduction to the Social Sciences* (1960).

Several factors underlie this long-term if perhaps now dissipating neglect of ethnographic fieldnotes. To begin with, ethnographers are often uneasy or embarrassed about fieldnotes. Many seem to regard fieldnotes as a kind of backstage scribbling—a little bit dirty, a little bit suspect, not something to talk about too openly and specifically. Fieldnotes seem too revealingly personal, too messy and unfinished to be shown to any audience. For these and other reasons, scholars do not have ready access to original, unedited fieldnotes but only to completed ethnographies with the selected, reordered fieldnotes they contain. As a result, how ethnographers write fieldnotes remains largely hidden and mysterious.

In contrast, later stages of ethnographic writing, centered around producing finished ethnographic monographs, are more theoretically driven and less obviously personal. With a body of fieldnotes assembled, the ethnographer withdraws from the field to try to weave some of these strands into an ethnographic story. At this point the ethnographer handles fieldnotes more impersonally as data—as objects to be studied, consulted, and reordered in developing a tale for other audiences. The issues and procedures that mark this phase of ethnographic writing—coding, developing an analytic focus, etc.—are closer to the finished, published product and, thus, more amenable to presentation to others.

Furthermore, field researchers show no consensus on what kinds of writing to term "fieldnotes," when and how fieldnotes should be written, and their value for ethnographic research. These diverse and at times discordant views of the nature and value of fieldnotes have stymied self-conscious consideration of how to write fieldnotes.

In the first place, field researchers may have a variety of different forms of written records in mind when they refer to "fieldnotes." A recent inventory (Sanjek 1990c) found that ethnographers talked about all of the following: "headnotes," "scratch notes," "fieldnotes proper," "fieldnote records," "texts," "journals and diaries," and "letters, reports, papers." Hence there is wide variation in what ethnographers characterize as fieldnotes. Some field researchers, for example, consider fieldnotes to be writings that record both what they learn and observe about the activities of others and their own actions, questions, and reflections. Others insist on a sharp distinction between records of what others said and did—the "data" of fieldwork—and those notes incorporating their own thoughts and reactions. Yet deep differences also exist between those who emphasize this distinction between writings about others and writings about oneself: some view only the former as fieldnotes and consider the latter as personal "journals" or "diaries"; others "*contrast* fieldnotes with data, speaking of fieldnotes as a record of one's reactions, a cryptic list of items to concentrate on, a preliminary stab at analysis, and so on" (Jackson 1990b:7).

Second, field researchers may write fieldnotes in very different ways. Many compose fieldnotes only as "a running log written at the end of each day" (Jackson 1990b:6). But others contrast such "fieldnotes proper" with "fieldnote records" that involve "information organized in sets separate from the sequential fieldwork notes" (Sanjek 1990c:101). Furthermore, some field researchers try to write elaborate notes as soon after witnessing relevant events as possible, typically sitting down to type up complete, detailed observations every evening. Others initially produce less detailed records, filling notebooks with handwritten notes to be elaborated and "finished" upon leaving the field. And still others postpone the bulk of writing until they have left the field and begun to grapple with writing a coherent ethnographic account.

Finally, ethnographers disagree about whether fieldnotes are a resource or barrier to understanding. While some see them as the core of the research enterprise, others suggest that they provide little more than crutches to help the field researcher deal with the stresses and anxieties of living in another world while trying to understand it from the outside. Indeed, some contend that fieldnotes stymie deeper understanding. As one anthropologist quoted by Jackson noted (1990b:13): "[Without notes there is] more chance to schematize, to order conceptually . . . free of niggling exceptions, grayish half-truths you find in your own data."

In sum, ethnographers have failed to closely examine the processes of writing fieldnotes. While this failure arises in part from differing views of what fieldnotes are, it also results from disagreements about the skills needed for ethnographic observation and writing and about how necessary skills can be acquired. At one extreme, many field researchers assume that almost any literate, adventurous person can simply go to the field and do fieldwork; technical skills, if any, can be learned on the spot in a "sink or swim" vein. At another extreme, others contend that ethnographic research, particularly writing fieldnotes, involves God-given talents and sensitivities that simply cannot be taught. Some argue, for example, that only those with the special abilities of an Erving Goffman can become insightful field researchers. Training is not an issue to those so innately skilled.

Still others seem to concede that aspects of field research should and can be learned, but they exclude writing fieldnotes from these teachable skills. They view fieldnotes as so deeply idiosyncratic and personal as to preclude formal instruction. Both what the fieldworker does with those under study and how she understands and recounts these events will vary from one person to another. Thus different researchers write very different notes, depending upon disciplinary orientation, theoretical interests, personality, mood, and stylistic commitments. Writing fieldnotes supposedly resists formal instruction because the sense and meanings of whatever ethnographers write draw upon "tacit knowledge" and direct experiences that are not explicitly included in the notes.

We reject both the "sink or swim" method of training ethnographers and the attitude that ethnography involves no special skills or no skills beyond those a college-educated person possesses. We take the position that writing fieldnotes is not simply the product of innate sensibilities and insights but also involves skills learned and sharpened over time. Indeed, we maintain that ethnographers *need* to hone these skills and that the quality of ethnography will improve with self-conscious attention to how to write fieldnotes.

Furthermore, we contend that ethnographers can move beyond the impasse created by differing conceptions of fieldnotes by making explicit the assumptions and commitments they hold about the nature of ethnography as a set of practical research and writing activities. Such assumptions and commitments have direct implications for how to understand and write fieldnotes. If, for example, one sees ethnography as collecting information that can be "found" or "discovered" in much the same way by any researcher, one can reasonably separate the "findings" from the processes of making them and "data" from "personal reactions." Similarly, the sense that fieldnotes get in the way of intuitive understanding and deeper analytic insight reflects a theoretical commitment to grasping the "big picture" and to identifying broad patterns of activity rather than to tracking day-to-day routines and processes. This view, in turn, assumes that achieving these qualities can get lost beneath "too many facts" or "too much detail."

Thus, while universal guidelines for writing fieldnotes are quixotic, one can develop specific guidelines appropriate to a particular understanding of ethnographic research. In this book we assume and draw upon an interactionist, interpretive understanding of ethnography that derives from the traditions of symbolic interaction and ethnomethodology in order to elaborate one approach to fieldnotes and to the processes of writing them. Clearly, we offer only one among many possible approaches; field researchers starting with more positivist commitments or informed by other traditions within ethnography would approach many of the issues and procedures we discuss very differently. Nonetheless, we expect that much of what we recommend will be useful and suggestive for anyone beginning to do field research and to write fieldnotes.

We pursue a further goal in this book: to demystify writing fieldnotes, giving explicit attention to the processes of transforming observation and experience into inspectable texts. To do so, it is critical to look at actual working, "unfinished" fieldnotes rather than at published, polished fieldnotes and to consider how such notes are composed, rewritten, and worked into finished texts. Thus we focus on writing fieldnotes in its own right, considering a variety of technical, interactional, personal, and theoretical issues that arise with such writing. We also examine the processes and the practicalities of working with fieldnotes to write analytic memos and final ethnographic accounts for wider audiences.

Our goal is not only practical. We also want to bridge the gap that divides reflections on ethnographic texts from the actual practice of ethnography. By examining the practices actually used to write fieldnotes, we hope to advance understanding of the nature of ethnography in calling attention to the fundamental processes entailed in turning talk, observations, and experiences into written texts. It is misleading to try to grasp the transformation of experience into text by looking only at finished ethnographies and the fieldnotes they rely on. The problems and processes of writing initial, unpolished accounts of observations and experiences differ significantly from those involved in reviewing, selecting from, editing, and revising fieldnotes in order to produce a finished ethnography. Published fieldnotes are not only polished; they are also highly selected because they have to be tied to the specific themes used to construct the ethnography as a whole. In contrast, unfinished fieldnotes, written more or less contemporaneously with the events depicted, are not theoretically focused or integrated, not consistent in voice or purpose, nor even always clear or stylistically compelling.

Our attention to issues of writing fieldnotes grew out of our own experiences in teaching field research to undergraduate and graduate students. In the early 1980s two of us—Robert Emerson and Linda Shaw—began teaching a UCLA undergraduate course on field research methods. Organized as a practicum focused on fieldnotes and the field experiences they depicted, the course insisted that all students go to a field setting and immediately begin to write fieldnotes about what they saw and heard. In addition to intensive small group discussions of students' notes, we devoted class time to examining a xeroxed page or two of students' "notes of the week"—excerpts selected to illustrate key issues in field relations, writing strategies, or theoretical focusing. Throughout the course, students posed endless questions about writing fieldnotes, beginning with such matters as "What do I write about?" and concluding with problems of "How do I write it all up in a final paper?" Emerson and Shaw increasingly sought the experience of faculty in the Writing Programs at UCLA for advice in these matters. They met with Rachel Fretz, a folklorist with extensive field experience in Africa. These consultations led to the decision to coordinate a course on writing ethnographic fieldnotes with the existing field research methods course.

This manuscript began to take shape while team teaching these courses as part of an Immersion Quarter program at UCLA in the mid-1980s. Students in this program participated in internships while enrolled in a cluster of three courses—field research methods, ethnographic writing, and a variable topic substantive course (mental illness; control of crime; gender, race, and ethnicity in schools). The field methods and writing courses were tightly integrated, with coordinated topic, readings, and field assignments. As instructors, we met regularly to discuss the problems and successes of our students. We pooled our experiences and problem-solved, giving one another ideas for better ways to work with students as they learned to subject real world experience to sociological analysis. The ideas that comprise the core of the manuscript developed early on as a result of these meetings and their collective processes.

Junker's *Field Work: An Introduction to the Social Sciences* (1960) provided a model for assembling and presenting our materials. *Field Work* resulted from a collection of materials, "Cases on Field Work," created at the University of Chicago in a project organized by Everett C. Hughes to conduct "field work on field work" (Hughes 1960:v). This project involved "putting together what we had learned from [having taught methods to] several hundred students about the learning and doing of field work" (vii). Similarly, in order to illustrate useful practices and alternate possibilities for writing fieldnotes, we saturate the chapters that follow with "raw" fieldnotes.

We rely heavily upon fieldnotes and ethnographic extracts written by both undergraduate and graduate students who have taken our courses on field research and ethnographic writing at UCLA, California State University, San Marcos, and Cornell University. Some might object to the use of student fieldnotes on the grounds that these are not the writings of professionally trained researchers. In part our preference for student notes reflects the way we began to develop this book—by reading and commenting upon such writings, clarifying and articulating what impressed us as effective, exciting notes, and collecting examples of particular issues for teaching purposes. But in addition, we desire to demystify fieldnotes, an end better achieved by showing what can be done by students like those who will read and use this book. And finally, every quarter we found ourselves impressed by the quality, excitement, and freshness of the fieldnote accounts our students provided on ordinary and exceptional events in a variety of social settings.

In addition to student fieldnotes, we also draw examples from our own unpublished fieldnotes, which were compiled during a number of different research projects. These projects include Robert Emerson's study of litigants applying for domestic violence restraining orders, carried out in the late 1980s and early 1990s;[2] Rachel Fretz's ethnographic fieldwork on storytelling among the Chokwe in Zaire in 1976, 1977, 1982, and 1983 and in Zambia in 1992–93;[3] and field research carried out in a psychiatric facility for ex-mental patients by Linda Shaw in the early 1980s.

We address issues of writing fieldnotes for two general audiences. One audience includes those concerned with ethnography and field research primarily for academic research purposes. Here we seek to develop practical guidelines for writing fieldnotes that will prove helpful to both undergraduate and graduate students in several academic disciplines. These disciplines include sociology, anthropology, folklore, oral history, education, and ethnomusicology, in which field research and ethnographic methods have a prominent place; and disciplines such as political science, business administration, communications, composition studies, social welfare, and public health, in which ethnography and field research may be offered as secondary methodological options.

But in this book we also address audiences who commonly recognize few links with ethnography—those committed to experiential education and service learning. In promoting learning through doing, experiential education places students in community service or in internships in some institutional setting. In these placements students confront practical challenges in carrying out real world activities; the task is then to relate these experiences to traditional academic concerns.

To this point the key to this integration has been the critical incident journal (Batchelder and Warner 1977). But service learning journals encourage writing about the students' perceptions and feelings more than about what others are doing and saying. Such journals often do not encourage students to write at length or in real detail about their observations. They tend to be "crisis focused," attending to the dramatic and remarkable rather than to the everyday and routine; therefore they lead to very general accounts or to decontextualized accounts of "critical incidents" that inhibit reflection and in-depth understanding of daily processes.

We maintain that writing ethnographic fieldnotes, rather than journal entries, promises to strengthen and deepen the integration of experience with classroom knowledge. Writing fieldnotes would encourage experiential education students to observe more finely and systematically, to consider both the mundane and the dramatic, and to attend to others' activities and concerns as closely as their own. Furthermore, systematic, contemporaneously written fieldnotes provide a means for capturing the distinct phases or stages of an intern's adaptation to a particular setting. Such fieldnotes allow close documentation of the explicit and implicit instruction given interns about what things are important and how things should be done. Such instructions are a major mechanism by which newcomers are socialized to any particular setting; instructions reveal both the working skills and knowledge and also the actual priorities, assumptions, and commitments of those in the setting.

Obviously, points of strain will remain between the practice of ethnographic field research and experiential education. For example, writing extensive fieldnotes may require more commitment to research than is common to many experiential education students, who are often motivated—at least initially—by a desire to serve others or to assess the attractions of a particular career. Yet a persuasive case can be made to those who hold such priorities that ethnography can contribute a deeper understanding of the personal, work, and organizational processes likely to be encountered. Thus, the approach to ethnographic participation and writing developed here opens up much common ground between two traditions that have long gone their separate ways; it does so by providing a means to convert experiences into textual forms that can be brought back into the classroom and closely examined for their bearing on broader issues of social and intellectual life (cf. Bleich 1993).

We have set ourselves a very specific task in this book: to examine the different processes of writing involved in producing and using ethnographic fieldnotes. Hence we do not intend this book to stand on its own as an introduction to the practice of ethnographic field research. In particular, we do not treat in any detail either the deeper theoretical groundings of ethnography or the intricacies and dilemmas of actually carrying out a field work project. Rather, we complement existing overviews of the premises and procedures of ethnographic inquiry[4] by looking specifically at key practical issues involved in writing and using fieldnotes. We do consider, moreover, how writing fieldnotes is inextricably intertwined with methodological and theoretical commitments.

The chapters that follow are organized in ways that reflect our dual concerns with learning to write ethnographic fieldnotes and with understanding the relevance of these practices for ethnographic research more broadly. We use as our point of departure the experience and practice of students actually learning to write fieldnotes rather than an idealized or prescriptive version of how fieldnotes "ought to be written." After an overview of the nature and place of fieldnotes in ethnographic research, successive chapters address step-by-step processes and practices for writing and working with fieldnotes. Each chapter concludes with "Reflections" on the implications of the practices and processes we have been examining for more general issues of ethnographic theory and method.

Substantively, we begin in chapter 1 by considering the centrality of writing fieldnotes to ethnographic research and by specifying the assumptions and commitments that underlie our approach. Chapter 2 examines the distinctive stance of the ethnographer—that of participating in and observing the ongoing life of a natural setting in order to produce written accounts of events observed there; it then considers issues of jotting phrases or notes while in the setting. Chapter 3 explores procedures for writing up fieldnotes, either from memory or from previous jottings. Chapter 4 discusses various writing strategies for envisioning scenes on a page, for describing observed events, for organizing extended descriptions, and for writing in-process analytic ideas about these scenes. In chapter 5 we address ways of writing notes and developing analyses that effectively capture and convey what events mean to participants. Chapter 6 turns to working with lengthy sets of "completed" fieldnotes, considering how to read, sort, and code notes and how to begin analysis. Chapter 7 considers the ethnographer's choices about how to organize and write more polished, coherent ethnographies for wider audiences. Finally, in chapter 8 we reflect on the need in ethnographic writing to balance often contradictory requirements and concerns—loyalties to those studied with obligations to future readers, self-conscious reflection with getting accounts written down on paper, and sensitivity to indigenous meanings with analytic relevance.

We wish to acknowledge our gratitude to the Field Studies Program at UCLA for encouraging and supporting the Immersion Quarter program from which this book emerged. We owe special thanks in this regard to Jane Permaul, Rob Shumer, and Parvin Kassaie. We also wish to thank the following colleagues for comments and suggestions on this manuscript: Timothy Diamond, Dianne Dugaw, Shelley Feldman, Jan Frodesen, George Gadda, Dwight Giles, Claudia Ingram, Michael O. Jones, Jack Katz, Susan McCoin, Anita McCormick, Melvin Pollner, Anita Pomerantz, Amanda Powell, Judith Richlin-Klonsky, Mike Rose, Ruth M. Stone, Carol Warren, Randy Woodland, and two anonymous reviewers for the University of Chicago Press. And we wish to thank our copyeditor, Richard Allen, who promised he would "give us a hard time" and who did so in ways that pushed us to clarify our concerns and specify our arguments.

Finally, we wish the thank the following students from our field research courses who have generously given us permission to use their fieldnote and ethnographic writings as exemplars and illustrations: Karin Abell, Teri Anderson, Jim Angell, Erin Artigiani, Ben Beit-Zuri, Nancy S. Blum, Paul Brownfield, Jennifer Cheroske, Rebecca Clements, Cabonia Crawford, John Cross, Maria Estrada, Julie Finney, Robert Garot, Mauricio A. Gormaz, Heather W. Guthrie, David Hillyard, Suzanne Hirsch, Ronald X. Kovach, Shawn Lemone, Wendy Lin, Storm Lydon,

Francisco "Chuck" Martinez, Martha Moyes, Deanna Nitta, Phil Oka-moto, Blair Paley, Kristin Rains, Lisa Ravitch, Joanna Saporito, Kristin D. Schaefer, Joe Scheuermann, Cliff Spangler, Lakshmi Srinivas, Martha Stokes, Kathryn L. Tatar, Laura Miles Vahle, Linda Van Leuven, Karina Walters, David Whelan, Nicholas H. Wolfinger, and Terri Young. We especially thank Lisa Holmes and Martha Millison, not only for allowing us to use excerpts from their fieldnotes, but also for providing a "student response" after reading an earlier draft of the manuscript.

chapter one

Fieldnotes in Ethnographic Research

Ethnographic field research involves the study of groups and people as they go about their everyday lives. Carrying out such research involves two distinct activities. First, the ethnographer enters into a social setting and gets to know the people involved in it; usually, the setting is not previously known in an intimate way. The ethnographer participates in the daily routines of this setting, develops ongoing relations with the people in it, and observes all the while what is going on. Indeed, the term "participant-observation" is often used to characterize this basic research approach. But, second, the ethnographer writes down in regular, systematic ways what she observes and learns while participating in the daily rounds of life of others. Thus the researcher creates an accumulating written record of these observations and experiences. These two interconnected activities comprise the core of ethnographic research: First-hand participation in some initially unfamiliar social world and the production of written accounts of that world by drawing upon such participation. In the following sections we examine in detail each of these activities and then trace out their implications for writing fieldnotes.

ETHNOGRAPHIC PARTICIPATION

Ethnographers are committed to going out and getting close to the activities and everyday experiences of other people. "Getting close" minimally requires physical and social proximity to the daily rounds of people's lives and activities; the field researcher must be able to take up positions in the midst of the key sites and scenes of other's lives in order to observe and understand them. But getting close has another, far more significant component: The ethnographer seeks a deeper *immersion* in others' worlds in order to grasp what they experience as meaningful and important. With immersion, the field researcher sees from the inside how people lead their lives, how they carry out their daily rounds of activities, what they find meaningful, and how they do so. In this way immersion gives the field-worker access to the fluidity of others' lives and enhances his sensitivity to interaction and process.

Furthermore, immersion enables the fieldworker to directly and forcibly experience for herself both the ordinary routines and conditions under which people conduct their lives, and the constraints and pressures to which such living is subject. Goffman (1989:125) in particular insists that field research involves "subjecting yourself, your own body and your own personality, and your own social situation, to the set of contingencies that play upon a set of individuals, so that you can physically and ecologically penetrate their circle of response to their social situation, or their work situation, or their ethnic situation." Immersion in ethnographic research, then, involves both being with other people to see how they respond to events as they happen and experiencing for oneself these events and the circumstances that give rise to them.

Clearly, ethnographic immersion precludes conducting field research as a detached, passive observer; the field researcher can only get close to the lives of those studied by actively participating in their day-to-day affairs. Such participation, moreover, inevitably entails some degree of *resocialization*. Sharing everyday life with a group of people, the field researcher comes "to enter into the matrix of meanings of the researched, to participate in their system of organized activities, and to feel subject to their code of moral regulation" (Wax 1980:272–73). In participating as fully and humanly as possible in another way of life, the ethnographer learns what is required to become a member of that world, to experience events and meanings in ways that approximate *members' experiences*.[1] Indeed, some ethnographers seek to do field research by doing and becoming—to the extent possible—whatever it is they are interested in learning about. Ethnographers, for example, have become skilled at work activities they are seeking to understand (Diamond 1993; Lynch 1985) or in good faith have joined churches or religious groups (Jules-Rosette 1975; Rochford 1985) on the grounds that by becoming members they gain fuller insight and understanding into these groups and their activities. Or villagers may assign an ethnographer a role, such as sister or mother in an extended family, which obligates her to participate and resocialize herself to meet local expectations (Fretz n.d.).

In learning about others through active participation in their lives and activities, the fieldworker cannot and should not attempt to be a fly on the wall.[2] No field researcher can be a completely neutral, detached observer, outside and independent of the observed phenomena (Pollner and Emerson 1988). Rather, as the ethnographer engages in the lives and concerns of those studied, his perspective "is intertwined with the phenomenon which does not have objective characteristics independent of the observer's perspective and methods" (Mishler 1979:10). The ethnographer cannot take in everything; rather, he will, in conjunction with those in the setting, develop certain perspectives by engaging in some activities and relationships rather than others. Moreover, it will often be the case that relationships with those under study follow political fault lines in the setting, exposing the ethnographer selectively to varying priorities and points of view. As a result, the task of the ethnographer is not to determine "the truth" but to reveal the multiple truths apparent in others' lives.[3]

Furthermore, the ethnographer's presence in a setting inevitably has implications and consequences for what is taking place, since the fieldworker must necessarily interact with and hence have some impact on those studied.[4] "Consequential presence," often linked to *reactive effects* (that is, the effects of the ethnographer's participation on how members may talk and behave), should not be seen as "contaminating" what is observed and learned. Rather, these effects are the very source of that learning and observation (Clarke 1975:99). Relationships between the field researcher and people in the setting do not so much disrupt or alter ongoing patterns of social interaction as reveal the terms and bases on which people form social ties in the first place. For example, in a village based on kinship ties, people may adopt a fieldworker into a family and assign her a kinship term which then designates her rights and responsibilities toward others. Rather than detracting from what the fieldworker can learn, first-hand relations with those studied may provide clues to understanding the more subtle, implicit underlying assumptions that are often not readily accessible through observation or interview methods alone.[5] Consequently, rather than viewing reactivity as a defect to be carefully controlled or eliminated in entirety, the ethnographer needs to become sensitive to and perceptive of how she is seen and treated by others.

To appreciate the unavoidable consequences of one's own presence strips any special merit from the highly detached, "unobtrusive," and marginal observer roles that have long held sway as the implicit ideal in field research. Many contemporary ethnographers advocate highly participatory roles (Adler, Adler, and Rochford 1986) in which the researcher actually performs the activities that are central to the lives of those studied. In this view, assuming real responsibility for actually carrying out core functions and tasks, as in service learning internships, provides special opportunities to get close to, participate in, and experience life in previously unknown settings. The intern with real work responsibilities or the researcher participating in village life actively engage in local activities and are socialized to and acquire empathy for local ways of acting and feeling.

Finally, close, continuing participation in the lives of others encourages appreciation of social life as constituted by ongoing, fluid processes. Through participation, the field researcher sees first-hand and up close how people grapple with uncertainty and confusion, how meanings emerge through talk and collective action, how understandings and interpretations change over time. In all these ways, the fieldworker's closeness to others' daily lives and activities heightens sensitivity to social life as process.

Inscribing Experienced/Observed Realities

Even with intensive resocialization, the ethnographer never becomes a member in the same sense that those "naturally" in the setting are members.[6] The fieldworker plans on leaving the setting after a relatively brief stay, and his experience of local life is colored by this transience. As a result "the participation that the fieldworker gives is neither as committed nor as constrained as the native's" (Karp and Kendall 1982:257). Furthermore, the fieldworker orients to many local events not as "real life" but as objects of possible research interest, as events that he may choose to write down and preserve in fieldnotes. In these ways, research and writing commitments qualify ethnographic immersion, making the field researcher at least something of an outsider and, at an extreme, a cultural alien.[7]

Fieldnotes are accounts *describing* experiences and observations the researcher has made while participating in an intense and involved manner. But writing descriptive accounts of experiences and observations is not as straightforward and transparent a process as it might initially appear. For writing description is not merely a matter of accurately capturing as closely as possible observed reality, of "putting into words" overheard talk and witnessed activities. To view the writing of descriptions simply as a matter of producing texts that *correspond* accurately to what has been observed is to assume that there is but one "best" description of any particular event. But in fact, there is no one "natural" or "correct" way to write about what one observes. Rather, because descriptions involve issues of perception and interpretation, different descriptions of "the same" situations and events are possible.

Consider, for example, the following descriptions of moving through express checkout lines in three different Los Angeles supermarkets, written by three student researchers. These descriptions share a number of common features: all describe events from the point of view of shoppers/observers moving through express checkout lines; all provide physical descriptions of the other major players in the lines—the checker, other shoppers—and of at least some of the items they are purchasing; and all attend closely to some minute details of behavior in express lines. Yet each of these fieldnote accounts takes a different tack in describing a supermarket express line. Each selects and emphasizes certain features and actions, ignoring and marginalizing others. Furthermore, these descriptions are written from different points of view, and they shape and present what happened on the express lines in different ways—in part because the researchers observe different people and occasions, but also in part because they make different writing choices:

Mayfair Market Express Line

There were four people in line with their purchases separated by an approx. 18″ rectangular black rubber bar. I put my frozen bags down on the "lazy susan linoleum conveyor belt" and I reached on top of the cash register to retrieve one of the black bars to separate my items. The cashier was in her mid thirties, approx., about 5′2″ dark skinned woman with curly dark brown hair. I couldn't hear what she was saying, but recognized some accent to her speech. She was in a white blouse, short sleeved, with a maroon shoulder to mid thigh apron. She had a loose maroon bow tie, not like a man's bow tie, more hangie and fluffy. Her name tag on her left chest side had red writing that said "Candy" on it.

[Describes the first two men at the front of the line.] The woman behind him was dark skinned with straight dark brown hair cut in a page boy. She was wearing a teal blue v-neck knit sweater with black leggings. In her section was juice, a can of pineapple juice, and a six-pack of V-8 tomato juice. The guy in front of me had a pink polo shirt on and tan shorts. He was about 6'2", slender, tan with blond short hair with a gold 18 gauge hoop in his left ear (I thought he was gay). In his triangle of space he had packaged carrots, a gallon of whole milk, and a package of porkchops.

Candy spent very little time with each person, she gave all a hello, and then told them the amount, money was offered, and change was handed back onto a shelf that was in front of the customer whose turn it was. Before Candy had given the dark-haired woman her change back, I noticed that the man in the pink shirt had moved into her spatial "customer" territory, probably within a foot of her, and in the position that the others had taken when it was their turn, in front of the "check writing" shelf. (I thought it was interesting that the people seemed more concerned about the proper separation of their food from one another's than they did about body location.) . . .

As I walk up to the shelf (where it all seems to happen), I say "Hi," and Candy says "Hi" back as she scans my groceries with the price scanner. . . .

This observer describes the line *spatially* in terms of individual people (particularly physical appearance and apparel) and their groceries as laid out before being rung up ("in his triangle of space he had . . . "). Indeed, this account notes as an aside the contrast between the care taken to separate grocery items and the seeming disregard of physical space that occurs at the "check writing shelf" as one shopper is about to move on and the next-in-line to move in.

Ralph's Express Line, Easter Morning

I headed east to the checkout stands with my romaine lettuce, to garnish the rice salad I was bringing to brunch, and my bottle of Gewurtztraminer, my new favorite wine, which I had to chill in the next half hour. As I approached the stands, I realized that the 10-items-or-less-cash-only line would be my best choice. I noticed that Boland was behind the counter at the register—he's always very friendly to me—"Hey, how you doing?"

I got behind the woman who was already there. She had left one of the rubber separator bars behind the things she was going to buy, one of the few personal friendly moves one can make in this highly routinized queue. I appreciated this, and would have thanked her (by smiling, probably), but she was already looking ahead, I suppose in anticipation of checking out. I put my wine and lettuce down. There was already someone behind me. I wanted to show them the courtesy of putting down a rubber separator bar for them too. I waited until the food in front of mine was moved up enough for me to take the bar, which was at the front of the place where the bars are (is there a word for that? bar bin?), so that I wouldn't have to make a large, expansive move across the items that weren't mine, drawing attention to myself. I waited, and then, finally, the bar was in sight. I took it, and then put it behind my items, looking at the woman behind me and smiling at her as I did so. She looked pleased, and a bit surprised, and I was glad to have been able to do this small favor. She was a pretty blonde woman, and was buying a bottle of champagne (maybe also for Easter brunch?). She was wearing what looked like an Easter dress—it was cotton, and pretty and flowery. She looked youngish. Maybe about my age. She was quite tall for a woman, maybe 5'10" or so.

The woman in front of me didn't take long at all. I've learned quite well how to wait in queues and not be too impatient. Boland, the checker, saw me, and said, "Hi! How's it going?" or something like that. . . .

This observer describes moving through the line as she experienced the process on a moment by moment basis, framing her accounts of others' behaviors as she received, understood, and reacted to them. This style of description gives the reader unique access to the observer's thoughts and emotions; for example, while space is an issue, it is framed in terms not of distance but of its implications for self and feelings (e.g., avoiding "a large expansive move across the items that weren't mine").

In the next excerpt, the writer shifts his focus from self to others:

Boy's Market Express Line

. . . I picked a long line. Even though the store was quiet, the express line was long. A lot of people had made small purchases today. I was behind a man with just a loaf of bread. There was a cart to the side of him, just sitting there, and I thought someone abandoned it (it had a few items in it). A minute later a man came up and "claimed" it by taking hold of it. He didn't really try to assert that he was back in line—apparently he'd stepped away to get something he'd forgotten—but he wasn't getting behind me either. I felt the need to ask him if he was on line, so I wouldn't cut him off. He said yes, and I tried to move behind him—we were sort of side by side—and he said, "That's okay. I know where you are."

An old woman was behind me now. She had her groceries in one of those carts that old people tend to use to wheel their groceries home. She was thumbing through the National Enquirer, and was clutching a coupon in her hand. She scanned a few pages of the paper, and then put it back in the rack. I looked ahead at the person whose groceries were being checked out—she was staring at the price for each item as it came up on the register.

At this point the guy who I'd spoken to earlier, the guy who was right in front of me, showed a look of surprise and moved past me, over to an abandoned cart at the end of the aisle. He was looking at what was in it, picking up the few items with interest, and then put them back. I thought he'd seen something else he wanted or had forgotten. He came back over to his cart, but then a supermarket employee walked by, and he called out to the man, walking over to the cart and pointing at it, "Do you get many items like this left behind?" The employee hesitated, not seeming to understand the question, and said no. The guy on line said, "See what's here? This is formula [cans of baby formula]. That's poor people's food. And see this [a copper pot scrubber]? They use that to smoke crack." The employee looked surprised. The guy says, "I was just wondering. That's very indicative of this area." The employee: "I live here and I didn't know that." The guy: "Didn't you watch Channel 28 last night?" Employee: "No." Guy: "They had a report about inner city problems." Employee, walking away as he talks: "I only watch National Geographic, the MacNeil-Lehrer Hour, and NPR." He continues away. . . .

Meanwhile the man with the bread has paid. As he waits momentarily for his change, the "guy" says, "Long wait for a loaf of bread." Man says, "Yeah," and then adds, jokingly (and looking at the cashier as he says it, as if to gauge his reaction), "these cashiers are slow." The cashier does not appear to hear this. Man with bread leaves, guy in front of me is being checked out now. He says to the cashier, "What's the matter, end of your shift? No sense of humor left?" Cashier says, "No. I'm tired." Guy: "I hear you." Guy then says to the bagger: "Can I have paper and plastic please, Jacob" (he emphasizes the use of the bagger's name)? Jacob complies, but shows no other sign that he's heard the man. Guy is waiting for transaction to be completed. He's sitting on the railing, and he is singing the words to the Muzak tune that's playing. Something by Peabo Bryson. Guy's transaction is done. He says thank you to the bagger, and the bagger tells him to have a good day.

Cashier says, "How are you doing?" to me. . . .

In these notes the observer initially writes himself into a prominent role in the line, but then he moves himself offstage by spotlighting another character who says and does a number of flamboyant things as he waits and then gets checked out. This express line becomes a mini-community, first marked by ongoing exchanges between those in line, then drawing in a passing store employee, and culminating in interactions between this character and the checker and bagger.

Writing fieldnote descriptions, then, is not so much a matter of passively copying down "facts" about "what happened." Rather, such writing involves active processes of interpretation and sense-making: noting and writing down some things as "significant," noting but ignoring others as "not significant," and even missing other possibly significant things altogether. As a result, similar (even the "same") events can be described for different purposes, with different sensitivities and concerns.

In this respect, it is important to recognize that fieldnotes involve *inscriptions* of social life and social discourse. Such inscriptions inevitably *reduce* the welter and confusion of the social world to written words that can be reviewed, studied, and thought about time and time again. As Geertz (1973:19) has characterized this core ethnographic process: "The ethnographer 'inscribes' social discourse; *he writes it down.* In so doing, he turns it from a passing event, which exists only in its own moment of occurrence, into an account, which exists in its inscription and can be reconsulted."

As inscriptions, fieldnotes are products of and reflect conventions for *transforming* witnessed events, persons, and places into words on paper.[8] In part, this transformation involves inevitable processes of *selection;* the ethnographer writes about certain things and thereby necessarily "leaves out" others. But more significantly, descriptive fieldnotes also inevitably *present or frame* objects in particular ways, "missing" other ways that events might have been presented or framed. And these presentations reflect and incorporate sensitivities, meanings, and understandings the field researcher has gleaned from having been close to and participated in the described events.

There are other ways of reducing social discourse to written form. Survey questionnaires, for example, record "responses" to pre-fixed questions, sometimes reducing these answers to numbers, sometimes preserving something of the respondents' own words. Audio and video recordings, which seemingly catch and preserve almost everything occurring within an interaction, actually capture but a slice of ongoing social life. What is recorded in the first place depends upon when, where, and how the equipment is positioned and activated, what it can pick up mechanically, and how those who are recorded react to its presence. Further reduction occurs with the representation of a recorded slice of embodied discourse as sequential lines of text in a "transcript." For while talk in social settings is a "multichanneled event," writing "is linear in nature, and can handle only one channel at a time, so must pick and choose among the cues available for representation" (Walker 1986:211). A transcript thus selects particular dimensions and contents of discourse for inclusion while ignoring others, for example, nonverbal cues to local meanings such as eye gaze, gesture, and posture. Researchers studying oral performances spend considerable effort in developing a notational system to document the verbal and at least some of the nonverbal communication; the quality of the transcribed "folklore text" is critical as it "represents the performance in another medium" (Fine 1984:3). The transcript is never a "verbatim" rendering of discourse, because it "represents . . . an analytic interpretation and selection" (Psathas and Anderson 1990:75) of speech and action. That is, a transcript is the product of a transcriber's ongoing interpretive and analytic decisons about a variety of problematic matters: how to transform naturally occurring speech into specific words (in the face of natural speech elisions); how to determine when to punctuate to indicate a completed phrase or sentence (given the common lack of clear-cut endings in ordinary speech); deciding whether or not to try to represent such matters as spaces and silences, overlapped speech and sounds, pace stresses and volume, and inaudible or incomprehensible sounds or words.[9] In sum, even those means of recording that researchers claim come the closest to realizing an "objective mirroring" necessarily make reductions in the lived complexity of social life similar in principle to those made in writing fieldnotes.[10]

Given the reductionism of any method of inscription, choice of method reflects researchers' deeper assumptions about social life and how to understand it. Fieldwork and ultimately the fieldnote are predicated on a view of social life as continuously created through people's efforts to find and confer meaning on their own and others' actions. Within this perspective, the interview and the recording have their uses. To the extent that participants are willing and able to describe these features of social life, an interview may prove a valuable tool. Similarly, a video recording provides a valuable record of words actually uttered and gestures actually made. But the ethos of fieldwork holds that in order to fully understand and appreciate action from the perspective of participants, one must get close to and participate in a wide cross-section of their everyday activities over an extended period of time. Ethnography, as Van Maanen (1988:ix) insists, is "the peculiar practice of representing the social reality of others through the analysis of one's own experience in the world of these others." Fieldnotes are distinctively a method for capturing and preserving the insights and understandings stimulated by these close and long-term experiences. Thus fieldnotes inscribe the sometimes inchoate understandings and insights the fieldworker acquires by intimately immersing herself in another world, by observing in the midst of mundane activities and jarring crises, by directly running up against the contingencies and constraints of the everyday life of another people. Indeed, it is exactly this deep immersion—and the sense of place that such immersion assumes and strengthens—that enables the ethnographer to inscribe the detailed, context-sensitive, and locally informed fieldnotes that Geertz (1973) terms "thick description."

This experiential character of fieldnotes is also reflected in changes in their content and concerns over time. Fieldnotes grow through gradual accretion, adding one day's writing to the next's. The ethnographer writes particular fieldnotes in ways that are not pre-determined or pre-specified; hence fieldnotes are not collections or samples in the way that audio recordings can be, i.e., decided in advance according to set criteria. Choosing what to write down is not a process of sampling according to some fixed-in-advance principle. Rather it is both intuitive, reflecting the ethnographer's changing sense of what might possibly be made interesting or important to future readers, and empathetic, reflecting the ethnographer's sense of what is interesting or important to the people he is observing.

IMPLICATIONS FOR WRITING FIELDNOTES

We draw four implications from our understanding of ethnography as the inscription of participatory experience: (1) What is observed and ultimately treated as "data" or "findings" is inseparable from the observational process. (2) In writing fieldnotes, the field researcher should give special attention to the indigenous meanings and concerns of the people studied. (3) Contemporaneously written fieldnotes are an essential grounding and resource for writing broader, more coherent accounts of others' lives and concerns. (4) Such fieldnotes should detail the social and interactional processes that make up people's everyday lives and activities.

Inseparability of "Methods" and "Findings"

Modes of participating in and finding out about the daily lives of others make up key parts of ethnographic methods. These "methods" determine what the field researcher sees, experiences, and learns. But if substance ("data," "findings," "facts") are products of the methods used, substance cannot be considered independently of method; *what* the ethnographer finds out is inherently connected with *how* she finds it out. As a result, these methods should not be ignored. Rather, they should comprise an important part of written fieldnotes. It thus becomes critical for the ethnographer to document her own activities, circumstances, and emotional responses as these factors shape the process of observing and recording others' lives.[11]

From this point of view, the very distinction between fieldnote "data" and "personal reactions," between "fieldnote records" and "diaries" or "journals" (Sanjek 1990c), is deeply misleading. Of course, the ethnographer can separate what he says and does from what he observes others saying and doing, treating the latter as if it were unaffected by the former.[12] But such a separation distorts processes of inquiry and the meaning of field "data" in several significant ways. First, this separation treats data as "objective information" that has a fixed meaning independent of *how* that information was elicited or established and by whom. In this way the ethnographer's own actions, including his "personal" feelings and reactions, are viewed as independent of and unrelated to the events and happenings involving others that constitute "findings" or "observations" when written down in fieldnotes. Second, this separation assumes that "subjective" reactions and perceptions can and should be controlled by being segregated from "objective," impersonal records. And finally, such control is thought to be essential because personal and emotional experiences are devalued, comprising "contaminants" of objective data rather than avenues of insight into significant processes in the setting.

Linking method and substance in fieldnotes has a number of advantages: it encourages recognizing "findings" not as absolute and invariant but as contingent upon the circumstances of their "discovery" by the ethnographer. Moreover, the ethnographer is prevented, or at least discouraged, from too readily taking one person's version of what happened or what is important as the "complete" or "correct" version of these matters. Rather, "what happened" is one account, made by a particular person to a specific other at a particular time and place for particular purposes. In all these ways, linking method and substance builds sensitivity to the multiple, situational realities of those studied into the core of fieldwork practice.

The Pursuit of Indigenous Meanings

In contrast to styles of field research which focus on others' behavior without systematic regard for what such behavior means to those engaged in it, we see ethnography as committed to uncovering and depicting indigenous meanings. The object of participation is ultimately to get close to those studied as a way of understanding what their experiences and activities *mean to them*.[13]

Ethnographers should attempt to write fieldnotes in ways that capture and preserve indigenous meanings. To do so, they must learn to recognize and limit reliance upon preconceptions about members' lives and activities. They must become responsive to what others are concerned about, in their own terms. But while fieldnotes are about others, their concerns and doings gleaned through empathetic immersion, they necessarily reflect and convey the ethnographer's understanding of these concerns and doings. Thus, fieldnotes are written accounts that filter members' experiences and concerns through the person and perspectives of the ethnographer; fieldnotes provide the ethnographer's, not the members', accounts of the latter's experiences, meanings, and concerns.

It might initially appear that forms of ethnography concerned with "polyvocality" (Clifford and Marcus 1986:15), or oral histories and feminist ethnographies (Stacey 1991) which seek to let members "speak in their own voices," can avoid researcher mediation in its entirety. But even in these instances, researchers continue to select what to observe, to pose questions, or to frame the nature and purpose of the interview more generally, in ways which cannot avoid mediating effects (see Mills 1990).

Writing Fieldnotes Contemporaneously

In contrast to views holding that fieldnotes are crutches at best and blinders at worst, we see fieldnotes as providing the primary means for deeper appreciation of how field researchers come to grasp and interpret the actions and concerns of others. In this respect, fieldnotes offer subtle and complex understandings of these others' lives, routines, and meanings.

As argued earlier, the field researcher comes to understand others' ways by becoming part of their lives and by learning to interpret and experience events much as they do. It is critical to document closely these subtle processes of learning and resocialization *as they occur;* continuing time in the field tends to dilute the insights generated by initial contact with an unknown way of life. Long-term participation dissolves the initial perceptions that arise in adapting to and discovering what is significant to others; it blunts early sensitivities to subtle patterns and underlying tensions. In short, the field researcher does not learn about the concerns and meanings of others all at once, but in a constant, continuing process in which she builds new insight and understanding upon prior insights and understandings. Researchers should document these emergent processes and stages rather than attempt to reconstruct them at a later point in light of some final, ultimate interpretation of their meaning and import. Fieldnotes provide a distinctive resource for preserving experience close to the moment of occurrence and, hence, for deepening reflection upon and understanding of those experiences.

Similar considerations hold when examining the ethnographer's "findings" about those studied and their routine activities. Producing a record of these activities as close to their occurrence as possible preserves their idiosyncratic, contingent character in the face of the homogenizing tendencies of retrospective recall. In immediately written fieldnotes, distinctive qualities and features are sharply drawn and will elicit vivid memories and images when the ethnographer rereads notes for coding and analysis. Furthermore, the distinctive and unique features of such fieldnotes, brought forward into the final analysis, create texture and variation, avoiding the flatness that comes from generality.

The Importance of Interactional Detail

Field researchers seek to get close to others in order to understand their ways of life. To preserve and convey that closeness, they must describe situations and events of interest in detail. Of course, there can never be absolute standards for determining when there is "enough detail." How closely one should look and describe depends upon what is "of interest," and this varies by situation and by the researcher's personality, orientation, and discipline. Nonetheless, most ethnographers attend to observed events in an intimate or "microscopic" manner (Geertz 1973:20–23) and in writing fieldnotes seek to recount "what happened" in fine detail.

Beyond this general "microscopic" commitment, however, our specifically interactionist approach leads us to urge writers to value close, detailed reports of interaction. First, interactional detail helps one become sensitive to, trace, and analyze the interconnections between methods and substance. Since the fieldworker discovers things about others by interacting with them, it is important to observe and minutely record the sequences and conditions marking such interactions. Second, in preserving the details of interaction, the researcher is better able to identify and follow *processes* in witnessed events and hence to develop and sustain processual interpretations of happenings in the field. Field research, we maintain, is particularly suited to documenting social life as process, as emergent meanings established in and through social interaction (Blumer 1969). Attending to the details of interaction enhances the possibilities for the researcher to see beyond fixed, static entities, to grasp the active "doing" of social life. Writing fieldnotes as soon and as fully as possible after events of interest have occurred encourages detailed descriptions of the processes of interaction through which members of social settings create and sustain specific, local social realities.

REFLECTIONS: WRITING FIELDNOTES AND ETHNOGRAPHIC PRACTICE

Ethnography is an active enterprise. Its activity incorporates dual impulses. On the one hand, the ethnographer must make her way into new worlds and new relationships. On the other hand, she must learn how to represent in written form what she has come to see and understand as the result of these experiences.

It is easy to draw a sharp contrast between these activities, between doing fieldwork and writing fieldnotes. After all, while in the field, ethnographers must frequently choose between "join(ing) conversations in unfamiliar places" (Lederman 1990:72) and withdrawing to some more private place to write about these conversations and witnessed events. By locating "real ethnography" in the time spent talking with and listening to those studied, many ethnographers not only polarize but also discount writing notes as a central component of fieldwork. "Doing" and "writing" should not be seen as separate and distinct activities, but as dialectically related and interdependent activities. Writing accounts of what happened during face-to-face encounters with others in the field is very much part of the doing of ethnography; as Geertz emphasizes, "the ethnographer 'inscribes' social discourse; he writes it down" (1973:19). This process of inscribing, of writing fieldnotes, helps the field researcher to understand what he has been observing in the first place and, thus, enables him to participate in new ways, to hear with greater acuteness, and to observe with a new lens.

While ethnographers increasingly recognize the centrality of writing to their craft, they frequently differ on how to characterize that writing and its relation to ethnographic research. Some anthropologists have criticized Geertz's notion of "inscription" as too mechanical and simplistic, as ignoring that the ethnographer writes not about a "passing event" but rather about "already formulated, fixed discourse or lore"; hence, inscription should more aptly be termed "transcription" (Clifford 1990:57). "Inscription" has also been criticized as being too enmeshed in the assumptions of "salvage ethnography," which date back to Franz Boas's efforts to "write down" oral cultures before they and their languages and customs disappeared (Clifford 1986:113). Indeed, ethnographers have suggested a number of alternative ways of characterizing ethnographic writing. Anthropologists frequently use "translation" (or "cultural translation") to conceptualize writing a version of one culture that will make it comprehensible to readers living in another. Clifford (1986) and Marcus (1986) use the more abstract term "textualization" to refer to the generic processes whereby an ethnography "translates experience into text" (Clifford 1986:115). And sociologists, notably Richardson (1990), describe the core of ethnographic writing as "narrating."

In general, however, these approaches conflate writing final ethnographies with writing ethnographic fieldnotes; thus, they fail to adequately illuminate the key processes and features of producing fieldnotes. Yet, each approach has implications for such contemporaneous writing about events witnessed in the field. First *translation* entails reconfiguring one set of concepts and terms into another; that is, the ethnographer searches for comparable concepts and analogous terms. In a sense, while writing fieldnotes an ethnographer is always interpreting and translating into text what she sees, even when writing notes for herself. Of course, in composing the final ethnography, the writer not only translates concepts but also a whole way of life for a future audience who may not be familiar with the world she describes. Second, *narrating* often aptly characterizes the process of writing a day's experiences into a fieldnote entry. However, not all life experiences are well represented as cohesive stories: a narrative could push open-ended or disjointed interactions into a coherent, interconnected sequence. Thus, while many fieldnotes tell about the day in a storytelling mode, recounting what happened in a chronological order, most entries lack any overall structure which ties the day's events into a story line with a point. As a result, the storytelling of fieldnotes is generally fragmented and episodic. Finally, *textualization* clearly focuses on the broader transformation of experience into text, not only in final ethnographies, but especially so in writing fieldnotes. Indeed, such transformation first occurs in the preliminary and varied writings in the field. Moreover, these fieldnotes often prefigure the final texts!

In sum, the fluid, open-ended processes of writing fieldnotes resonate with the imagery of all these approaches. Never a simple matter of inscribing the world, fieldnotes do more than record observations. In a fundamental sense, they constitute a way of life through the very writing choices the ethnographer makes and the stories she tells; for, through her writing she conveys her understandings and insights to future readers unacquainted with these lives, people, and events, In writing a fieldnote, then, the ethnographer does not simply put happenings into words. Rather, such writing is an interpretive process: it is the very first act of textualizing. Indeed, this often "invisible" work—*writing ethnographic fieldnotes*—is the primordial textualization that creates a world on the page and ultimately shapes the final ethnographic, published text.

chapter two

In the Field: Participating, Observing, and Jotting Notes

Ethnographers ultimately produce some sort of written account of what they have seen, heard, and experienced in the field. But different ethnographers, and the same ethnographer at different times, turn experience and observation into written texts in different ways. Some maximize their immersion in local activities and their experience of others' lives, deliberately suspending concern with the task of producing written records of these events. Here the field researcher decides where to go, what to look at, what to ask and say, so as to experience fully another way of life and its concerns. She attends to events with little or no orientation to "writing it down" or even to "observing" in a detached fashion. Indeed, an ethnographer living in rather than simply regularly visiting a field setting, particularly in non-Western cultures where language and daily routines are unfamiliar, may have no choice but to participate fully and to suspend immediate concerns with writing. A female ethnographer studying local women in Africa, for example, may find herself helping to prepare greens and care for children, leaving no time to produce many written notes. Yet in the process of that involvement she may most clearly learn how women simultaneously work together, socialize, and care for children. Only in subsequent reflection might she fully notice the subtle changes in herself as she learned to do and see these activities as the women do.

Field researchers using this style value relating naturally to those encountered in the field; they focus their efforts on figuring out—holistically and intuitively—what these people are up to. Any anticipation of writing fieldnotes is postponed (and in extreme cases, minimized or avoided altogether) as diluting the experiential insights and intuitions that immersion in another social world can provide.[1] Only at some later point does the ethnographer turn to the task of recalling and examining her experiences in order to write them down.

But the ethnographer may also participate in ongoing events in ways that directly and immediately involve inscription. Here the field worker is concerned with "getting into place" to observe interesting, significant events in order to produce a detailed written record of them. As a result, participation in naturally occurring events may come to be explicitly oriented toward writing fieldnotes. At an extreme, the field worker may self-consciously look for events that should be written down for research purposes; he may position himself in these unfolding events to be able to observe and write; and he may explicitly orient to events in terms of "what is important to remember so that I can write it down later."

Both modes of participation have strengths and drawbacks. The former allows an intense immersion in daily rhythms and ordinary concerns, increasing openness to others' ways of life. The latter can produce a more detailed, closer-to-the-moment record of that life. In practice, most field researchers employ both styles at one time or another, now participating without thought about writing up what is happening, now focusing closely on events in order to write about them. Indeed, the fieldworker may experience a shift from one mode to another as events unfold in the field. Caught in some social moment, for example, the field researcher may come to see deep theoretical relevance in a mundane experience or practice. Conversely, a researcher in the midst of observing in a more detached, writing-oriented mode may suddenly be drawn directly into the center of activity.[2]

In both styles, the ethnographer writes fieldnotes more or less contemporaneously with the experience and observation of events of interest, in the spirit of the ethnographer who commented, "Anthropologists are those who write things down at the end of the day" (Jackson 1990b:15). In the experiential style, writing may be put off for hours or even days, until the field researcher withdraws from the field and, relying solely on memory, sits down at pad or computer to reconstruct important events.[3] In the participating-to-write style, writing—or an orientation to writing—begins earlier, when the researcher is still in the field, perhaps in the immediate presence of talk and action that will be inscribed. The ethnographer may not only make mental notes or "headnotes"[4] to include certain events in full fieldnotes, but he may also write down, in the form of jottings or scratch notes, abbreviated words and phrases to use later to construct full fieldnotes.

Furthermore, in both styles field researchers are deeply concerned about the quality of the relationships they develop with the people they seek to know and understand. In valuing more natural, open experience of others' worlds and activities, field researchers seek to keep writing from intruding into and affecting these relationships. They do so not only to avoid distancing themselves from the ongoing experience of another world, but also because writing and research commitments more generally may engender feelings of betraying those with whom one has lived and shared intimacies. Ethnographers who participate in order to write, in contrast, pursue and proclaim research interests more openly as an element in their relationships with those studied. But these field researchers too experience moments of anguish, of uncertainty about whether to include intimate or humiliating incidents in their fieldnotes. Moreover, they often become very sensitive to the ways in which the stance and act of writing are very visible to and can influence the quality of their relationships with those studied.

In the remainder of this chapter we focus on a participating-in-order-to-write fieldwork style which confronts writing issues directly and immediately in the field. This style brings to the fore the interconnections between writing, participating, and observing as a means of understanding another way of life: this approach focuses on learning how to look in order to write, while it also recognizes that looking is itself shaped and constrained by a sense of what and how to write. In examining these issues, we initially consider choices confronting field researchers in deciding how, where, and when to make jottings in field settings. Next we offer suggestions on what to observe when participating with an eye to writing fieldnotes. We then present illustrations of actual jottings made in different field settings and discuss a number of considerations that might guide the process of making jottings.

MAKING JOTTINGS: HOW, WHERE, AND WHEN

In attending to ongoing scenes, events, and interactions, field researchers take mental note of certain details and impressions. For the most part these impressions remain "headnotes" only. In some instances, the field researcher makes a brief written record of these impressions by jotting

down key words and phrases. Jottings translate to-be-remembered observations into writing on paper as quickly rendered scribbles about actions
and dialogue. A word or two written at the moment or soon afterwards
will jog the memory later in the day and enable the fieldworker to catch
significant actions and to construct evocative descriptions of the scene.
Or, more extensive jottings may record an ongoing dialogue or a set of
responses to questions. Particularly when learning a new language, the
ethnographer should jot key expressions and terms.

Through trial and error field researchers evolve distinctive practical
styles for writing jottings. An initial choice involves the selection of writing materials. Many fieldworkers use small notepads that fit easily in
pocket or purse. Others prefer even less obtrusive materials, using folded
sheets of paper, to record jottings about different topics on specific sides.
Writers also frequently develop idiosyncratic preferences for particular
types of pens or pencils.

Field researchers actually write jottings in different ways. It is time-
consuming and cumbersome to write out every word fully, and many
fieldworkers develop their own private systems of symbols and abbrevia-
tions. Some even learn a formal transcribing system such as shorthand or
speedwriting. These procedures not only facilitate getting words on a
page more quickly; they also make jotted notes incomprehensible to
those onlookers who ask to see them and hence provide a means for
protecting the confidentiality of these writings.

Field researchers must also decide when, where, and how to write
jottings. Far from simply mundane matters, such decisions can have tre-
mendous import for relations with those in the field. The researcher
works hard to establish close ties with participants so that she may be
included in activities that are central to their lives. In the midst of such
activities, however, she may experience deep ambivalence: on the one
hand, she may wish to preserve the immediacy of the moment by jotting
down words as they are spoken and details of scenes as they are enacted;
on the other hand, she may feel that taking out a note pad and writing
jottings will ruin the moment and plant seeds of distrust. Participants may
now see her as someone whose primary interest lies in discovering their
secrets and turning their most intimate and cherished experiences into
objects of scientific inquiry.[5]

Nearly all ethnographers feel torn at times between their research
commitments and their desire to engage authentically those people whose
worlds they have entered. Attempting to resolve these thorny relational

and moral issues, many researchers hold that conducting any aspect of the research without the full and explicit knowledge and consent of those studied violates ethical standards. In this view, local assistants must be understood as collaborators who actively work with the researcher to tell the outside world about their lives and culture. Such mutual collaboration requires that the researcher ask permission to write about events and also respect people's desire not to reveal aspects of their lives.

Other field researchers feel less strictly bound to seek permission to conduct research or to tell participants about their intention to record events and experiences. Some justify this stance by insisting that the field researcher has no special obligations to disclose his intentions; all social life involves elements of dissembling, as no one ever fully reveals all his deeper purposes and private activities. Other researchers point out that jottings and fieldnotes written for oneself as one's own record will do no direct harm to others. This approach, of course, puts off grappling with the tough moral and personal issues until facing subsequent decisions about whether to publish or otherwise make these writings available to others. Finally, some advocate withholding knowledge of their research purposes from local people on the grounds that the information gained will serve the greater good. Researchers, for example, can only describe and publicize the conditions under which undocumented factory workers or the elderly in nursing homes live if they withhold their intentions from the powerful who control access to such settings.

Many beginning researchers, wanting to avoid open violations of trust and possibly awkward or tense encounters, are tempted to use covert procedures and to try to conceal the fact that they are conducting research or to wait until they leave the field to jot notes. While these decisions involve both the researcher's conscience and pragmatic considerations, we recommend as a general policy that the fieldworker inform people in the setting of the research, especially those with whom he has established some form of personal relationship. In addition to making these relations more direct and honest, openness avoids the risks and likely sense of betrayal that might follow from discovery of what the researcher has actually been up to. Concerns about the consequences—both discovery and ongoing inauthenticity—of even this small secret about research plans may mount and plague the fieldworker as time goes on and relations deepen.

Of course, strained relations and ethical dilemmas are not completely avoided by informing others of one's research purposes. While participants may have consented to the research, they might not know exactly what the research involves or what the researcher will do to carry it out.[6] They might realize that the fieldworker is writing fieldnotes at the end of the day, but they become used to his presence and "forget" that this writing is going on. Furthermore, marginal and transient members of the setting may not be aware of his research identity and purposes despite conscientious efforts to inform them.

By carrying out fieldwork in an overt manner, the researcher gains flexibility in when, where, and how to write jottings. In many field situations it may be feasible to jot notes openly. In so doing the fieldworker should act with sensitivity, trying to avoid detracting from or interfering with the ordinary relations and goings-on in the field. If possible, the fieldworker should start open jottings early on in contacts with those studied. If one establishes a "note-taker" role, jotting notes comes to be part of what people expect from the fieldworker. Here it helps to offer initial explanations of the need to take notes; an ethnographer can stress the importance of accuracy, of getting down exactly what was said. People often understand that such activities are required of students and, therefore, tolerate and accommodate the needs of researchers who, they believe, want to faithfully represent what goes on. When learning a new language in another culture, the field researcher can explain that she is writing down local terms in order to remember them. By saying the word as she writes, people might offer new terms and become further interested in teaching her.

Although taking down jottings may at first seem odd or awkward, after a time it often becomes a normal and expected part of what the fieldworker does. In the following excerpt from a Housing and Urban Development [HUD] office, the office manager and a worker jokingly enlist the fieldworker as audience for a self-parody of wanting to "help" clients:

Later I'm in Jean's office and Ramon comes up and waxes melodramatic. Take this down, he says. Jean motions for me to write, so I pull out my notepad. "I only regret that I have but eight hours to devote to saving" . . . He begins to sing "Impossible Dream," in his thick, goofy Brooklyn accent. . . . "Feel free to join in," he says. . . .

Here, the ethnographer and his note-taking provide resources for a spontaneous humorous performance.[7]

Yet even when some people become familiar with open writing in their presence, others may become upset when the researcher pulls out his pad and begins to write down their words and actions. Ethnographers may try to avoid the likely challenges and facilitate open, extensive note-taking by positioning themselves on the margins of interaction. Even then, they may still encounter questions, as reflected in the following comment by a field researcher observing divorce mediation sessions:

I tried to take notes that were as complete as possible during the session. My sitting behind the client had probably more to do with wanting to get a lot of written notes as unobtrusively as possible as with any more worthy methodological reason. While taking copious amounts of notes (approximately 50 pages per session) did not seem to bother the clients, a few mediators became quite defensive about it. One mediator wanted to know how I "decided what to write down and what not to write down." At staff meetings this same mediator would sit next to me and try to glance over to see what I had written in my notebook.

Given the delicacy of this and similar situations, fieldworkers must constantly rely upon interactional skills and tact to judge whether or not taking jottings in the moment is appropriate.[8]

Furthermore, in becoming accustomed to open jotting, people may develop definite expectations about what events and topics should be recorded. People may question why the fieldworker is or is not taking note of particular events, and they may feel slighted if she fails to make jottings on what they are doing or see as important. Consider the following exchange, again described by the field researcher studying divorce mediation, which occurred as she openly took notes while interviewing a mediator about a session just completed:

On one occasion when finishing up a debriefing, . . . [the mediator] began to apply some eye make-up while I was finishing writing down some observations. She flashed me a mock disgusted look and said, "Are you writing *this* down too!" indicating the activity with her eye pencil.

Open jotting, then, has to be carefully calibrated to the unfolding context of the ongoing interaction.[9]

Open jottings not only may strain relations with those who notice the writing; jottings can also distract the ethnographer from paying close attention to talk and activities occurring in the setting. A field researcher will inevitably miss fleeting expressions, subtle movements, and even key content in interactions if his nose is in his notepad. Taking open jottings is not always advisable for other reasons as well. In some settings the fieldworker's participation in ongoing interaction may be so involving as to preclude taking breaks to write down jottings; in such instances, he may have to rely more upon memory, focusing on incidents and key phrases that will later trigger a fuller recollection of the event or scene. For example, in a setting where only a few people write and do so only on rare occasions, an ethnographer who writes instead of participating in an all-night village dance may be perceived as failing to maintain social relationships—a serious offense in a close-knit village.

As a result of these problems, even ethnographers who usually write open jottings may at other times make jottings privately, out of sight of those studied. Waiting until just after a scene, incident, or conversation has occurred, the ethnographer can then go to a private place to jot down a memorable phrase. Here it is often useful for the fieldworker to adopt the ways members of the setting themselves use to take "time out" or "get away." Fieldworkers have reported retreating to private places such as a bathroom (Cahill 1985), deserted lunchroom, stairwell, or supply closet to record such covert jottings. Depending upon circumstances, the fieldworker can visit such places periodically, as often as every half hour or so, or immediately after a particularly important incident. Other researchers avoid all overt writing in the field setting; but immediately upon leaving the field, they pull out a notebook to jot down reminders of the key incidents, words, or reactions they wish to include in full fieldnotes. This procedure allows the fieldworker to signal items that she does not want to forget without being seen as intrusive.

An ethnographer may write jottings in ways intermediate between open and hidden styles, especially when note-taking becomes a part of her task or role. Those in the field may or may not know explicitly that the fieldworker is writing jottings for research purposes. In one instance, for example, a student in a law office who was asked to take notes during client interviews used the assignment as an opportunity to take down research jottings. This student reported that while she did not make explicit when she wrote jottings, both the attorney and clients knew of her research. Though many activities do not so easily lend themselves to writing jottings, fieldworkers can find other naturally occurring means to incorporate jottings. For example, fieldworkers often learn about settings by becoming members. For the fieldworker who assumes the role of a novice. the notes which as a beginner he is permitted or even expected to write may become the jottings for his first fieldnotes.

Strategies for how, where, and when to jot notes change with time spent in the field and with the different relationships formed between fieldworker and people in the setting. Even after the ethnographer has established strong personal ties, situations might arise in fieldwork when visibly recording anything will be taken as inappropriate or out of place; in these situations, taking out a notebook would generate deep discomfort to both fieldworker and other people in the setting.[10] One student ethnographer studying a campus bookstore who had grown quite friendly with bookstore workers—with whom she had spoken openly about her study—nonetheless reported the following incident:

> One of the younger cashiers came up to me after having seen me during two of my last observation sessions. She approached me tentatively with a question about me being a "spy" from the other campus bookstore or possibly from the administration. Trying to ease the situation with a joke, I told her I was only being a spy for sociology's sake. But she didn't understand the joke, and it only made the situation worse.

Sometimes people may be uncomfortable with a jotting researcher because they have had little experience with writing as a part of everyday life. Especially in oral cultures, watching and writing about people may seem like a strange activity indeed. In other instances, people have unpleasant associations with writing and find jottings intrusive and potentially dangerous. On one occasion an elder in a Zambian village became very hesitant to continue speaking after the ethnographer jotted down his name on a scrap of paper, simply to remember it. She later learned that government officials in colonial times used to come by and record names for tax purposes and to enlist people into government work projects.

Finally, even with permission to write openly, the tactful fieldworker will want to remain sensitive to and avoid jotting down matters which participants regard as secret, embarrassing, too revealing, or which puts them in any danger. In other instances, the people themselves may not object and in fact urge the researcher to take notes about sensitive matters. Even though she thinks they may be embarrassing or bring them harm if they were to be made public, the researcher might take jottings but then later decide not to use them in any final writing.

All in all, it is a defining moment in field relations when an ethnographer takes out a pad and begins to write down what people are saying and doing in the presence of those very people. Therefore, fieldworkers take very different approaches to jottings, their strategies both shaping and being shaped by their setting and by their relationships. Hence, decisions about when and how to take jottings must be considered in the context of the broader set of relations with those in the setting. In some situations and relations, taking open jottings is clearly not advisable. In others, fieldworkers decide to take jottings but must devise their own unique means to avoid or minimize awkward interactions that may arise as a result. When deciding when and where to jot, it is rarely helpful or possible to specify in advance one "best way." Here, as in other aspects of fieldwork, a good rule of thumb is to remain open and flexible, ready to alter an approach if it adversely affects people.

PARTICIPATING IN ORDER TO WRITE

Deciding whether or not to make jottings presupposes some sense for what to observe and write about in the first place. But in the flux of their field settings, beginning students are often hesitant and uncertain about what they should pay attention to as potential issues for writing. We have found a number of procedures to be helpful in advising students how initially to look-in-order-to-write.[11]

First, ethnographers should take note of their *initial impressions*. These impressions may include those things available to the senses—the tastes, smells, and sounds of the physical environment, the look and feel of the locale and the people in it. Such impressions may include details about the physical setting, including size, space, noise, colors, equipment, and movement, or about people in the setting, such as number, gender, race, appearance, dress, movement, comportment, and feeling tone. Recording these impressions provides a way to get started in a setting that may seem overwhelming. Entering another culture where both language and customs are incomprehensible may present particular challenges in this regard. Still, the ethnographer can begin to assimilate strange sights and sounds through writing about them.[12]

Furthermore, this record preserves these initial and often insightful impressions, for observers tend to lose sensitivity for unique qualities of a setting as these become commonplace. Researchers who are familiar with the setting they study, perhaps already having a place in that setting as workers or residents, have lost direct access to these first impressions. However, such fieldworkers can indirectly seek to recall their own first impressions by watching any newcomers to the setting, paying special attention to how they learn, adapt, and react.

Second, field researchers can focus on observing *key events or incidents*. Fieldworkers may at first have to rely on their own experience and intuition to select noteworthy incidents out of the flow of ongoing activity. Here, for example, the fieldworker may look closely at something that surprises or runs counter to her expectations, again paying attention to incidents, feeling tones, impressions, and interactions, both verbal and nonverbal.

Similarly, field researchers may use their own personal experience of events that please, shock, or even anger them to identify matters worth writing about. A fieldworker's strong reaction to a particular event may well signal that others in the setting react similarly. Or a fieldworker may experience deeply contradictory emotions—for example, simultaneously feeling deep sympathy and repulsion for what he observes in the field. These feelings may also reflect contradictory pressures experienced by those in the setting.

To use personal reactions effectively, however, requires care and reflection. Many beginning ethnographers take note of such experiences, but tend to judge the actions of people in the setting, for better or worse, by their own rather than the others' standards and values. Prejudging incidents in outsiders' terms makes it difficult to cultivate empathetic understanding and to discover what import local people give to them (see chapter 5). The field researcher should be alive to the possibility that local people, especially those with very different cultures, may respond to events in sharply contrasting ways. For example, an ethnographer in a Chokwe village may react with alarm to an unconscious man drugged by an herbal drink in a trial-for-sorcery court, only to realize that others are laughing at the spectacle because they know he will soon regain consciousness.

Yet fieldworkers should not go to the other extreme and attempt to manage strong personal reactions by denial or simply by omitting them from fieldnotes. Rather, we recommend that the ethnographer register her feelings, then step back and use this experience to increase sensitivity to the experiences of others in the setting. Are others in the setting similarly surprised, shocked, pleased, or angered by an event? If so, under what conditions do these reactions occur, and how did those affected cope with the incidents and persons involved? Whether an ethnographer is working in a foreign or familiar culture, she needs to avoid assuming that others respond as she does.

Third, field researchers should move beyond their personal reactions to an open sensitivity to what those in the setting experience and react to as "significant" or "important." The sorts of actions, interactions, and events that catch the attention of people habitually in the setting may provide clues to these concerns. The field researcher watches for the sorts of things that are meaningful to those studied. Specifically: What do they stop and watch? What do they talk and gossip about? What produces strong emotional responses for them? "Troubles" or "problems" often generate deep concern and feelings. What kinds occur in the setting? How do people in the setting understand, interpret, and deal with such troubles or problems? Such "incidents" and "troubles" should move the field researcher to jot down "who did what" and "how others reacted." Since a researcher in an unfamiliar setting often pays close attention to others' actions in order to imitate and participate, she can augment her learning by writing down what others do and how they respond. A follow-up strategy that we strongly recommend is to talk to those involved and those witnessing the incident about their impressions.

In this way, the field researcher attends not only to the activities local people engage in but also to the particular meanings they attribute to these activities. She seeks and discerns local knowledge and meanings, not so much by directly asking actors what matters to them, but more indirectly and inferentially by looking for the perspectives and concerns embedded and expressed in naturally occurring interaction. A field researcher, for example, might give close attention to evaluations and distinctions made by members in the course of their daily activities. By way of illustration, those in a work setting may regularly contrast "good" workers and "bad" workers. By noting such distinctions, the researcher learns something about what matters to those in the setting. In addition, by attending closely to how, in conversation, people apply these distinctions to particular workers, the fieldworker may learn how these reputations become resources used to find meaning.

In this sense, the ethnographer is concerned not with members' indigenous meanings simply as static categories but with how members of settings invoke those meanings in specific relations and interactions. This requires, then, not just that the ethnographer describe interactions, but that she consistently attend to "when, where, and according to whom" in shaping all fieldnote descriptions. Those in different institutional positions (e.g., supervisors and workers, staff and clients), for example, may evaluate different workers as "good" (or "bad") and may do so by invoking different evaluative criteria. Indigenous meanings, then, rarely hold across the board but rather reflect particular positions and practical concerns that need to be captured in writing fieldnotes.

When first venturing into a setting, field researchers should "cast their nets" broadly; they should observe with an eye to writing about a range of incidents and interactions. Yet forays into a setting must not be viewed as discrete, isolated occasions that have little or no bearing on what will be noted the next time. Rather, observing and writing about certain kinds of events foreshadow what will be noticed and described next. Identifying one incident as noteworthy should lead to considering what other incidents are similar and hence worth noting. As fieldwork progresses and becomes more focused on a set of issues, fieldworkers often self-consciously collect a series of incidents and interactions of the "same type" and look for regularities or patterns in them.

Even when looking for additional examples of a similar event, the field researcher is open to and indeed searches for *different forms* of that event, for *variations from or exceptions to an emerging pattern*. Beginning field researchers are often discouraged by such discoveries, fearing that exceptions to a pattern they have noted will cast doubt upon their understanding of the setting. This need not be the case, although noting differences and variations should prod the field researcher to change, elaborate, or deepen her earlier understanding of the setting. The field researcher, for example, may want to consider and explore possible causes or conditions that would account for difference or variation: Are the different actions the result of the preferences and temperaments of those involved or of their different understandings of the situation because they have different positions in the local context? Or the ethnographer may begin to question how she decided similarity and difference in the first place, perhaps coming to see how an event that initially appeared to be different is actually similar on a deeper level. In these ways, exploring what at least initially seem to be differences and variations will lead to richer, more textured descriptions and encourage more subtle, grounded analyses in a final ethnography (see chapter 7).

In summary, ethnographic attention involves balancing two different orientations. Especially on first entering the field, the researcher identifies significant characteristics gleaned from her first impressions and personal reactions. With greater participation in some local social world, however, the ethnographer becomes more sensitive to the concerns and perspectives of those in the setting. She increasingly appreciates how people have already predescribed their world in their own terms for their own purposes and projects. A sensitive ethnographer draws upon her own reactions to identify issues of possible importance to people in the setting but privileges their "insider" descriptions and categories over her own "outsider" views.

Two Illustrations of Jottings

In order to convey how field researchers actually write and use jottings, we provide two illustrations. Both focus on scenes, observed actions, and dialogue rather than on evaluation or psychological interpretation. The two researchers approach interaction in their settings in very different ways, noting different sensory and interpretive details.

"they're not very good"

The following jotted notes focus on meeting a would-be promotor of Spanish-language rock music in a club:

> Jorge = at table   doesn't introduce me to anyone
> now only speaks in Spanish
>   chit chat — who's playing
>   "they're not very good" — apology

These jottings preserve a number of incidents in the club, including where Jorge is seated and the fact that he has switched to Spanish after having previously spoken English. A general sequence of events is laid out: Jorge does not introduce the observer, who has come in his company; there is general conversation ("chit chat"); someone (not specified here) asks "who's playing" (presumably the name of the band is given, but is mentally marked as easily remembered and not recorded); someone (*not the field worker!*) makes an evaluative comment about the band, and the observer notes her sense that this remark was an "apology" (for having brought her to this club), thus providing interactional context for interpreting its import.

"you can call his doctor"

The following jottings concern a woman who is seeking a temporary restraining order against her two landlords, one of whom is not present in the courtroom. The landlord who is present disputes the woman's testimony that the missing landlord is "well enough to walk" and hence could have come to court:

> you can call his doctor at UCLA and
> he can verify all this
> I just don't call people on the
> telephone — courts don't operate that way —
> it has to be on paper or
> (in person)

These jottings represent a fragment of dialogue between the landlord defendant (the first two lines) and the judge (the last four lines; see chapter 3 for the full fieldnote written from this jotting). The jotting reflects an interest in the judge's insistence on legal procedure: he as judge ("courts") will not independently investigate litigants' claims; rather, litigants are responsible for presenting any evidence in the courtroom. Note that only spoken words are recorded; specific speakers are not indicated but can be identified by content or from memory. The words represent direct quotes, written down as accurately as possible when spoken; an exception occurs in the last line, where the observer missed the judge's exact words ending this sentence (because of jotting down the preceding dialogue) and inserted a paraphrase "in person" (indicated by parentheses).

JOTTINGS AS MNEMONIC DEVICES: WHAT WORDS AND PHRASES?

Each of the jottings in the previous illustrations is "a mnemonic word or phrase [written] to fix an observation or to recall what someone has just said" (Clifford 1990:51). As preludes to full written notes, jottings capture bits of talk and action from which the fieldworker can begin to sketch social scenes, recurring incidents, local expressions and terms, members' distinctions and accounts, dialogue among those present, and his own conversations.

Making jottings, however, is not only a writing activity; it is also a mind-set. Learning to jot down details which remain sharp and which easily transform into vivid descriptions on the page results, in part, from envisioning scenes as written. Writing jottings that evoke memories requires learning what can be written about and how. We have found the following recommendations helpful for making jottings useful for producing vivid, evocatively descriptive fieldnotes.

First, jot down details of what you sense are key components of observed scenes or interactions. Field researchers record immediate fragments of action and talk to serve as focal points for later writing accounts of these events in as much detail as can be remembered. The field researcher studying Spanish rock music, for example, jotted that the promoter she accompanied to a club "now only speaks in Spanish" while he had spoken English in their prior, less public contacts. She also wrote down a key direct quote—"they're not very good"—along with the term "apology" to remind her of the context and meaning of this remark.

Second, avoid making statements characterizing what people do that rely on generalizations. Many novice field researchers initially tend to jot down impressionistic, opinionated words which lend themselves better to writing evaluative summaries than to composing detailed, textured descriptions. For example, it is problematic for a field researcher to characterize the way someone works as "inefficient." Such cryptic, evaluative jottings are likely to evoke only a vague memory when the fieldworker later on attempts to write a full description of the social scene. Such jottings also convey nothing of how people in the setting experience and evaluate worker performance. Similarly, jottings that a probation officer "lectures about school" and that a youth is "very compliant—always agrees" during a probation interview are overly generalized; such summary statements are not helpful for writing close descriptions of how probation officer and youth actually talked and acted during a particular encounter.

Third, jot down concrete sensory details about actions and talk. Field researchers note concrete details of everyday life which *show* rather than tell about people's behavior (see chapter 4). By incorporating such details, jottings may provide records of actual words, phrases, or dialogue that the field researcher wants to preserve in as accurate a form as possible. It is not enough, for example, to characterize an emotional outburst simply as "angry words." Rather the ethnographer should jot the actually spoken words, along with sensual details such as gestures and facial expressions suggesting that the speaker's emotional experience involved "anger."

Jotting these words should evoke recall not only of the details about what happened but also of the specific circumstances or context involved: who was present, what they said or did, what occurred immediately before and after, etc. In this way jottings may be used to reconstruct the actual order or sequence of talk, topics, or actions on some particular occasion.

Beginning ethnographers sometimes attempt to identify motives or internal states when recording observed actions. Having witnessed an angry exchange, for example, one is often tempted to focus on the source or reason for this emotional outburst, typically by imputing motive (e.g., some underlying feeling such as "insecurity") to one or both of the parties involved. Such psychologized explanations, however, highlight only one of a number of possible internal states that may accompany or contribute to the observed actions. Anger could, for example, result from frustration, fatigue, the playing out of some local power struggle, or other hidden factors; the ethnographer who simply witnesses a scene has no way of knowing which factors are involved.[13]

Field researchers do not ignore emotions; they may well note feelings such as anger, sadness, joy, pleasure, disgust, loneliness, but they do so as such emotions are expressed and attended to by those in the setting. For example, in describing the emotional consequences of routinely "having to say no" to clients coming to a HUD office in desperate need of housing, an ethnographer wrote the following:

Laura to me, slouched down on her desk, head in hands: "Sometimes I just don't feel like helping people, you know? You have to say no so often. That's a big part of this program. It gets to you psychologically. (How?) I didn't study psychology, but it affects you" (rolling her eyes).

Here the ethnographer writes not to explain *why* this HUD worker experienced or reported these emotions (although she herself points to a feature of her work—"You have to say no so often"), but to highlight *how* she expressed her feelings. He does so not only by direct quotation in her own words but also by providing vivid details of her body posture ("slouched," "head in hands") and by noting her accenting eye movements.

When witnessing social scenes, then, the ethnographer's task is to use his own sensibilities to learn how others understand and evaluate what happened, how they assess internal states and determine psychological motivation. Useful jottings should correspondingly reflect and further this process of writing textured, detailed descriptions of interactions rather than of individual motivation.

Fourth, jot down sensory details which you could easily forget but which you deem to be key observations about the scene. Jottings are devices intended to encourage the recall of scenes and events in the construction of some broader, fuller fieldnote account. Since jottings must later jog the memory, each field researcher must learn which kinds of details they best remember and make jottings about those features and qualities they easily forget. Thus, fieldworkers come to develop their own jotting styles reflecting their distinctive recall propensities, whether visual, kinetic, or auditory. Some focus on trying to capture evocative pieces of broader scenes, while some jot down almost exclusively dialogue; others record nonverbal expression of voice, gesture, movement; still others note visual details of color and shape. Through trial and error, field researchers learn what most helps them to recall field experiences once they sit down to write up full notes.

Jottings may serve more generally to remind the ethnographer of what was happening at a particular time, in this sense providing a marker around which to collect other remembered incidents. For example, one field researcher teaching in a Headstart Program described a series of incidents that occurred while supervising children playing in a sandbox. Included in her jottings but not in her full fieldnotes was the phrase, "Three new bags of sand were delivered to the sandbox." In discussing this scratch note later she commented: "I don't think it is so important as I would want to include it in my notes because I think it is just—I wrote it down to remind me more what the day was like, what was happening."[14]

Fifth, jottings can be used to signal general impressions and feelings, even if the fieldworker is unsure of their significance at the moment. In some cases, the ethnographer may have only a vague intuitive sense about how or why something may be important. Such feelings might signal a key element that in the future could enable the field researcher to see how incidents "fit together" in meaningful patterns. For example, at another point the ethnographer in the Headstart Program made a jotting about a student, "Nicole showing trust in me," which she decided not to write up in her full notes: "It was just an overall feeling I had throughout the day; . . . at that point when I wrote the jottings I couldn't remember an exact incident." But this jotting served as a mental note, subsequently stimulating her to appreciate (and record) the following incident as a revealing example of "children trusting teachers":

At one point, Nicole got on the swings without her shoes on and asked me for a push. I told her that I would push her after she went and put her shoes on. Nicole paused and looked at me. I repeated my statement, telling her that I would save her swing for her while she was gone. Nicole then got off of the swing and put her shoes on. When she came back to the swing, I praised her listening skills and gave her a hug. I then gave her a push. I found this incident to be a significant accomplishment for Nicole, as usually she doesn't listen to the teachers.[15]

Having thought about whether or not to write this jotting up as full notes made this student sensitive to the issue of "trust." The jotting later acted as a stimulus to observe and write up a "concrete event" involving such "trust."

In summary, by participating in a setting with an eye to making jottings, an ethnographer experiences events as potential subjects for writing. Like any other writer, an ethnographer learns to recognize potential writing material and to see and hear it in terms of written descriptions. Learning to observe in order to make jottings thus is keyed to both the scene and to the page. Ethnographers learn to experience through the senses in anticipation of writing: to remember dialogue and movement like an actor; to see colors, shapes, textures, and spatial relations as a painter or photographer; and to sense moods, rhythms, and tone of voice like a poet. Details experienced through the senses turn into jottings with active rather than passive verbs, sensory rather than analytic adjectives, and verbatim rather than summarized dialogue.

REFLECTIONS: WRITING AND ETHNOGRAPHIC MARGINALITY

While a primary goal of ethnography is immersion in the life-worlds and everyday experiences of a group of people, the ethnographer inevitably remains in significant ways an outsider to the worlds of those studied. Immersion is not merging; the field researcher who seeks to "get close to" others usually does not become one of these others but rather continues to be a researcher interested in and pursuing research issues, albeit in close proximity to the ordinary exigencies of life that these others experience and react to (see Bittner 1988; Emerson 1987).[16] The ethnographer, then, stays at least a partial stranger to the worlds of the studied, despite sharing in many aspects of their daily lives. The student-ethnographer working in a bookstore noted that the pull toward involvement as an insider was particularly strong and the researcher's stance difficult to maintain:

There were times when I wanted to be free to listen to other individuals talk or to watch their activities, but friends and acquaintances were so "distracting" coming up and wanting to talk that I wasn't able to. Also, there was this concern on my part that, as I got to know some of the staff people better, their qualities as human beings would become so endearing that I was afraid that I would lose my sociological perspective—I didn't want to feel like in studying them, I was exploiting them.

Field researchers respond to these tensions in a variety of ways. Some try to maintain a detached, observational attitude even toward people whom they like and respect, seeking to keep research commitments somewhat separate from personal attachments.[17] Others find themselves unable to sustain an invariably watching, distancing stance toward people they are drawn to and toward events which compellingly involve them. These ethnographers then take time out, either implicitly or self-consciously, by not observing and/or writing fieldnotes about selected portions of their field experience while continuing to do so about other portions. And finally, some ethnographers may decide that the relationships they have formed in the field are more valuable and enduring than any research product, and eventually they come to abandon entirely the project as research activity.

But the ethnographer remains a stranger as long as, and to the extent that, she retains commitment to the exogenous project of studying or understanding the lives of others—as opposed to the indigenous project of simply living a life in one way or another. When living in a village on a long-term basis, the ethnographer may feel drawn into daily, intimate relations as a neighbor or perhaps even as a part of a family. On these occasions she may participate "naturally"—without a writing orientation or analytic reflection—in ongoing social life. But on other occasions, she participates in local scenes in ways directed toward making observations and collecting data. Here her actions incorporate an underlying commitment to write down and ultimately transform into "data" the stuff and nuances of that life. In this way, efforts to observe in order to write about shared experiences and witnessed events induce a distinctive ethnographic stance. In this sense, we can suggest that the ethnographer's strangeness is created and maintained exactly by writing fieldnotes; such notes reflect and realize this socially close but experientially separate stance.[18]

This ethnographic marginality is often manifested interactionally when the fieldworker ceases simply doing what other people are doing and begins openly writing about these doings. In this sense, overtly writing jottings is a critical, consequential ethnographic activity, publicly proclaiming and reaffirming fieldworkers' research commitments and hence their status as outsiders, as persons in the setting who have clearly delineated tasks and purposes that differ from those of members.[19] Writing down jottings not only reminds ethnographers of their marginal social standing in settings but creates it as well, increasing immediate feelings of isolation and alienation.

It should come as no surprise, then, that many ethnographers, both students and experienced practitioners, feel deeply ambivalent about jottings. Jottings interfere with their interactions with people in the field; they create difficulties in interacting with others while at the same time observing and writing down what is happening. Indeed, students who come back from the field without jottings usually report that taking jottings on the spot would have made others uncomfortable. These students, then, directly experience the distracting, alienating consequences of jotting notes.

Most ethnographers, however, try to balance and juggle these tendencies, sometimes participating without immediate thought about writing down what is occurring, sometimes temporarily withdrawing to some private place to write covert jottings, at other times visibly jotting notes. Several practical writing conflicts arise from these opposing pressures. The inclination to experience daily events either as a "natural" participant or as a researcher shows up in writing as shifts in point of view as well as in varying kinds of details considered significant for inscription. Even where and when to jot notes depends on the person's involvement at a particular moment as a participant or observer. Whether a researcher-as-neighbor in the village and researcher-as-intern on a job, the tension between the present-oriented day-to-day role and the future-oriented ethnographer identity appears in the practical choices in writing both jottings and more complete notes.

In sum, in most social settings writing down what is taking place as it occurs is a strange, marginalizing activity, marking the writer as an observer rather than as a full, ordinary participant. But independently of the reactions of others, participating in order to write leads one to assume the mind-set of an observer, a mind-set in which one constantly steps outside of scenes and events to assess their "write-able" qualities. It may be for this reason that some ethnographers try to put writing out of mind entirely by opting for the more fully experiential style of fieldwork. But this strategy puts off rather than avoids the marginalizing consequences of writing, for lived experience must eventually be turned into observations and reduced to textual form.

chapter three

Writing Up Fieldnotes I:
From Field to Desk

After hours participating in, observing, and perhaps jotting notes about ongoing events in a social setting, most fieldworkers return to their desks and their computers or typewriters to begin to write up their observations into full fieldnotes. At this point, writing becomes the explicit focus and primary activity of ethnography: momentarily out of the field, the researcher sits down to the task of turning recollections and jottings into detailed written accounts that will preserve as much as possible what she noticed and now feels is significant.

In this chapter, we are concerned with the processes of writing up full fieldnotes; we focus on how ethnographers go about the complex tasks of remembering, elaborating, filling in, and commenting upon fieldnotes in order to produce a full written account of witnessed scenes and events.

At the Desk

Writing up fieldnotes requires a block of concentrated time. Incidents that span a few minutes may take the ethnographer several hours to write up; she tries to recall just who did and said what, in what order, and to put all that into words and coherent paragraphs. Indeed, an ethnographic maxim holds that every hour spent observing requires an additional hour to write up. Over time, fieldworkers evolve a rhythm that balances time spent in the field and time writing notes. In some situations, the field researcher may put a cap on time devoted to observing in order to allow a substantial write-up period on leaving the field. Limiting time in the field in this way lessens the likelihood that the fieldworker will forget what happened or become overwhelmed by the prospect of hours of composing fieldnotes. For beginning ethnographers, we recommend, when possible, leaving the field after three to four hours in order to begin writing fieldnotes.

In other situations the fieldworker might find it more difficult to withdraw for writing. Anthropologists working in other cultures generally spend whole days observing and devote evenings to writing. Field researchers who fill roles as regular workers must put in a full work day before leaving to write notes. In both cases, longer stretches of observation require larger blocks of write-up time and perhaps different strategies for making note-writing more manageable. For example, once having described basic routines and daily rhythms in the first sets of notes, the ethnographer who spends hours in the field may focus subsequent notes on significant incidents that occurred throughout the day. At this stage longer periods spent in the field may in fact prove advantageous, allowing greater opportunities for observing incidents of interest.

Alternatively, the field researcher with regular workday responsibilities may find it useful to designate certain hours for observing and taking jottings, giving priority to these observations in writing up full fieldnotes. Varying these designated observation periods allows exploration of different patterns of activity throughout the day. Of course, while using this strategy, the fieldworker should still write notes on important incidents that occur at other times.

Perhaps more crucial than how long the ethnographer spends in the field is the timing of writing up fieldnotes. Over time, people forget and simplify experience; notes composed several days after observation tend to be summarized and stripped of rich, nuanced detail. Hence we strongly encourage researchers to sit down and write full fieldnotes as soon as possible after the day's (or night's) research is done.

Writing fieldnotes *immediately* after leaving the setting produces fresher, more detailed recollections that harness the ethnographer's involvement with and excitement about the day's events. Indeed, writing notes immediately on leaving the field offers a way of releasing the weight of what the researcher has just experienced. It is easier to focus one's thoughts and energies on the taxing work of reviewing, remembering, and writing. In contrast, those who put off writing fieldnotes report that with the passage of time the immediacy of lived experience fades and writing fieldnotes becomes a burdensome, even dreaded experience.

Often, however, it is impossible for an ethnographer to find time to write up notes immediately upon leaving the field. Long or late hours, for example, may leave him too tired to write notes. Under these circumstances, it is best to get a good night's sleep and turn to writing up first thing in the morning. Sometimes even this is impossible: a village event may last through several days and nights, confronting the anthropological researcher with a choice between sleeping outside with the villagers or taking time out periodically to sleep and write notes.

Whether written immediately or soon after returning from the site, the fieldworker should go directly to computer or typewriter, not talking with intimates about what happened until full fieldnotes are completed. Such "what happened today" talk can rob note-writing of its psychological immediacy and emotional release; writing the day's events becomes a stale recounting rather than a cathartic outpouring.[1]

Ethnographers use a variety of different means to write up full notes. While the typewriter provided the standard tool for many classic ethnographers, some handwrote their full notes on pads or in notebooks. Contemporary ethnographers strongly prefer a computer with a standard word processing program. Typing notes with a word processing program not only has the advantage of greater speed (slow typists will soon notice substantial gains in speed and accuracy), but also allows for the modification of words, phrases, and sentences in the midst of writing without producing messy, hard-to-read pages. And fieldnotes written on the computer are easily reordered; it is possible, for example, to insert incidents or dialogue subsequently recalled at the appropriate place. Finally, composing with a word processing program facilitates coding and sorting fieldnotes as one later turns to writing finished ethnographic accounts.

The researcher who has been in the field for a long period and has limited time immediately afterward for writing full fieldnotes has several alternatives. First, he may make extensive, handwritten jottings about the day's events, relying on the details of these notes to postpone writing full fieldnotes, often for some time.[2] Secondly, she may dictate fieldnotes into a tape recorder. One can "talk fieldnotes" relatively quickly and can dictate while driving home from a field setting. But while dictation preserves vivid impressions and observations immediately on leaving the field, dictated notes eventually have to be transcribed, a time-consuming, expensive project. And in the meantime, the field researcher does not have ready access to these dictated notes for review or for planning her next steps in the field.

In summary, beginning ethnographers should not be surprised to experience deep ambivalence in writing fieldnotes. On the one hand, after a long, exciting, or draining stint in the field, writing up notes may seem a humdrum, extra burden; on the other hand, writing fieldnotes may bring expressive release and reflective insight. Having seen and heard intriguing, surprising things all day long, the fieldworker is finally able to sit down, think about, and relive events while transforming them into a permanent record. Writing fieldnotes may bring on an outpouring of thoughts and impressions as the writer reviews and re-experiences the excitement and freshness of the day's events.

STANCE AND AUDIENCE IN WRITING FIELDNOTES

Sitting down to write full fieldnotes involves a turning away from the field scene toward "getting it down on the page," toward the worlds of research and writing. In making this turn, the field researcher does not grapple simply with what to write down; she also decides *how* she is going to present and convey what she has seen and observed. While some of these decisions are relatively straightforward, others are more implicit, arising from the particular *stance* adopted in writing fieldnotes, that is, from the author's orientation toward and attitudes about the topic or people studied. Whether her stance is primarily influenced by a theoretical position within a discipline or by her personal, moral, and political commitments, the ethnographer expresses this fundamental stance in a distinctive tone which can be heard and sensed in specific writing choices throughout her fieldnotes.

At a fundamental level, a researcher's stance in fieldwork and note-writing originates in his outlook on life. *Prior experience, training, and commitments* influence the fieldworker's stance in writing notes; these influences predispose him to feel, think, and act toward people in more or less patterned ways. Whether it be from a particular gender, social, cultural, or intellectual position, the fieldworker not only interacts and responds to people in the setting from that orientation but also writes his fieldnotes by seeing and framing events accordingly. The effects of this fundamental stance appear in fieldnote writing in subtle ways: these range from how he identifies with (or distances himself from) those studied and thus writes about them sympathetically (or not), to the kinds of local activities which draw his attention and result in more detailed descriptions, to the way he prioritizes and frames certain topics and thus writes more fully about any events he sees as relevant.

By self-consciously recognizing his fundamental orientation, the fieldworker may be able to write fieldnotes that highlight and foreground issues and insights made available by that orientation. This recognition may also make him more sensitive to the ways his orientation shapes key interactions with others. For example, in writing up fieldnotes about a school for gays and lesbians, one heterosexual male often wrote about the ways students pressed him to reveal his sexual orientation and watched for his responses to their jokes and teasing. But an openly identified gay male researcher in the same field-site became sensitive to how students "sexualized" stories about their experiences as they constructed gay identities in everyday talk. Indeed, he then began to ask and write about students' talk about sexual activities, as in the following fieldnote:

"Wait," I said, interrupting his story. "Where was this?" "Over by Circus Books," Adam said. "And what was he doing?" I asked as I leaned forward smiling slightly. "He was cruising," Adam said. . . . "What's that?" I asked. . . . "It's a meeting place," answered John. "And this is at a bookstore," I said sounding a bit confused. "Yeah," they both said reassuringly.

The more the field researcher acknowledges those factors influencing his fundamental stance toward people in the setting, the more he can examine and use the insights and appreciations opened up by this stance in fieldnote writing. Furthermore, he can better guard against any overriding, unconscious framing of events—for example, by avoiding evaluative wording or by focusing on members' views of events.

As fieldwork progresses, the researcher's stance toward people and issues may change. As she learns through interactions with individuals in the setting to look at activities, events, and issues in new ways, she may adjust her prior views and reorient herself vis-à-vis others. Having readjusted her stance toward people in the setting, she will more frequently write fieldnotes in ways which not only highlight members' views but which also reveal her ongoing resocialization. Over time, a fieldworker's personal views and theoretical commitments often change; her stance in writing fieldnotes shifts as she more frequently comes to see and respond to events as members do.

Another key component determining the stance expressed in written fieldnotes is *intended or likely audience*. How a field researcher writes about observed events is linked to often unacknowledged assumptions about whom he is writing for. We first consider anticipated actual readers and then turn to the subtle but significant relevance of more diffusely envisioned audiences.

Under most circumstances, a researcher writes fieldnotes immediately for herself as a future reader. This absence of an actual reader allows the researcher to write in relaxed and shifting styles, moving from stance to stance, from audience to audience without worrying (at that point) about consistency or coherence. In this sense, fieldnotes should be written "loosely" and flowingly. If and when fieldnotes are shown to another reader—usually in a more comprehensive paper or article—the field researcher can at this time take control of this process; she can select, focus, and edit any notes before making them available to others. As future reader of her own fieldnotes, the researcher anticipates a detailed reading in order to code and analyze the notes for a paper or article.

Fieldnotes are also written differently depending upon how far in the future the field researcher projects himself as reader. Student field researchers, for example, may write notes for themselves as readers in the near future—e.g., at the end of the quarter or semester when working on a final paper. Experienced ethnographers envision themselves as readers in a more distant future, recognizing that notes should include details and background sufficient for making sense of them several years hence, when the immediacy of the field experience has faded.

In practice, however, the researcher-writer may have in mind actual readers other than herself. Student researchers in particular must ordinarily submit their fieldnotes to an instructor and write notes for that reader. Similarly, field researchers in team projects (Douglas 1976) will write notes to be read by co-workers and colleagues. Here field researchers may self-consciously write with actual readers in mind, producing accounts explicitly oriented to these others' knowledge and concerns. One common effect of writing with such readers in mind is to include more details of background and context to make fieldnotes more accessible. The ethnographer should nonetheless try to maintain a loose, flowing, and shifting approach, not trying to write with consistency of voice and style.[3]

The effects of envisioned audiences on how fieldnotes are written are more subtle and complex than those of actual readers.[4] The ethnographer's stance in writing fieldnotes involves trying to convey something about the world she has observed to outside audiences made up of those who are unfamiliar with that world. In this sense fieldnotes are ultimately intended for outsiders of one sort or another. Indeed, it is in this respect that fieldnotes differ from a personal diary: fieldnotes are not merely the personal reactions of the writer, intended to heighten self-awareness and self-insight; they are more fundamentally accounts framed and organized to be read by some other, wider audience.

Many ethnographers envision and write for a professional audience, forming their fieldnotes with eventual publication in mind. These sorts of notes may need some polishing and smoothing, but the writing is intended to be comprehensible to other professionals who are unfamiliar with the people and customs being written about. To the extent that the researcher-writer is self-conscious about writing for an ultimate, broader audience, notes will be richer; they will provide more background, context, and detail.

This is not to say that fieldnotes in "raw" form would be immediately comprehensible to professional or other outside readers. Fieldnotes are an accumulating body of writings in which the sense of later portions will depend upon what has been written earlier. People or events described in earlier notes, for example, need not be described in later ones. And indeed, just who the people are in particular incidents may not be evident to outside readers because of abbreviated names and lack of socially identifying information.[5] Only with filling in and contextualizing would such a fieldnote actually become comprehensible to someone other than the writer. Thus, accumulating fieldnote entries have an open-endedness which allows for new information and insights and an unfinished in-progress quality which calls for editing later on.

In writing fieldnotes most ethnographers probably shift between self and professional others as envisioned future audiences. When writing in the first person about one's own direct involvement in field events or when reflecting on one's emotional reactions or intuitions about next steps to take in the field, for example, the ethnographer may assume that these accounts will only be read by and hence need only to be comprehensible to oneself. In contrast, when writing up an event that was deeply "important" to those in the setting and that is likely to be excerpted for the final ethnography, the writer may strive for completeness and detail.

In sum, stance and envisioned audiences significantly prefigure the way a researcher composes fieldnotes, even though both take on heightened salience when the field researcher self-consciously prepares texts for wider audiences. For writing fieldnotes involves a series of intricate, moment by moment choices in abstracting and processing experience. These choices involve not only what to look at and perhaps jot down, but also *for whom and hence how* to write up full fieldnotes. For student ethnographers, this audience is usually an instructor who reads and comments on fieldnotes, although more ultimate audiences—e.g., professional readers in one's own discipline—may also have an influence even at this point. These intended and anticipated audiences and the theoretical commitments they reflect linger as an influential presence over every ethnographer's shoulder.

THE PROCESS OF WRITING UP

At first glance, writing up may appear to be a straightforward process to the fieldworker. It may seem that with sufficient time and energy, she can simply sit down and record her observations with little attention to her writing process. While having enough time and energy to get her memories on the page is a dominant concern, we suggest that the fieldworker can benefit by considering several kinds of writing choices. In this section we discuss "purposes and styles," "recalling in order to write," "turning jottings into full fieldnotes," "multiple voices and points of view," and "real-time and end-point descriptions" as these influence the process of writing.

Multiple Purposes and Styles

Ethnographers have multiple purposes in writing their fieldnotes, and these aims shape their choices and styles of writing.[6] The most urgent purpose is to record experiences while they are still fresh. Thus ethnographers write hurriedly, dashing words "down on the page"; their notes read like an outpouring, not like polished, publishable excerpts. Knowing that a memorable event fades and gets confused with following ones as time passes, a fieldworker writes using whatever phrasing and organization seems most accessible, convenient, and do-able at the time. She need not worry about being consistent, and she can shift from one style, one topic, one thought to another, as quickly as the fingers can type.

In that initial writing, the field researcher concentrates on a remembered scene more than on words and sentences. Focusing too soon on words produces an internal "editor" that distracts attention from the evoked scene and stops the outpouring of envisioned memory. The goal is to get as much down on paper in as much detail and as quickly as possible, holding off any evaluation and editing until later. As one student commented at one point in her process for writing up notes: "I might just type this in and go back later on and decide that's not exactly how I wanted to word that or that's not exactly the way that I was feeling at that time, but for now, I just like to get them down and then go back over."

In writing up, ethnographers strike a balance between describing fully and getting down the essentials of what happened. As one student said while struggling to describe an incident:

Here I'm going to stop and go back later because I know what I'm trying to say but it isn't coming out. . . . So there's a little more to it than that, but I have to think about how to say it, so I'm just going to leave it. When I write my fieldnotes, I just try to get it all down and I go back through and edit, take time away from it and then come back and see if that's really what I meant to say or if I could say that in a better way, a clearer way.

Fieldworkers may write down all the words that come to mind and later choose a more evocative and appropriate wording. Many writers produce a first round quickly, knowing that they will make additions, polish wording, or reorganize paragraphs at some other time. Thus, in that first rush of writing, finding the absolutely best word or phrase to persuade a future audience should not be of such concern that it slows down the flow of getting words to paper.

All in all, while ethnographers develop a variety of styles and strategies for writing fieldnotes, we encourage initial writing that is as spontaneously organized as conversation about a day's experiences, with changes in topic and focus that reflect shifts in the writer's attention; as varied in language and sentence patterns as the voices of individual speakers; and as unevenly and loosely phrased as the hurried flow of writing dictates. Such writing sounds quite unpolished because fieldnotes in-the-making are not yet edited for readers.

After "getting it down," ethnographers can give more attention to other purposes for writing fieldnotes. After finishing a day's entry, a fieldworker may quickly reread what he has written, filling in with additional phrases and comments as he does so.[7] Such additions may describe

an experience as fully as possible; reflect on and express the field researcher's sense of the meaning or import of that experience; or self-consciously
try to persuade an envisioned, future reader to see that experience in a
particular way.

These different purposes and additions may produce even more
marked stylistic shifts in a set of fieldnotes. Getting it down results in a
loose, sporadic flow of writing; reflecting and making sense leads to an
entry with comments and questions; imagining an interested reader who
wishes to know more encourages longer and more vividly detailed notes.

Recalling in Order to Write

Ethnographers seem to rely upon a few standard ways of recalling and
organizing the day's events when writing full fieldnotes. One strategy is
to trace one's own activities and observations in chronological order, recalling noteworthy events in the sequence in which one observed and
experienced them. Another strategy is to begin with some "high point"
or an incident or event that stands out as particularly vivid or important,
to detail that event as thoroughly as possible, and then to consider in
some topical fashion other significant events, incidents, or exchanges. Or
the ethnographer may focus more systematically on incidents related to
specific topics of interest in order to recall significant events. Often ethnographers combine or alternate between strategies, proceeding back and
forth over time in stream of consciousness fashion.

As emphasized in the previous chapter, field researchers do not always
produce abbreviated, jotted accounts of what happened in a setting prior
to sitting down to write full fieldnotes. Under these circumstances, recalling witnessed events for writing begins from memory alone. Here the
ethnographer may simply pick some starting place—a key incident, the
beginning of her day in the field—and begin writing. Or she may start
by reviewing the day, event by event, and make decisions at each point
as to whether this or that is noteworthy. Finally, in beginning the writing-
up session, the fieldworker may employ any of these procedures to develop a listing or outline of events and topics to be covered.

Writing fieldnotes from jottings (or from a listing of topics developed
in preparation for writing) may follow a different course. Particularly if
the jottings are extensive, they can be used to organize the fieldnotes: the
fieldworker simply turns to the start of that day's jottings and moves

through in the order recorded, filling in and making connections between jotted segments on the basis of memory. In this sense, jottings anchor the writing process, providing a link back to the field. Ethnographers thus rely upon key words and phrases from their jottings to jog their memories. The issue, however, is not simply that, with jottings to rely on, fieldworkers can remember "everything." Rather, they can feel more secure about their ability to recall and to write about those scenes they found noteworthy while in the field.

Turning Jottings into Full Fieldnotes

Producing full fieldnotes from jottings is not a mechanical process. The fieldworker must construct something out of these bits and pieces of information together with the recollections of events, incidents, and experiences they inspire. The description that results must make sense as a logical, sensible series of incidents and experiences, even if only to an audience made up of the fieldworker herself.

In writing fieldnotes from jottings, the ethnographer moves back and forth between these jottings and the fuller, richer recollection of the events that occurred. To appreciate these processes, note the contrasts in content, texture, and comprehensibility between the initial jottings and the full fieldnotes concerning the court hearing on a requested temporary restraining order in the landlord-tenant dispute.

Jottings:[8]

[case number]
Snow, Marcia
Thomas   atty - AIDS Mike
                                               Murphy
                                               legal guardian

---

are you prepared to proceed against
the one individual — (both)
massive doses of chemother(apy)
I don't think he's ever going to come in
                                               here
I know he's well enough to walk —
came in (returned heater) — when?

you can call his doctor at UCLA and
he can verify all this
I just don't call people on the
telephone — courts don't operate that way — it has to be on paper or (in
person)

———

Mr. M returned my heaters —
was walking

———

Let me be clear
You dont want to proceed against
only one of these individuals?
I want to proceed against (no, but)
— if he is his guardian both — but

———

unravel it
Dept 10 —J(udge) Berkoff
Ms. S, hold on just a

Full Fieldnotes:

Marcia Snow has longish, curly, dark brown hair, in her 20s, dressed informally
in blue blouse and pants. No wedding ring, but with a youngish looking guy
with glasses. Robert Thomas is in his 40s, light brown hair, shaggy mustache,
jacket with red-black checked lining.

Judge begins by asking RT if he has an atty; he does, but he is not here. He
explains that his business partner, Mike Murphy, who is also named in the TRO,
is not here today; he has AIDS, and is very ill. "I'm his legal guardian," so I can
represent his concerns. J asks MS: "Are you prepared to proceed against the one
individual?" MS answers that she wants the order against both of them. RT then
explains that MM has had AIDS for three years, has had "massive doses of chemo-
therapy," and adds: "I don't think he's ever going to come in here." J asks MS if
from what she knows that MM is this sick. MS hesitates, then says: "I know he's
well enough to walk." I saw him walking when he returned the heaters that they
stole. J: When was this? (I can't hear her answer.) RT: He's had AIDS for three
years. He's very sick. "You can call his doctor at UCLA and he can verify this."
J: "I just don't call people on the telephone. Courts don't operate that way. It has
to be on paper" or testified to in person. RT repeats that MM is very ill, that he
has to take care of him, and he is not getting better. But MS again counters this,
saying again: "Mr. Murphy returned my heaters—he was walking then. . . ."

J then looks to MS, asking: "Let me be clear—you don't want to proceed
against only one of these individuals?" MS: "No, I want to proceed against both.
But if he is his guardian," then I can go ahead today with it. J agrees to this, saying
he will let another judge "unravel it," and assigns the case to Dept. 10, Judge
Berkoff. MS and RT turn to leave, but J says: "Ms. Snow, hold on just a minute
until the clerk has your file." MS waits briefly, then gets file and goes out with
the guy with her.

Compared to the highly selected, partial, and abbreviated jottings, the full fieldnotes tell a coherent, step-by-step story of what was observed in the courtroom. Most of this story consists of details that have been filled in from memory. The brief "background" of the case provided by the jottings, for example, has been fleshed out into relatively full descriptions of the two litigants (but not of the judge or other regular courtroom personnel). In addition, the notes tell a story about one specific topic—the problems arising from the absence of a co-defendant, the questions the judge raises about this absence, and a sequence of responses to this problem by the petitioner and defendant. The story, however, is missing key elements (for example, the fact that this case involves a tenant-landlord dispute) and contains elements of unknown meaning (for example, Marcia's comment about how the absent defendant "returned the heaters that they stole").

Also consider the handling of direct quotations in moving from jottings to fieldnotes. Only those words actually taken down at the time are placed in quotes; a portion of the direct speech missed at the time is paraphrased outside the direct quotes. Thus, the jotted record of the judge's remark, "it has to be on paper or (in person)" is written in fieldnote form as: "'It has to be on paper' or testified to in person." As a general practice, speech not written down word for word at the time should either be presented as indirect quotation or paraphrased (see chapter 4).

In general, writing fieldnotes from jottings is not a straightforward remembering and filling in; rather, it is a much more active process of constructing relatively coherent sequences of action and evocations of scene and character (see chapter 4). In turning jottings and headnotes into full notes, the fieldworker is already engaged in a sort of preliminary analysis whereby she orders experience, both creating and discovering patterns of interaction. This process involves deciding not simply *what to include* but also *what to leave out,* both from remembered headnotes and from items included in jottings. Thus, in writing full fieldnotes, the ethnographer may clearly remember or have jottings about particular incidents or impressions but decide for a variety of reasons not to incorporate them into the notes. The material may seem to involve matters that are peripheral to major activities in the setting, that members appear to find insignificant, or that the ethnographer has no interest in.

However, in continuing to write up the day's fieldnotes or at some later point in the fieldwork, the ethnographer may see significance in jottings or headnotes that initially seemed too unimportant or uninterest-ing to include in full fieldnotes. The student ethnographer who, in writ-ing full notes, had initially passed over a jotting about the "delivery of three new bags of sand" to the sandbox at a Headstart Program (chapter 2) saw relevance and meaning in this incident as she continued to write up and reflect on the day's observations:

Now that I'm thinking back, when we got the sand, it was a really hot day so that actually that jotting did help me remember because it was so warm out that Karen, the teacher, said that the children could take their shoes off in the sand box. This became a really tough rule to enforce because the children aren't al-lowed to have shoes off anywhere else. They would just run out of the sand box and go into the parking lot and so it was a really tough rule to enforce. And I have an incident about that.

In the comments made here, the student comes to appreciate (and con-struct) a linkage between the three new bags of sand included in her jottings and what she sees as significant issues of rule enforcement and control in the setting; with this appreciation, she decides to incorporate the delivery of the sand as an incident in her notes. Moreover, this focus on enforcement and control leads her to review her memory for "rele-vant" events or "incidents"; here she recollects "an incident about that," signaling her intent to write up this incident in her notes.

In light of the ways "significance" shifts and emerges in the course of writing notes and thinking about their import, we encourage students to write about as many of these "minor" events as possible, even if they seem insubstantial or only vaguely relevant at the moment. They may signal important processes relevant to other incidents or to emerging ana-lytic themes in ways the ethnographer may only appreciate at some later point. Even when writing the story of one rather cohesive event, writers should include apparently tangential activities and comments, for they may turn out to provide key insights into the main action.

Multiple Voices and Points of View

In writing fieldnotes, an ethnographer not only remembers and envisions a scene; he also presents that scene from a selected angle which highlights some of its features more than others. This angling results in part from theoretical concerns of the researcher's discipline; it also results in part from the nature of his participation in the field—for example, from his inevitably selective positioning and from identifying with certain members' experiences. In writing, the ethnographer thus reconstructs memories—prompted by jottings and headnotes—which privilege certain observational perspectives and certain members' experiences over others.

The selective tendencies of field participation and memory construction are supplemented by the fact that ethnographers, like all writers recounting events, must unavoidably tell their story through a particular "point of view." By convention, "point of view" refers to the written perspective on events, i.e., through whose eyes events are seen as well as through whose voice they are described. Point of view refers to the perspective through which the story gets told, through whose view the characters, actions, setting, and events will be presented to the reader. Although authors have developed varied and complex ways to tell a story, the most general distinctions are between first-person, third-person, and omniscient points of view (Abrams 1988:144–48).

The First-person Point of View

A first-person mode "limits the point of view to what the first-person narrator knows, experiences, infers, or can find out by talking with other characters" (Abrams 1988:146). In fieldnotes, the first-person "I" telling the story is the ethnographer himself. Since this perspective most readily encourages the writer to recount his own experiences, responses, and commentary as well as the actions and talk of others, we suggest that an ethnographer often write in the first person. In writing fieldnotes in the first person, the researcher presents the details he saw, experienced, and now remembers from his own perspective and in his own voice.

Writing in the first person is particularly effective when the ethnographer is also a member of the group she is studying. Seeing incidents through her eyes allows us to see an insider's view of actions, as filtered through her concerns as an ethnographer. In addition, the first-person point of view allows the ethnographer to present the natural unfolding of experience as seen from her participant's viewpoint.

The following fieldnote, written in the first person, illustrates these qualities. In this excerpt, an observer employed in an upscale eyeglass establishment recounts an upsetting incident of sexual harassment by one of the owners of the store:

About halfway through the day, I am standing in the front section with Richard, one of the owners, and Al, the manager, who's on door duty. I reach down to get a sunglass to try on and say, "Oooo, these are great," as I pull out the plastic stop-sign shaped frames. Richard mutters something like "no" to tell me that they won't be good on me. I notice that they are Lunettes, the manufacturer of VVO glasses, and am surprised that I've never seen these and that Richard is so quick to judge the result. I put them on and ask Richard, "What do you think?" He looks at me and says, "You've got really great tits, don't you." I think he has said, "You've got really great taste, don't you," so I say, "Yeah, these are great," as I look at myself in the mirror. (I also believe that when I don't have my glasses on and I can't see, that I also cannot hear. I have reconstructed Richard's words as he said them, from his next clarifying statement, and did not just put in my interpretation.) I look at Richard. He says, "They're really great tits." I utter a low "Huh?" (I now go back to his first statement in my mind, and understand that I had misheard his suggestion of my great taste in eyeglasses. Maybe on some level I heard him correctly the first time, but recast it as something else; denial restores equilibrium.) He continues, "Really firm and high—really firm," gesturing at this point with his hands like he's feeling breasts. I am stunned and cross my arms across my chest. (I did this unconsciously, as it wasn't until Richard's next line that I had realized I had done this gesture of protection.) He continues, "You cover yourself up." He folds his arms: "Never seen you get shy before." He then puffs up his chest as if to strut (as if to show me what I usually do, or what he expects me to usually do). "That's not appropriate," I say softly.

By writing in the first person, this ethnographer not only can present what the offender, Richard, said and what she said and did in response; but also she can reveal how she felt and thought about her experience: "I am stunned. . . ." In this instance of abusive remarks inserted into an otherwise innocuous conversation, the ethnographer's expression of her feelings of withdrawal and self-protection reveal, more fully than any mere record of his words ever could have, how truly distasteful and offensive his remarks were to her. Were it written in the third person, the fieldnote would have lost her insider's view—her inner thoughts and feelings changing as the incident unfolded. Nor would the fieldnote have revealed the way the owner's insistence in repeating the offensive remark transforms her earlier hearing of the comment and causes her "to cross my arms across my chest" in a "gesture of protection." This insistent repetition accentuates and makes the offensiveness of these remarks pointed and unescapable.

Moreover, by using the first person, the fieldnote can portray both the author's experience as a member and her reflections as a writing ethnographer. For example, she reconstructs and presents her experience of sexual harassment so that we see how she initially experienced it as a salesperson talking to the store owner—mishearing him to say, "You have great taste," a remark more appropriate to their work relationship and to presenting glasses to customers. But we also hear her commentary on her experience, inserted in an aside as she writes the fieldnote, on why she initially misheard his offensive comment: "Maybe on some level I heard him correctly the first time, but recast it as something else; denial restores equilibrium."

The Third-person Point of View

Although such first-person fieldnotes allow the researcher to express her thoughts and feelings well, the primary aim of ethnography is to describe what others are doing and saying. Writing in the third-person point of view is particularly effective for conveying others' words and actions. We suggest that the ethnographer write many of his fieldnotes from this perspective to report what he sees others doing and saying.

Writing fieldnotes from the third-person point of view does not demand that the writer entirely avoid first-person pronouns or invariably absent herself from her fieldnotes. Within primarily third-person fieldnote accounts of others, the writer can include herself as a participant-observer in the scene and insert her own responses in first-person asides. For example, in observing and participating in the *mukanda* rituals (initiations for boys) in Kabompo District, Northwest Province of Zambia, Rachel Fretz often wrote fieldnotes which described the activities of others.[9] These descriptions are primarily third-person accounts, though she occasionally inserts her first-person perspective. In the following excerpt, for example, she looks out at what others are doing and occasionally inserts "I" statements in recounting moments of active participation and in describing her responses.

That afternoon we heard the women and children hollering as though a *Iyishi* had come and we [another researcher and I] ran down [to the center of the village] with our cameras. It was *Kalulu,* the rabbit mask. He is a small, lithe figure dressed in a grass skirt and grass shirt around his neck. On his arms and legs he wears the usual fiber costume, a net-like fitted body "overall," and his mask is a small red and white painted face with two large cloth ears. He calls out a nasalized, "Wha, wha." It sounds like a child's cry. He hopped around the yard and half-ran toward the children. Then the Headman told the women to dance with him; so D, his daughter, called some women and children together and they turned their backs toward the Rabbit, *Kalulu,* and sang and danced. . . . Now and then Kalulu rather listlessly chased a woman or child. And then all of a sudden, he used his small

switch and ran right up to a girl and switched her. The children ran away shriek-
ing and the Rabbit ran over to J's house. Shortly it came back.

And then it seems that the Headman called John over and gave him some
directions because after that John went and found Kianze, the eight-year-old girl
who lives with N (she's her grandchild) and grabbed her firmly by the arm and
held on and dragged her screaming over toward *Kalulu*, the Rabbit, who reached
to catch her.

She ran screaming in the other direction and John went after her again and
grabbed her and pulled her toward the Rabbit. Kianze, looking over her shoulder,
seemed thoroughly terrified and screamed and screamed with tears running down
her face. (I felt horrified as I watched.) This time the Rabbit swatted her and she
ran still screaming into her house. And the mask ran after her and entered the
house. But she managed, I was told later, to hide under a bed.

Then, *Kalulu* ran after Jinga and he caught her and picked her up in his arms.
Jinga screamed too, but she did not seem so terrified and did not cry. Someone
said later that N [her grandmother] yelled at him to get her back, for the mask
had started to carry her down the path toward the *mukanda* camp.

Around this time, I noticed that Ana [the other young girl] had disappeared.
(Someone said she ran out into the bush and hid.) It seemed the Rabbit thought
she was hiding in her house, for he started to chase her mother, Nyana, who ran
swiftly into the house and slammed the door shut. Since it was a solid wooden
door which she held shut, the Rabbit could not push it open. . . .

(Truly, *Kalulu* Rabbit is a trickster who plays and dances and then turns on
people.) The next day I asked John why he grabbed Kianze and Jinga; he said it
was because they were supposed to go to school, but that they just left home but
did not actually go into the school every day. After a while, the mask ran off
down the *mukanda* path and I went home, still shocked by the mask's treatment
of the two girls.

Although the ethnographer in writing these fieldnotes focuses primarily on others—the masked dancer, the screaming girls, the grandmother—she occasionally includes her responses to the frightened girls
as "I" remarks inserted within her description. Had she quoted the out-
cries of the young girls and of the grandmother calling for someone to
rescue her granddaughter, she could have augmented the sense of seeing
the chase from a more immediate, close-up position. However, since she
was doing her research in the Chokwe language in a multilingual area
and these particular people were speaking Lunda and Luvale, she could
not provide direct quotes. Thus, her descriptions report their actions,
screams, and what others speaking Kichokwe told her. Indeed, ethnographers should only write what they actually see and hear others do and
say; they should write as reported speech what others repeat to them.

When an ethnographer tracks closely the activities of one person for a period of time, he can write from a *focused third-person* perspective in which he limits his descriptions to what that member saw, did, and said. Field researchers may self-consciously write from the point of view of a person directly involved in the scene or action. They may do so by describing an event from that person's actual physical location, by selecting details the person seems to notice, and by including the person's own words describing the event. For example, in telling about a fight between parents from the child's point of view, a writer might not only narrate using many of the child's words but also describe only those details a child might notice, such as the loud voices, threatening movements, and the large size of those fighting. Though the researcher might make inferences about thoughts and feelings, he would base them on observable facial expressions, gestures, and talk, and describe these from the child's perspective.

Use of the focused third person in writing often enables the field researcher to more fully sense an individual member's outlook and to pursue questions and issues of interest to that person. For example, while studying traditional healing methods in an African culture, the researcher might track the activities of a healer for a day: going with him to make his medicines, sitting beside him as he treats his patients, and resting with him after his duties (cf. Yoder 1982). By staying closely involved in one member's activities and then describing what that person pays attention to, does, and says, the ethnographer is more likely to get a sense of his perspective. However, the researcher should not attribute motives or try to depict what the healer is thinking; rather, the writer limits her fieldnotes to what she observed the healer do and actually heard him say. Indeed, verbatim quoting, along with accompanying gestures and facial expressions, is one of the most effective means of portraying a person's views.

Clearly, the field researcher who actually takes different observational positions and participates empathetically with different people can more effectively write from different focused third-person perspectives and document the multiple voices in the setting.[10] For example, in writing notes on a check-out line in a grocery store, the fieldworker might describe activities, at different times, from the position and perspective of the checker, the bagger, a customer being served, and customers waiting in line. Members' voices and views most clearly are heard by faithfully recording their accounts and dialogues.

The Omniscient Point of View

An ethnographer can also write in the third person but adopt an omniscient point of view. In this point of view a writer assumes "privileged access to the characters' thoughts and feelings and motives, as well as to their overt speech and action" (Abrams 1988:145). Ethnographers who write from this point of view use an "objective" tone and style to report events as "realist tales" (Van Maanen 1988). In adopting this all-knowing stance, the writer can freely move from one time and place to another and readily shift between characters. Indeed, with an omniscient perspective a writer may describe not only characters' observable movements and talk but also their innermost thoughts, feelings, and motivations. And because this point of view positions the writer as a detached observer above or outside events, she then can depict characters and actions with near-divine insight into prior causes and ultimate outcomes.

Had the fieldworker studying *mukanda* rituals in Zambia taken an omniscient perspective, she would have recounted the intense and frenzied dancing, drumming, and singing of the whole village throughout the prior night. Then she might have described the feelings of the young boys—perhaps fear and excitement—waiting to be rushed at dawn into the camp for circumcision. Certainly, the masked figure dancing to the drumming would also have drawn her attention, and she would have described his raffia costume and the black-and-red decorations on the mask. From her unlimited perspective, she also might have described the circumcision taking place in the boy's camp out in the bush, with the fathers, brothers, and uncles attending. (Her descriptions of this gender-delineated, all-male place would have had to be based on interviews.) Next, she might have turned to the mothers, other women, and children, back in the village, to report not only the singing and the ritual pouring of water on the mothers' heads, but also to describe their thoughts—whether nervousness or joy—as they waited to hear from the camp leader that their sons had been successfully circumcised.

This ethnographer, of course, did not actually write her fieldnotes in such an omniscient manner, although she did describe many of these ritual actions as she saw them or as others reported them to her. Indeed, it would have been practically impossible to have written an omniscient account of every aspect without having devoted many hours to interviewing people about events she was unable to witness directly and about their thoughts and feelings about these matters. Moreover, an interactionist and interpretive stance generally militates against using an omniscient perspective in writing fieldnotes. An omniscient style produces fieldnotes that: merge the ethnographer's participatory experience with reports from others; conceal the complex processes of uncovering the varied understandings of what an event is about; reduce and blend multiple perspectives into accounts delivered in a single, all-knowing voice; and ignore the highly contingent interpretations required to reconcile and/or prioritize competing versions of the event.[11]

Combining and Varying Points of View

Regardless of the point of view assumed in writing fieldnotes, conscientious ethnographers always keep their writing circumscribed by what they saw and heard, sticking to actual details they witnessed and to actual accounts they received. Thus, whether the author takes a first-person, a third-person, or an omniscient point of view, the writing inevitably comes from that ethnographer's experience; she inevitably represents her knowledge and understanding of others' experiences. But the degree to which the researcher becomes involved in people's doings implicitly shapes the perspective from which she can write about some incidents. Involvement allows the writer to write from a "near" perspective and to present details as seen by a member and, by quoting, to present a member's voice. In contrast, even when writing in the first person, a physically or emotionally "distant" perspective often results in more generalized descriptions presented in a reportorial tone of voice.

Fieldnotes can also move from one perspective to another, in part because the researcher constantly shifts her attention between self and others. Fieldnotes should balance sensitivity to people's experiences of events with self-conscious awareness of the observer's own perceptions and reactions to these others. This shifting back and forth readily shows up in changing voices and points of view.

On the one hand, the field researcher attends to and writes about what events mean to members. He gives special attention to routine events that occur frequently in that setting; even if people take these events for granted and show little explicit interest in them, such events occupy a great deal of their time and energy. The ethnographer also attends to issues or incidents that seem of special interest or significance to members; the goal is both to discover what such issues are and to discern the specific meanings that members attach to them. In writing with this intention, the fieldworker often uses a limited third-person point of view and frequently quotes members so that their voices can be heard.

On the other hand, the ethnographer cannot neglect her own involvement in observed scenes, in making the observations, and in writing them up. We expect an ethnographer's presence to be not only seen but heard in the day-to-day descriptions. Thus, the goal is not merely a picture of the daily life and concerns of others, but rather a picture of this life and these concerns as seen, understood, and conveyed by the ethnographer. Here, for example, the ethnographer includes features and occurrences that are unexpected, that stand in contrast with what she is used to, or that generate strong emotional reactions. In writing such fieldnotes, she often writes in the first person because she focuses on her reactions to events and people. Including herself in the interactions, she quotes both herself and others.

In sum, while an ethnographer writes particular segments from a single point of view, the fieldnotes as a whole shift. The fieldworker moves from describing events observed at one position, point in time, and perspective to descriptions constructed from other points of view.

"Real-Time" and "End-Point" Descriptions

In writing descriptive accounts, ethnographers face an additional choice: whether to describe an event "in real time" from a perspective of incomplete or partial knowledge, or to describe it from some end point of more complete knowledge.

In real-time descriptions, the writer seeks to characterize events using only what is known at discrete points as the event unfolds; thus, the writer tries to avoid using information that will ultimately come out but as of yet is not available for describing what happened at those prior moments. By way of illustration, consider the way in which the following description of approaching a skid row mission excludes key meanings until they are actually discovered by the writer:

The whole area around the Mission, including the alley, was dense with people, more so than the surrounding blocks. Probably eighty percent of these people were black; about ninety percent were male. People lay, sat or stood all along the aqua colored walls of the Mission. . . . The people on the left-hand side of the door gave the impression of being in line: they all were standing at fairly uniform distances, and the same people were standing in line throughout the several hours

I was around the Mission. When I later read the Mission's literature, I realized that these people were likely waiting in line for the privilege of spending the night in the Mission. The literature noted that "sleep tickets" were given out at 12:30 pm and that the line formed early. Interesting, there were many more people in back of the Mission in what I perceived to be the lunch line than were in the sleep line.

This real time account preserves the writer's experience of seeing an assemblage of people and not quite knowing what they were doing. That they were "in line" is not initially used to characterize the scene, but is presented as an in-process discovery; some effort is made to specify initial grounds for describing these people as "in line," e.g., "uniform distance," continuity over time. The later discovery of the "purpose" of these activities—to get a "sleep ticket" allowing one to spend the night in the Mission—is explicitly described; only then is this assemblage characterized as "the sleep line."

In contrast, field researchers may also describe events by making full use of what they ultimately came to know and understand about them. This procedure incorporates "facts" or understandings subsequently established in order to describe or characterize what was going on at earlier stages. In describing a formal business meeting in this way, for example, an observer would from the very start of the notes describe participants by name and position, even though she had only come to learn these matters over the course of the meeting.

In general, this procedure for writing about events uses understandings obtained only at some "end point" as a resource for describing what happened at earlier moments. In observing new scenes, we often use what we ultimately come to know to describe events and meanings that we had initially not understood or had understood partially or incorrectly. Indeed, observation involves continuous processes of such *retrospective reinterpretation,* as the observer shapes into more definitive form what at some earlier point had been hazy, ambiguous, or downright confusing (Garfinkel 1967). Written ethnographic descriptions may also incorporate such retrospective reinterpretations. A fieldworker observing on a bus, for example, may note that a "crazy woman" boarded and talked to the driver. If this woman's "craziness" only became apparent as she talked to the driver and other passengers, it represents an evaluation inferred from an ongoing course of interaction; to characterize her as "crazy" from her initial appearance in the scene obscures these processes and strips the written account of any consideration of how her disorientation became visible to the observer. On the other hand, it might have been that her presenting appearance and initial demeanor made this passenger's "craziness" evident "at a glance" to the fieldworker (and presumably to any culturally competent member of American urban society). In this case to characterize this person as "crazy" right from the start raises an issue of adequate description rather than of retrospective interpretation; "crazy" is a highly evaluative term that should be accompanied by some description of whatever observable features led to such a judgment in the first place. In general, descriptively effective fieldnotes will enable a reader to distinguish initial understandings from retrospective reinterpretations.

Some retrospective reinterpretation of this sort is practically unavoidable. For many purposes, we are not interested either in the initial interpretations an observer made of people based on woefully incomplete information or in just how the observer figured out who and what these people were and what they were doing. Yet there are times and occasions when the field researcher may want to preserve initial understandings— however misguided—and the actual process of determining meaning.

One such occasion is when the ethnographer wants to highlight the natural unfolding of experience. For example, the account of the sexual harassment incident presented earlier in this chapter uses the owner's subsequent comment to reconstruct the writer's actual hearing of his first abusive comment as "what he must have said." This tactic compels the writer to backtrack to explain how such a "mishearing" could have occurred, thus emphasizing the separation and contrast between "what actually occurred" from "what the observer/writer experienced." An alternative would have been to present the incident exactly as experienced: report the owner's first comment as "you've got really great taste, don't you?"; then indicate how his second comment, "you've got great tits," transformed the previous hearing. This descriptive procedure would allow the reader to share the observer's shock in ways that more closely reflect the temporal unfolding of the experience.

An ethnographer may also want to minimize the degree of retrospective reinterpretation in order to highlight his own processes for determining meaning. To return to our earlier example: if a fieldworker were interested in how participants in a business meeting come to figure out who the others present are, then he might focus on describing just how he came to figure out these identities, writing the notes in a way that preserved the initial lack of definiteness in these matters. These descriptive procedures allow the reader to share at least part of the observer/

writer's actual experience of discovering meaning. It also brings the observer/writer to the center of the process of establishing meaning and hence "de-objectivizes" the description; a description of how a "sleep line" outside a skid row mission came to be discovered as such shows the observer/writer to be an active interpreter of the social world.

In summary, whether writing in "real time" in order to reveal the process or in an "end-point" storytelling mode, the writer learns through writing about her experiences. In the process of writing up, an ethnographer assimilates and thereby starts to understand an experience: she makes sense of that moment by intuitively selecting, highlighting, and ordering details and by beginning to appreciate their linkages with or contrasts to previously observed and described experiences. In these respects, writing fieldnotes is more than a process of remembering and getting it down. Rather, writing fieldnotes promotes learning and deepens understanding about what has been seen and heard in the field.[12] Especially when learning an entirely unfamiliar way of life, researchers benefit from writing about their experiences, for through writing they learn to understand what may seem, at first, unusual and overwhelming. Indeed, ethnographers often want to write because they realize that writing is a way of seeing, that a lived experience is not only preserved but also is illuminated through writing about it.

REFLECTIONS: "WRITING" AND "READING" MODES

To characterize fieldnotes as descriptions initially conveys the prospect of simple, straightforward writing. But once we recognize that description involves more than a one-to-one correspondence between written accounts and what is going on, writing fieldnotes raises complex, perplexing problems. Descriptions are grounded on the observer/writer's participation in the setting, but no two persons participate in and experience a setting in exactly the same way. Moreover, there is always more going on than the ethnographer can notice, and it is impossible to record all that can be noticed. Description inevitably involves different theories, purposes, interests, and points of view. Hence, fieldnotes contain descriptions that are more akin to a series of stories portraying slices of life in vivid detail than to a comprehensive, literal, or objective rendering.[13]

The ethnographer, however, needs to avoid getting drawn into the complexities of fieldnote descriptions while actually writing fieldnotes.

She must initially work in a *writing mode,* putting into words and on paper what has been seen and heard as quickly and efficiently as possible. In this text-producing mode, the ethnographer tries to "get it down" as accurately and completely as possible, avoiding too much self-consciousness about the writing process itself. She stays close to the events at issue, rekindling her excitement about these events, getting on with the task of inscribing them before memory fades. The writing ethnographer tries to "capture what is out there," or more accurately, to construct detailed accounts of her own observations and experience of what is "out there." At this point, too much reflection distracts or even paralyzes; one tries to write without editing, to produce detailed descriptions without worry about analytic import and connections, to describe what happened without too much self-conscious reflection.

Only subsequently, once a text has actually been produced, can the ethnographer really step back and begin to consider the complexities which permeate fieldnote descriptions; only with fully detailed fieldnotes can the ethnographer adopt a *reading mode* and begin to reflect on how these accounts are products of his own often implicit decisions about how to participate in and describe events. That is, only with full notes in hand does it make sense to view these writings as texts that are truncated, partial, and perspectival, products of the ethnographer's own styles of participating, orienting, and writing. It is at this point that the ethnographer can begin to treat fieldnotes as constructions, to read them for the ways they *create* rather than simply record reality.

One key difference between initially working in a writing mode and subsequently in a reflexive reading mode lies in how the ethnographer orients to issues of "accuracy," to "correspondence" between a written account and what it is an account of. In the moment of writing the ethnographer must try to create some close correspondence between the written account and his experiences and observations of "what happened." The immediate task in writing fieldnote descriptions is to create a detailed, accurate, and comprehensive account of what has been experienced. But once notes have been written, this correspondence criterion may lose salience. "What happened" has been filtered through the person and writing of the observer onto the written page. The resulting text "fixes" a social reality in place, but in a way that makes it difficult to determine its relationship with realities outside that text. Readers may attempt to do so by invoking what they know from having "been there" or from experience with a similar reality. But readers are heavily constrained by what is on the page; they usually lack any effective means of gaining access to "what actually happened" independently of the written account. In such a reading mode, then, self-conscious, self-critical reflection on how writing choices have helped construct specific texts and textual realities becomes both possible and appropriate.

chapter four

Writing Up Fieldnotes II: Creating Scenes on the Page

To view writing fieldnotes simply as a matter of putting on paper what a field researcher has heard and seen suggests that it is a transparent process; in this view, field researchers "mirror" observed reality in their notes. They describe without elaborate rhetoric, intricate metaphors, or complex, suspenseful narration. Writing detailed description, this view suggests, requires only a sharp memory and conscientious effort.

A contrasting view insists that all writing, even seemingly straightforward descriptive writing, is a construction. Through his choice of words and method of organization, a writer presents a *version* of the world. As a selective and creative activity, writing always functions more as a filter than a mirror reflecting the "reality" of events. Ethnographers, however, have only recently come to appreciate this view, and to see how even "realist" ethnographies are constructions which rely upon a variety of stylistic conventions. Van Maanen (1988:47), for example, has identified "studied neutrality" as a core convention in realist ethnography; through this convention "the narrator . . . poses as an impersonal conduit, who unlike missionaries, administrators, journalists, or unabashed members of the culture themselves, passes on more-or-less objective data in a measured intellectual style that is uncontaminated by personal bias, political goals, or moral judgments."

As with completed ethnographies, descriptive fieldnotes also draw on a variety of writing conventions. Ethnographers construct their fieldnote descriptions from selectively recalled and accented moments. Whether it be an incident, event, routine, interaction, or visual image, ethnographers reconstruct each moment from selected details which they remember or had jotted down: words, gestures, body movements, sounds, background setting, etc. While writing, they further highlight certain actions and statements more than others in order to portray their sense of an experience. In other words, ethnographers create scenes on a page through highly selective and partial descriptions of observed and reevoked details. These scenes—that is, moments recreated on a page—represent ethnographers' perceptions and memories of slices of life, enhanced or blurred by their descriptive writing skills.

In this chapter, we explore the relations between an ethnographer's attention to people's sayings and doings, immediate purposes for recalling these moments, and writing options for presenting and analyzing them. Of course, no writing technique enables an ethnographer to write up life exactly as it happened or even precisely as she remembers it. At best, the ethnographer "recreates" her memories as written scenes which authentically depict people's lives through selected, integrated details. But in mastering certain descriptive techniques, she can write up her notes more easily in that first dash of getting everything down; and she can depict more effectively those scenes which she intuitively selects as especially significant. Whether she writes up key scenes first or goes back to them to fill in details, learning descriptive writing strategies will enable her to more vividly and fully create those scenes on the page.

We begin this chapter by examining writing strategies for *depicting* slices of observed and remembered life in fieldnotes; specifically, we consider strategies for *describing* basic settings, for *presenting dialogue* between people, and for *characterizing* the main individuals who appear in the account. Second, we present options for *organizing* fieldnote descriptions: *sketches* and then two forms of narrative, *episodes* and *fieldnote tales*. (Although we discuss depicting and organizing strategies separately, in actual fieldnote writing one does both at the same time.) Third, we examine several *strategies of analysis* which, in contrast to descriptive writing, allow for in-process reflection through *asides* and *commentary* about the fieldnotes being written. Such reflection about fieldnotes not only spurs the ethnographer to envision scenes more clearly the next time he sees similar events, but it also facilitates tracing out potential interconnections between events recounted in the fieldnotes.

Throughout the chapter, we focus our suggestions on increasing fieldworkers' awareness of their options for writing. For example, first-time fieldworkers typically have little difficulty in writing snippets about brief interactions; however, they are often uncertain about how to write about more complex, key scenes by sequencing interactions, creating characters, reporting dialogue, and contextualizing an action or incident with vivid, sensory details. Failing to write in-process commentary, they overlook obvious connections which they might pursue. But though we offer many concrete suggestions and examples, we do not attempt to prescribe a "correct" style or to cover all the writing options an ethnographer might use. Yet, we do suggest that one's writing style does often influence how one envisions what can be written. An ethnographer committed to an "objective" writing style presented in the passive voice and with neutral, colorless wording will often overlook human agency and will more likely skip over the more messy (and often most interesting) details of human experience. Learning to envision scenes as vivid, detailed writing on a page is as much a commitment to a lively descriptive style of writing as it is to an intellectual honesty in recording events fully and accurately.

WRITING DETAILED NOTES: DEPICTION OF SCENES

The ethnographer's central purpose is to describe a social world and its people. But often beginning researchers produce fieldnotes lacking sufficient and lively detail. Through inadvertent summarizing and evaluative wording, a fieldworker fails to adequately describe what she observed and experienced. The following strategies enable a writer to coherently depict an observed moment through vivid details: these strategies are description, presentation of dialogue, and characterization. As is evident in several of the included excerpts, fieldworkers often merge several strategies.

Description

"Description" is a term used in more than one way. Thus far, we have referred to writing fieldnotes as descriptive writing in contrast to analytic argumentation.[1] Here we refer more specifically to description as a means of picturing through concrete sensory details the basic scenes, settings, objects, people, and actions the fieldworker observed. In this sense, writing descriptive images is just one part of the ethnographer's storytelling about a day's events.

As a writing strategy, description calls for concrete details rather than abstract generalizations, for sensory imagery rather than evaluative labels, and for immediacy through details presented at close range. Goffman (1989:131) advises the fieldworker to write "lushly," making frequent use of adjectives and adverbs to convey details. For example, details present color, shape, and size to create visual images; other details of sound, timbre, loudness, and volume evoke auditory images; those details describing smell or fragrance recreate olfactory images; and details portraying gestures, movements, posture, and facial expression convey kinetic images. While visual images tend to predominate in many descriptions, ethnographers find that they often combine these various kinds of images in a complete description.

When describing a scene, the writer selects those details which most clearly and vividly create an image on the page; consequently, he succeeds best in describing when he selects details according to some purpose and from a definite point of view. For example, the writer acquires a clearer sense of what details to accent if he takes as his project describing not the office setting for his observations, but the office environment as a cluttered place to work, perhaps as seen from the secretary's perspective who struggles with her boss's disorder every day. However, frequently the fieldworker sits down to write about a setting he does not yet understand. In fact, the beginning ethnographer often faces the dilemma of not knowing what counts as most important; under these circumstances his purpose is simply to document the impression he has at that time. Wanting to recall the physical characteristics and the sensory impressions of his experiences, a fieldworker often describes the setting and social situations, characters' appearances, and even some daily routines.

Ethnographers often select details to describe the ambience of a setting or environment that is important for understanding subsequent action. For example, during initial fieldwork in a village in southeastern Zaire, an ethnographer might reflect on the spacial arrangement and social relations as she has observed them thus far. In her fieldnotes, she might describe how the houses all face toward an open, cleared area; that the village pavilion where men visit is situated in the center; that the women cook by wood fires in front of their houses, often carrying babies on their backs as they work and are assisted by younger girls; that some men and boys sit under a tree in the yard near two other men weaving baskets. How she perceives these details and the way she frames them as contextualizing social interactions determines, in part, the details she selects to create this visual image of a small village in the late afternoon.

An ethnographer should also depict the appearance of characters who arc part of described scenes in order to contextualize actions and talk. For example, in looking at how residents adapted to conditions in a psychiatric board-and-care home, Linda Shaw described someone who others living in the home thought was especially "crazy":

Robert and I were sitting by the commissary talking this afternoon when a new resident named Bruce passed by several times. He was a tall, extremely thin man with straggly, shoulder-length, graying hair and a long bushy beard. I had heard that he was only in his thirties, even though he looked prematurely aged in a way that reminded me of the sort of toll that harsh conditions exact from many street people. He wore a long, dirty, gray-brown overcoat with a rainbow sewn to the back near the shoulder over a pair of torn blue jeans and a white tee shirt with what looked like coffee stains down the front. Besides his disheveled appearance, Bruce seemed extremely agitated and restless as he paced from one end of the facility to the other. He walked with a loping gait, taking very long strides, head held bent to his chest and his face expressionless, as his arms swung limply through the air, making a wide arc, as though made of rubber. As Bruce passed by on one of these rounds, Robert remarked, "That guy's really crazy. Don't tell me he's going to be recycled into society."

Here the ethnographer provides a detailed description of a newcomer to the home to provide the context necessary to understand a resident's comment that this person was too crazy to ever live outside of the home.

While describing appearance might initially seem easy, in fact many observers have difficulty doing so in lively, engaging ways. Part of the problem derives from the fact that when we observe people whom we do not know personally, we initially see them in very stereotyped ways; we normally notice and describe strangers in terms of gender, age, race, along with other qualities of their physical appearance.[2] Thus, beginning fieldworkers invariably identify characters by gender. They frequently add one or two visible features: "a young woman," "a young guy in a floral shirt," "two Latina women with a small child," "a woman in her forties," "a white male with brown/blond medium length hair." Indeed, many fieldnotes present characters as *visual cliches,* relying on worn out, frequently used details to describe others, often in ways that invoke common stereotypes: a middle-aged librarian is simplistically described as "a bald man wearing thick glasses," a youth in juvenile hall as having "slicked back hair," a lawyer as "wearing a pin-striped suit" and "carrying a brief-case." Such cliches not only make for boring writing, but also more dangerously blind the writer to specific attributes of the person in front of him.

The description of a character's appearance is frequently "categoric" and stereotyped for another reason as well: fieldworkers rely upon these cliches not so much to convey anothers' appearance to envisioned readers, but to label (and thus provide clarity about) who is doing what within the fieldnote account. For example, a fieldworker used the phrase "the floral shirt guy" a number of times to specify which character he was talking about when he described the complicated comings and goings occurring in a Latino street scene. Thus the initial description does not provide many details about this character's appearance, but merely tags him so that we can identify and follow him in the subsequent account.

However, the ethnographer must train herself both to notice more than these common indicators of general social categories and to capture distinctive qualities that will enable future readers (whether herself in re-reading notes or others who read excerpts) to envision more of what she saw and experienced. A *vivid image* based on actual observation depicts specific details about people and settings so that the image can be clearly visualized. For example, one fieldworker described a man in a skid row mission as "a man in the back who didn't have any front teeth and so spoke with a lisp." Another described a boy in a third-grade classroom as "wiggling his butt and distorting his face for attention" on entering the classroom late. Such images use details to paint more specific, lively portraits and avoid as much as possible vague, stereotypic features.

Ethnographers can also write more vivid descriptions by describing how characters dress. The following excerpt depicts a woman's clothes through concrete and sensory imagery:

Today Molly, a white female, wore her African motif jacket. It had little squares on the front which contained red, yellow, green, and black colored prints of the African continent. Imposed on top was a gold lion of Judah (symbol of Ethiopian Royal Family). The sleeves were bright—red, yellow, and green striped. The jacket back had a picture of Bob Marley singing into a microphone. He is a black male with long black dreadlocks and a little beard. Written in red at the top was: "Rastafari."

This description advances the ethnographer's concern with ethnic identity and affiliation. The initial sentence, "Today Molly, a white female, wore her African motif jacket," sets up an unexpected contrast: Molly is white, yet she wears an item of clothing that the researcher associates with African-American culture. "African motif" directs attention to particular attributes of the jacket (colors, insignia, and symbols) and ignores other observable qualities of the jacket, e.g., its material, texture, style, cleanliness, or origins. Consequently, this description frames the jacket as an object publicly announcing its wearer's affiliation with African-Americans.[3]

Furthermore, rather than simply *telling* the reader what the ethnographer infers, this passage *shows* affiliation with African-Americans in immediate detail, through actions and imagery. Contrast this descriptive strategy with the following (hypothetical) abstract and evaluative depiction which generalizes rather than specifies details: "Today, Molly, a white girl, *assertively* wore her *bright African* jacket. She always *shows off* in these clothes and *struts* around *like a black*." Not only does this summary rely on a vague adjective (bright), but it also obscures the actions with evaluative adverbs and verbs (assertively, struts, and shows off) and categorizing labels (like a black).

Because an ethnographer wishes to depict a scene for a reader, he does not condense details, avoids evaluative adjectives and verbs, and never permits a label to stand for description. While all writing entails grouping and identifying details, the ethnographer resists the impulse to unselfconsciously label others according to received categories from his own background. Nonetheless, it is not enough to avoid evaluative wording. In descriptions, the writer's tone of voice unavoidably reflects his personal attitude toward the people described. A better-than-thou attitude or an objectifying of the other (as odd, a foreigner, from a lower class, from a less civilized culture) always "shows" in subtle ways: tone, like a slip-of-tongue, appears in word choice, implicit comparisons, and even in rhythms as in the staccato of a curt dismissal. A self-reflective ethnographer should make his judgments explicit in written asides. But, the best antidote to these evaluative impulses is to keep in mind that the ethnographer's task is to write description that leads to an empathetic understanding of the social worlds of others.

In addition to describing people, places, and things, an ethnographer might also depict a scene primarily through action. For example, she might portray a character's talk, gesture, posture, and movement. In contrast to describing a person's appearance, action sequences highlight a character's agency to affect her world; a character acts within a situation, in response to a condition or to interactions with others in ways that shape future interactions. Through actions, characters move through space and time; thus writers aim to capture the dynamic quality of action and its forward movement—something happens!

The following exchange between teacher and student focuses on the student's actions and the teacher's responses in a class for the "deaf and hard-of-hearing":

> Bobbie walks in, swaying from side to side, and looks around. The teacher asks him where he had been and Bobbie mumbles something. Then he starts walking over to the computer and says that he wants to work on it, but the teacher replies, "No, Bobbie I want you to sit down here and see if you can play with us." Bobbie sits down at one end of the board [to a game]. He notices a crack in the board and folds it upward while asking, "Why did you put a crack in the board?" The teacher frowns and tells him curtly, "It was made that way. Put it back." Bobbie continues to move all the pieces around. The teacher tells him, "Okay, Bobbie, why don't you go work on the computer." Bobbie gets up quickly and walks over to the computer where he sits down and starts working immediately.

Here, the writer presents the sequence of interactions with almost no descriptive detail about appearances. Yet he conveys the scene by describing actions sequentially, using active verbs which allow the reader to see the back-and-forth movement of the interaction. We get a clear sense of movement from the lively, vividly worded actions: walks in, swaying, looks around, asks, starts walking, sits down, tells him, does not cooperate, moves, gets up quickly, walks over, starts working.

By convention, writers present action as progressing through time. In the above scene, the interactions are so clearly linked that the writer uses only one transitional word—"then." In a longer scene, or in one with less obviously interconnected actions, a writer needs to orient the reader with transitional markers to indicate shifts in time, place, and person as the action unfolds. Writers sequence actions in an order (e.g., first, second, third), and mark action shifts with transitions (e.g., now, then, next, afterwards, the next morning). They also locate action with situational markers (e.g., here, there, beyond, behind). In the following excerpt, a researcher studying an outpatient psychiatric treatment facility connects actions through transitional phrases ("as he continues talking") and transitional words ("then," "as"):

> I sat down on the bench in the middle of the hall. And as I sat waiting for something to gain my attention, I heard the director yell out, "Take off your clothes in the shower!" as he shuts the door to the shower room. . . . Remaining outside

the door of the shower room, the director speaks with Roberta, one of the staff members assigned to look over the clients. Then Karen approaches them with a small, dirty Smurf that she found outside. "Look at it, how pretty, kiss it," she says talking to the director, but he doesn't pay any attention to her. As he continues talking to Roberta, he glances over and notices that I am observing them. As our eyes lock, he opens up his arm toward Karen and requests a hug. Karen, in her usual bashful way, giggles as she responds to his hug.

In this action-oriented paragraph, the writer focuses on movement—sat, shuts, approaches, glances, opens—interspersed with talk: "the director yell[s] out, 'Take off your clothes in the shower!'" In observing and reporting actions, ethnographers interested in social interactions view action and talk as interconnected features of what people "do." They write about "talk" as a part of people's actions.

Dialogue

Ethnographers also reproduce dialogue—conversations that occur in their presence or that members report having had with others—as accurately as possible. They reproduce dialogue through direct and indirect quotation, through reported speech, and by paraphrasing. We hold that only those phrases actually quoted verbatim should be placed between quotation marks; all others should be recorded as indirect quotations or paraphrases.

The following example illustrates how direct quotation, indirect quotation, and reported speech work together to convey back-and-forth conversation:

For a minute or so before I left, I talked with Polly, the black woman who guards the front school entrance. As we were talking, a black girl, wearing dark blue sweats, walked by. Polly pointed to her. "Did you see that girl?" she asked me. I told her I had, and Polly confided that the girl had hassled her. Polly said the girl tried to leave school without permission and had started arguing. She said the principal had been walking by and he had tried to deal with the disturbance. And the girl had answered, "This is my school. You can't control me!" and then she called the principal a "white MF." Polly told me, "It's usually a black MF, but she changed it." She said that girl has a "bad attitude" and shook her head.

Writing up this conversation as predominately indirect quotation preserves the back-and-forth flow of the spoken interaction. Interspersing quoted fragments livens up the dialogue and lends a sense of immediacy. By clearly marking the direct quotation, indirect quotation, and reported speech, we can see how they work together:

Direct: "Did you see that girl?"
Indirect: I told her I had . . .
Indirect: . . . and Polly confided that the girl had hassled her. Polly said that the
  girl tried to leave school without permission and had started arguing. She
  said the principal had been walking by and he had tried to deal with the
  disturbance.
Reported speech, direct:
  And the girl had answered, "This is my school. You can't control me!" and
  then she called the principal a "white MF."
Direct: "It's usually a black MF, but she changed it."
Indirect: She said that that girl has a
Direct: "bad attitude". . .

Indirect quotation more closely approximates dialogue than paraphrasing does. Paraphrasing this conversation with Polly might have preserved the basic content. But in paraphrasing, a writer translates speech into her own words and too readily starts to summarize. For example, a paraphrase of the last portion of this excerpt might read: "The girl talked back to the principal and called him names. . . . She has some attitude problems." This paraphrasing obscures the flavor of chatting and offering confidences, and it fails to voice the student's remarks to the principal which thus would have been unheard.

Members' own descriptions and "stories" of their experiences are invaluable indexes to their views and perceptions of the world (see chapter 5) and should be documented verbatim when possible. Writing this exchange as a "story" told verbatim to the fieldworker preserves two different kinds of information. First, it shows that "something happened" between a student, a guard, and the principal. Second, the account provides the guard's experience of that something. As the guard's story, this fieldnote conveys more about the teller and her concerns than it does about the girl and her trouble.

Writing up dialogue is more complicated than simply remembering talk or literally replaying every word. People talk in spurts and fragments. They accentuate or even complete a phrase with a gesture, facial expression, or posture. They send complex messages through incongruent, seemingly contradictory and ironic verbal and nonverbal expression as in sarcasm or polite put-downs. Thus ethnographers must record the meanings they infer from the bodily expression accompanying words—gesture, movement, facial expression, tone of voice. Furthermore, people do not take turns smoothly in conversations: they interrupt each other, overlap words, talk simultaneously, and respond with ongoing comments and murmurs. Such turn-taking can be placed on a linear page by bracketing the overlapping speech.

Although accurately capturing dialogue in jottings and full fieldnotes requires considerable effort, ethnographers have a number of reasons for peppering their notes with verbatim quoted talk. Such dialogue conveys character traits, advances action, and provides clues to the speaker's social status, identity, personal style, and interests. Dialogue allows the field researcher to capture members' terms and expressions as they are actually used in specific situations. In addition, dialogue may point to key features of a cultural world view. The following excerpt comes from a discussion in an African-American history course:

Deston, a black male with Jheri curls, asked Ms. Dubois, "What's a sell-out? I hear that if you talk to a white person—you sell-out. If you go out with a white girl—you sell-out." She replied that some people "take it to the extreme." She said that a sell-out could even be a teacher or someone who works at McDonalds. Then she defined a sell-out as "someone who is more concerned about making it . . . who has no racial loyalty, no allegiance to people."

The writer uses direct quotation to capture a back-and-forth exchange about racial identity, and also retains a key members' term.

Since such verbatim quoting persuasively convinces a reader that one "was there" and overheard as an insider, it can be tempting to approximate remembered talk. However, we urge jotting down verbatim quotes as often as possible while in the field and then punctuating with quotation marks only those phrases that are actually written down. Such consistency not only avoids accidental misrepresentation but also keeps a fieldworker more alert to presenting members' views.

These issues and choices in writing dialogue become complex when the local language differs from the researcher's. How well the researcher knows the language certainly determines the extent of verbatim quoting. For example, when a fieldworker does research in a second language, not only will she frequently miss what someone said because she did not understand a particular word, but she also will have difficulty capturing the verbatim flow of a dialogue even when she does understand. By working with a local assistant and checking to make sure she understands correctly what people are saying, she can compensate for some of her difficulty. Similar problems arise when working in English in a setting with much technical lingo or other in-group expressions such as slang. Unable to follow all the talk, the researcher paraphrases as much as she can and occasionally includes the snippets of verbatim talk she heard and remembered clearly.

In response to these language difficulties, many ethnographers supplement their fieldnotes by tape recordings. They might also make recordings in order to preserve as detailed a record of naturally occurring talk as possible so that they can pursue particular theoretical issues. For example, field researchers interested in recurrent patterns of interaction between staff and clients may make special efforts to tape-record at least some such encounters.[4] Still, most ethnographers do not regard recordings as their primary or exclusive form of data; rather, they use them as one way among others for closely examining the meaning events and experiences have for those studied.

By way of illustration, consider how Rachel Fretz worked with recordings of storytelling performances among the Chokwe people in Bandundu, Zaire. She recorded and carefully transcribed all verbal expressions of both narrators and audience, since listeners actively participate in the storytelling session. The following is an excerpt from the beginning of one such performance; the narrator (N), a young man, performs to an audience (A) of women, men, and children one evening around the fire (Fretz forthcoming).

N: Once upon a time, there were some young boys, myself and Fernando and
    Funga and Shamuna.
A: Is it a story with a good song?
N: They were four persons. They said, "Ah. Let's go hunting."
    Pia they went everywhere. *Pia* they went everywhere.
A: Good.
N: They went this way and that way, this way and that way. No game. "Let's
    return. Let's go." They saw a large hut. Inside there was a container with
    honey in it.
    "My friends, this honey, *mba,* who put it here?"
    He said, "Who?"
    Another said, "Who?"
    [Another said,] "Let's go. We can't eat this."

Then, *fwapu,* Funga came forward and said, "Ah! You're just troubled. Even though you're so hungry, you won't eat this honey?"

"Child. The man who put the honey here is not present. You see that this house was built with human ribs, and you decide to eat this honey." He [Funga] said, "Get out of here. I'll eat it. Go on ahead. Go now." He took some honey; he ate it.

"Shall we wait for him? We'll wait for him."

He came soon. "Let's go."

Liata, liata, liata, they walked along. "We're going a long way. We came from a great distance." They arrived and found, ah! *Kayanda* [my goodness], a large river.

"My friends, what is this?"

"My friends, such a large river. Where did it come from?"

He said, "Ah! Who can explain it?"

"We can't see its source or where it's going."

"Let's cross the river. I'll go first."

First Singing

N: Oh Papa. Eee, Papa, it's I who ate honey.
A: This large river God created, I must cross it.
N: Papa! Eee, Papa, I'm going into the water.
A: This large river God created, I must cross it.
N: Papa! Eee, Papa, I didn't eat it.
A: This large river God created, I must cross it.
N: Papa! Eee, Papa, I'm crossing to the other side.
A: This large river God created, I must cross it.

Transcribing a performance involves catching all the teller's words and audience responses (often requiring the help of a native speaker) despite such interfering sounds as a dog barking and children crying. Accurate transcription also requires close attention to the rhythm and pauses in speaking so that the punctuation and line breaks reflect the storytelling style (cf. Hymes 1991; Tedlock 1983).

But transcribing and translating the tape is only one part of the ethnographer's efforts to learn about and understand storytelling performances. She also wrote extensive fieldnotes describing the situation and participants.[5] For example, she noted that the storytelling session took place by the fire in the chief's pavilion at an informal family gathering including the chief, his seven wives, and their children and grandchildren. She observed that the women participated primarily by singing the story-songs and by answering with exclamations and remarks. The ethnographer also recorded her conversations with these participants and the general comments Chokwe people offered about telling such stories, called *yishima.* She found out that in this performance, listeners know that the house-made-of-human-ribs probably belongs to a sorcerer, that eating his honey is dangerous because it will cast a spell over them, that the river which appeared from nowhere across their path had been created by the sorcerer, and that Funga who ate the honey most likely will drown as a consequence of not listening to his older brother. She learned that the recurring song, sung four times during the performance, created a tension between hope and panic about the consequences of eating the honey, and between trusting that it was a natural river created by God ("This large river God created") and fearing that it was a sorcerer's invention ("Eee, Papa, it's I who ate the honey.")

Thus, a transcription of recorded speech is not a straightforward and simple means of documenting an event. The ethnographer needs to observe and listen to more than the words; she needs to ask many follow-up questions and write down what she learns. As a result, much field research uses a variety of recording and encoding processes, combining fieldnotes with audio and video recording.[6]

Characterization

Ethnographers describe the persons they encounter through a strategy known as *characterization*. While a simple description of a person's dress and movements conveys some minimal sense of that individual, the writer more fully characterizes a human being through also showing how that person talks, acts, and relates to others. An ethnographer most effectively characterizes individuals in context as they go about their daily activities rather than by simply listing their characteristics. Telling about a person's traits never is as effective as showing how they live. This entails presenting characters as fully social beings through descriptions of dress, speech, gestures, and facial expression, which allow the reader to infer traits. Traits and characteristics thus appear in and through interaction with others rather than by being presented as isolated qualities of individuals. Thus, characterization draws on a writer's skills in describing, reporting action, and presenting dialogue.

In the following set of fieldnotes, Linda Shaw describes an encounter with a couple living in the kitchen area of an apartment in a psychiatric board-and-care facility. The woman in particular emphasizes the efforts they have made to create a "normal" living environment and the futility they feel in doing so:[7]

I went with Terri and Jay today as they offered to show me the "apartment" they had created out of the small converted kitchen area that was their room. Terri escorted me from one space to another, taking great pride in showing me how they had made a bedroom area at one end, a living room next to it, and a kitchen area next to that. They had approximated an entire apartment in this tiny space, and she showed me features of each "room" in detail. The bed, they said, had a real mattress, not like the foam pads on all the other beds. There was a rug on the living room floor and a TV at the foot of the bed. Then Terri opened the cupboards. She pointed out the spice rack and counted each glass out loud. She took particular pride in the coffee pot she uses to fix Jay's morning coffee and a warmer oven where they sometimes heat take-out pizza.

Terri tried very hard to demonstrate all they had done to make their apartment like one that any married couple might have; yet, the harder she tried, the more apparent it became how different their lives really were. Terri spoke of the futility she felt in spite of all these efforts: "All the noise, the screaming, the tension really bothers me. I'm married, and I can't even be a normal wife here. I want to get up in the morning, fix my husband breakfast—a cup of coffee, eggs, bacon, orange juice—before he goes to work, clean the house, take care of the kids and then fix him a nice dinner and drink or whatever he wants when he gets home. Here, I get up and can fix him a cup of instant coffee. You know, it's not as good to just pick up the apartment, but then there's nothing else to do."

Terri comes across as a fully human individual whose actions and talk reveal her character. She has done her best to create the normal way of life she wishes for but cannot sustain in this quasi-institutional setting. Through her actions and words, we see her struggle in vain to construct this private space as a refuge against the debilitating forces of institutional life.

Pressed to finish his notes, a writer might be tempted to use some convenient label ("a retarded person," "a homeless person," a black/white/Asian, etc.) rather than looking closely at that person's actual appearance and behavior. Such quick characterization, however, produces a stock character who, at best, comes across as less than fully human and, at worst, appears as a negative stereotype. For example, one student, in describing people in a shopping mall, characterized an older woman as a "senile bag lady" after noting that she muttered to herself while fumbling absent-mindedly in a shabby, oversized purse. Such labeling sketches only a pale type and closes the writer's attention to other relevant details and actions.

An ethnographer, however, does include members' remarks and actions which stereotype or mock others. The following excerpt describes a student who mockingly acts out typical gestures and postures of a Latino "cholo" before some classmates:

As the white male and his friend walked away, he said "chale homes" [eh! homies] in a mock Spanish accent. Then he exaggerated his walking style: he stuck his shoes out diagonally, placed his arms at a curved popeye angle, and leaned back. . . . Someone watching said, "Look at you fools."

In this group of bantering young men, the white teenage male enacts a ludicrous caricature of a Latino "cholo." Ethnographers take care to distinguish members' characterizations from their own by providing details which clearly contextualize the talk and behavior as delivered from a member's point of view.

An individual already well known through previous entries does not need to have a full introduction each time he enters a scene. Even for a main character, one describes only those actions and traits relevant to the current interaction. In other words, a fieldworker not only considers an individual's qualities but also earlier appearances and relative impact in this moment. Each entry is only a partial record, and as notes accumulate, fieldworkers will notice that they have assembled enough observations to present some persons as full-fledged individuals ("rounded" characters), others as less well-known figures ("flat" characters), and a few individuals as types such as a bus driver or a policeman ("stock" characters).

Furthermore, continuing contacts with people greatly expand the field researcher's resources for writing fuller, richer characterizations. No longer limited to the surface features visible to any observer, the researcher can note and write about qualities that are harder to detect, that become evident only with repeated contact and greater familiarity. One problem here is that ethnographers often describe even main characters only upon first encountering them, leaving that first characterization unchanged despite coming to know more about that person. Hence we would suggest taking time as research progresses to periodically reflect on and try to capture on paper the appearance and feel of major characters, now known as persons with unique features and special qualities.

An ethnographer usually characterizes in detail those persons who act centrally in a scene. Although the full picture of any person develops through time in a series of fieldnotes, each description presents vivid and significant details which show a primary character as completely as possible: through appearance, body posture, gesture, words, and actions. In contrast, a peripheral figure might indeed be referred to simply with as few details as necessary for that person to be seen doing his small part in the scene.

A number of criteria shape the field researcher's decision about who is central and who is peripheral. First, the researcher's theoretical interests will focus her attention toward particular people. For example, the central characters in a study of teamwork among "support staff" in a courtroom were courtroom clerks and bailiffs rather than attorneys, witnesses, or the judge. Similarly, methodological strategies also focus the ethnographer's attention. For example, a strategy for depicting a social world by describing distinctive interactional patterns may shape the ethnographer's decision to focus on someone who presents a particularly vivid illustration of such a pattern.

In addition, the person's centrality and function for those in the social setting determine the degree of detail in characterization. If members in a scene orient to a particular person, then a description that makes that person central to the scene is called for. Conversely, even those who may be central figures in a setting might get slight attention from the field researcher if they are so treated by those in the scene. For example, in a scene focusing on students talking in the quad at lunchtime, the "principal walking across the courtyard and looking from side to side" might not be described in much more detail if no one seems to notice him.

Fieldnotes should also include the ethnographer as a character in the interactions. The presence of the ethnographer who truly stands at the side watching might only be noted to identify the position from which the event is seen. But an ethnographer who directly participates in the action becomes a relevant character in the fieldnote, especially when a member clearly interacts with her. Indeed, a researcher may act as a central character in the incident in unanticipated ways. He might shift from his stance as an outside observer and become fully engaged in the interactions. In the following excerpt, students playing an educational game in a class for the deaf and hard of hearing encourage each other to speak. The fieldworker, having had a stuttering problem all of his life, clearly empathizes with the students. Though essentially an outsider in the class, the fieldworker becomes a pivotal figure at one juncture:

> Lynn keeps on telling Caesar to say what the answers are by speaking (rather than through sign language). The teacher says, "Very good Lynn. . . . That's right, Caesar, you should try to speak what the answers are as well so that we can all understand you." Caesar looks over at me a little red in the face and looks down

at his desk with a half smile. The teacher asks him (while pointing at me), "Are you afraid of speaking because he is here?" Lynn and Jackie and Caesar all seem to answer at once in sign that he is afraid of having me hear him speak. I tell Caesar, "You don't have to be afraid of what I think. I have a hard time speaking too."

Caesar seems interested by my statements and points a finger at me questioningly. The teacher says, "Yes, it's okay, you speak fine. You don't have to be afraid of what anybody thinks about you. Just say one sentence and he'll tell you if he can understand you."

Caesar reluctantly says something and then looks at me, his head still slightly down and his face still red. A faint smile lines his lips as he waits for my answer. I had not understood a single word and was feeling desperate. What if they asked me to repeat what he had said? I reply, "Yes, that was fine. I understood you." The teacher quickly turns to Caesar and gives him the appropriate signs for my answer and goes directly into saying that he shouldn't be so intimidated by what other people think. Caesar looks at me and smiles. The game continues, and Caesar starts answering in both sign and speech. And I began to understand some of the things they were saying.

Clearly, this ethnographer's past experiences and presence played a central role in this scene, and his empathetic responses color the description in essential ways. Had he tried to write up these notes without including himself—his own interactions and feelings—the scene would have been deeply distorted.

When describing their own participation in scenes, field researchers generally write in the first person. If this observer had described the scene in the third person, referring to himself by name, much of the impact would have been lost:

Caesar reluctantly says something and looks at Paul, his head still slightly down and his face still red. A faint smile lines his lips as he waits for his answer. . . . He replies, "Yes, that's fine. I understood you." The teacher quickly turns to Caesar and gives him the appropriate signs for Paul's answer and goes directly into saying that he shouldn't be so intimidated by what other people think. Caesar looks at Paul and smiles. The game continues, and Caesar starts answering in both sign and speech.

In the original segment, the writer carefully stuck to Caesar's observable behavior ("looks over at me with a red face" and "looks down at his desk with a half smile") and did not attribute nervousness. But in the third person account, we miss an essential part of Caesar's struggle to speak. This struggle was conveyed through the ethnographer's empathetic and self-revealing comment, "I had not understood a single word. . . ," and by his closing observation, "And I began to understand some of the things they were saying." Through the writer's careful attention to details of behavior and talk as well as though his own revealed personal feelings, readers may sense the fear and later the relief in speaking and in being understood.

WRITING EXTENDED ENTRIES: ORGANIZATION

Not only can ethnographers improve their descriptive writing by learning strategies for depicting moments of lived experience, but they also can write more clearly by organizing their writing into coherent units. Clear organizational strategies enable them to conceptualize units and more easily write up an extended and complicated memory as a coherent set of fieldnotes.

Initially, field researchers may find it difficult to sustain a concentrated attention when writing. They may recall disconnected incidents and rush through their writing, thereby producing scattered details and unreadable fragments that will make it difficult to "see" or "hear" a coherent slice of life and therefore hard to subsequently use their fieldnotes. Or, they press on for pages, meandering through endless minutiae which also make their later rereading and analysis of fieldnotes difficult. However, remembering any observed scene as a series of moments and then sustaining that memory as a perceived whole will help one write up a "complete" scene. In addition, by drawing on conventional strategies for organizing their notes, field researchers can more easily sustain a focused attention while writing all the details remembered.

Field researchers frequently attempt to write detailed descriptions which fully document events from beginning to end. They want to be sure, later on, that they have not accidentally skipped writing up an important feature of an observed event or incident. Consequently, fieldworkers write up their fieldnotes in ways which indicate that they have recorded the "entire" scene. They do so not only by providing full details but also by writing in units which create and mark beginnings and endings. Details grouped in a paragraph form one such unit.

By convention, a *paragraph* coheres because the writer's attention focuses on one idea or insight. That means he perceives some actions as a gestalt and concentrates on them. While writing, he shifts attention from one recalled moment to another: for example, from one person or activity to another within a classroom. These slight shifts are often indicated by a paragraph break. Thus, in most fieldnotes, a paragraph presents a coherent moment and thereby structures the description.[8]

Ethnographers also organize their writing into units extending beyond a paragraph. They organize memories into larger wholes by sustaining their attention throughout an entire situation or event, so that the separate moments cohere to create a "complete" description of a scene. That larger whole becomes an extended entry, which may include a series of paragraphs. Though the largest unit of writing is that day's entire set of fieldnotes, the ethnographer often finds that she organizes her recollections and jottings to write up several discrete units within that day's entry.

These extended entries within a day's fieldnotes often concern an incident or event which the writer has noted to herself as especially important. Many fieldworkers sit down to write these events first. Especially when working on a computer, one can order the sequence of the day's activities and then scroll down to begin with that key event. In a sense, the ethnographer juggles two competing purposes: to get down all activities as quickly as possible and to write as fully and vividly as possible those scenes she intuits as most vital to her research project. When first in the field, the ethnographer might be more concerned with getting everything down: such writing is often more fragmented and spontaneous. Later on as her research progresses, she may be more invested in writing extended entries about incidents and events she selects as particularly revealing of members' experiences. Such fieldnotes require sustained concentration through longer passages and benefit from the extra effort to write vivid, detailed, and coherent sequences of action.

In writing such extended entries, ethnographers work with a number of different organizing units. In the following section, we consider three such options: sketches which describe a slice of life as an observed scene; and two forms of narrative entry, episodes and more extended fieldnote tales, which recount interactions, incidents, and events as dynamic actions in an unfolding scene.

Sketches

In a sketch, the fieldworker, struck by a vivid sensory impression, describes a scene primarily through detailed imagery. Much as in a photograph, sequencing of actions does not dominate. Rather the writer, as a more distanced observer looking out on a scene, describes what he or she senses. Presenting a more or less static snapshot contrasts with writing narrative, where the writer has the sense of moving through time, recounting one action after another.

While the term "sketch" employs a visual metaphor, this form of organizing writing need not rely only on visual details but can also incorporate auditory or kinetic details as well. For example, not appearance but the sense of smell might be the primary criteria for recalling and conveying the merits of a particular food. In describing people, settings, objects, and so forth, the writer must evoke all those senses which recall that moment as she perceived it. Often the sense of vision dominates, however, simply because the fieldworker observes at a distance or aims to give a brief overview of the setting. It also dominates, in part, because the English language for vision is much more detailed and developed than it is for the other senses.[9] Hence the ethnographic writer may have to expend special effort to evoke and write about nonvisual sensory images.

A sketch typically is a brief segment, which unifies descriptive details about a setting, an individual, or a single incident. Because it is primarily static, it lacks any sense of consequential action (of plot) and any full characterization of people. Consider the following sketch of a Latino street market, which focuses on a single character at a stall with toys:

An older Latina woman is bent over looking at the toys on the ground. Behind her she holds two plastic bags of something, which she uses to balance as she leans over. She picks up several toys in succession from the ground, lifting them up several inches to turn them over and around in her hand, and then putting them down. After a minute, she straightens up and walks slowly away.

Organizing details into a sketch in this way permits the writer to give a quick sense of the setting by presenting a close-up picture of one particular character's engagement with it.

Often, sketches contextualize subsequent interactions, placing them into a larger framework of events or incidents, and allow the reader to visualize more readily the setting or participants involved. On some occasions, however, these entries may stand as independent units of writing. In the following sketch, for example, another writer describes the scene in a high school during an uneventful, uncrowded lunch hour in a way that documents how students group themselves:

Even though it was cold and windy, there were still about one hundred black students clustered in the central quad. On the far left, one short black male wearing a black starter jacket was bouncing a ball. Next to him, seven black females and two black males were sitting on a bench. Further to the right stood a concentrated group of about thirty or forty black students. I counted about twenty who were wearing different kinds of starter jackets. Further up the quad stood another group of fifteen blacks, mostly females. At the foot of quad, on the far right, was — another group of maybe twenty black students, about equally male and female. Some were standing, while others were sitting on a short concrete wall against the auditorium. To the right of this group, I noticed one male, listening to a yellow walkman, dancing by himself. His arms were flung out, pulling as though he were skiing, while his feet ran in place.

This ethnographer was especially concerned with ethnic relations and wanted to track how, when, and where students socialized and with whom. Even when he could not hear or see exactly what the students were doing, he depicted these groupings in an almost snapshot fashion; although the paragraph includes visual and kinetic details, it creates the scene as a still-life rather than as an event in which actions could be sequenced.

In general, sketches are useful for providing an overall sense of places and people that sometimes stands as a background for other fieldnote descriptions. Descriptive sketches of people standing around or of a person's expression and posture as she looks at someone, for example, can reveal qualities of social relations even when apparently nothing much is happening.

Episodes

Unlike a sketch, which depicts a "still-life" in one place, an episode recounts action and moves in time. When recounting a brief incident which does not extend over a long period of time or involve many characters, one can organize and write it effectively as a single episode. In an episode, a writer tells an incident as one continuous action or interaction and thus constructs a more or less unified entry. Consequently, when ethnographers perceive actions as interrelated, they often write up that memory as a one- or two-paragraph episode.[10]

The following excerpt consists of a one-paragraph episode in which the writer describes an interaction between two students during the beginning of class time:

A black female came in. She was wearing a white puffy jacket, had glasses and straight feathered black hair. She sat down to my right. Robert and another male (both black) came in and sat down. They were eating Kentucky Fried Chicken which they took out of little red and white boxes. Robert's friend kept swiping at the black female, trying to slap her. She kept telling him in an annoyed voice to leave her alone. After a minute of this exchange, the black teacher said to the guy, "Leave her alone, brother." He answered Ms. Dubois with a grin on his face, "Don't worry. She's my sistah." The girl said, "Chhh," looking briefly at him. He had gone back to eating his chicken.

Here, the students' and teacher's actions are presented as a sequence, each seeming to trigger the next; the girl responds to the boy's swiping and the teacher responds to him, etc. Thus, these actions are linked and appear as one continuous interaction, producing a unified episode.

Not every episode needs to build to a climax as the one above does. Many fieldnote episodes minutely recount one character's routine, everyday actions. In fact, in many entries, ethnographers find themselves writing primarily about mundane activities. In the following excerpt, for example, the ethnographer recounts the way several students in an ESL class worked together to complete a group activity:

One group consisted of six people: two Korean girls, one Korean boy, two Mexican boys, and one Russian girl. Like all of the other groups, they arranged their chairs in a small circle for the assigned activity. Ishmael, a Mexican boy, held the question card in his hand and read it to the rest of the group: "List five things that you can do on a date for less than $10.00 in Los Angeles." (His English was heavily marked by his Mexican accent, but they could understand him.) Placing his elbows on the desk and looking directly at the group, he said, "Well?" He watched them for a minute or two; then he suggested that one could go for drinks at Hard Rock Cafe. The others agreed by nodding their heads. Ishmael again waited for suggestions from the group. The other Mexican boy said "going to the beach" and the Russian girl said "roller skating." The Koreans nodded their heads, but offered no other suggestions. (I think that Ishmael waited for others to respond, even though he seemed to know the answers.)

In describing this classroom scene, the ethnographer filled six pages with a series of such more or less isolated episodes occurring during that hour. Thus, she was able to present the small groups as working simultaneously on various activities. The episodes belong together only because they are situated in the same class during the same hour. When describing concurrent actions during one hour, for example, fieldworkers often write them up as a series of discrete episodes, loosely linked by time and place.

Many fieldnote episodes stand on their own, barely associated with others. Ethnographers write many such episodic entries because they rarely can track a sequence of actions and learn of all its outcomes within one day. They may write an episode about an interaction simply because it bears upon a topic they are interested in. They often write without knowing whether that fieldnote will later be important in the full analysis. Yet writing these episodes over time will enable the ethnographer to find patterns of behavior and connections between people's actions through many different fieldnotes.

Fieldnote Tales

Within a day's entry, ethnographers sometimes recount a series of episodes as interconnected because they are describing the same characters or similar activities. The writer might also perceive the episodes as linked because "something happens": actions progress, develop over time, and seem to lead to immediate outcomes. In telling these episodes, ethnographers draw on the conventions of narration and write the unfolding actions as "fieldnote tales." These tales often become the most extended units of writing embedded within a day's entry.

Writing fieldnote tales, however, differs from crafting a dramatic narrative. Well-crafted stories not only describe actions chronologically so that a reader can follow them, but they also build suspense into the unfolding action. These stories make "something happen." Characters act in ways that have consequences and that lead to an instructive, often dramatic outcome.[11] Ethnographers, however, are wary of imposing a unified narrative structure on events. Most everyday life incidents and events do not happen like dramatic stories in which one action neatly causes the next and results in clear-cut consequences; instead, much of life unfolds rather aimlessly. Describing life in a narrative form is highly interpretive writing; in doing so, the ethnographer might overdetermine the connections between actions and their movement toward an outcome. Making all experiences fit the formal demands of a story falsifies them.

Ethnographers, then, generally write fieldnote tales as a series of related episodes rather than as a unified narrative. We suggest that they resist crafting events into complex, dramatic sequences or into better sounding, more convincing stories: they should not revise or rearrange actions to make them lead (inevitably) to a particular ending or a climactic outcome; nor should they build suspense into everyday events that lack this quality. Rather, an ethnographer should try to recount action as it unfolded, to tell the event as she saw it happen. As a consequence, fieldnote tales tend to be episodic, a string of action chunks put down on the page one after another.

Though not highly-crafted or polished stories, fieldnotes tales nevertheless range from loosely to more cohesively integrated units within a day's entry. Inevitably, most fieldnote tales are loosely structured: the writer reports only what she saw and as much as she remembers. For instance, the ethnographer might write a series of episodes which highlight several characters or which concentrate on similar activities. She constructs them as an episodic fieldnote tale because she infers the actions to be loosely interconnected. Nevertheless, resisting the urge to write a cohesive story, she writes one episode after another, including all actions she observed and remembers, whether or not she sees how they fit in while writing about them. Often the import of an "extraneous" detail or episode becomes clear only when rereading the tale. When getting the scene on the page, the researcher makes what connections she can at the moment, guided by an intuitive sense for what belongs in this tale, for "what goes with what."

Sometimes, of course, an ethnographer may intend to write fieldnote tales as more tightly structured narratives—for very good ethnographic reasons. Committed to members' perception of events, the ethnographer should write cohesive tales about events which members enact or present as a unified series of actions. For example, the field researcher may observe activities that have more or less clear-cut beginnings, progression in which one action causes the next, and consequential endings. Many criminal court hearings in American society are structured to progress thus, and the ethnographer can felicitously write a cohesive tale about them. Similarly, the researcher may hear people telling coherent stories and should write these tales as the tellers narrate them. For example, people tell stories to each other about their day's experiences; they narrate past incidents in response to the researchers queries; and, they recount myths and legends learned from their elders. In writing about such events and stories, the ethnographer appropriately writes fieldnotes that have a unified narrative structure, in which one action leads to the next and builds to an outcome.[12]

In the following pages, we present two extended fieldnote tales. Though both tales present a series of episodes as the researchers saw and remembered them, the first tale presents the activities of two characters, a policeman and policewoman, and only loosely interconnects them. This episodic tale coheres only because the writer has a thematic interest in the activities of the two officers; that is, the episodes hang together by a thematic thread. The second tale, in contrast, achieves a tighter narrative structure by linking a series of episodes about a dean disciplining a student and, thereby, tells a single, unfolding incident. The writer clearly depicts a school incident in which one action leads to another; the fieldnote tale moves through a sequence of actions toward some sort of resolution.

In this first tale, a student ethnographer writes about events he observed while riding, one night, on patrol with two police officers, Sam and Alisha. He recounts a series of consecutive but otherwise fairly discrete episodes; although these episodes all involve police activities, they are only loosely related to one another and contain several possible "somethings that happened."

(a) As we were driving, Alisha was telling Sam about women officers in another department. "I can't believe what some of the women and the women trainees have done and I hate it cause it's always the women that do the stupidest things. And that's what gives a bad name to the women officers. So—"

"You know what the problem is, don't ya?" Sam says. "Women think on the wrong side of the brain."

"What?"

"They think out of the wrong side of their brain."

"Or is it because we don't have a penis to think from?" Alisha burst out laughing.

"NOOO!"

"Is that what you think, Sam?"

"No. I'll probably tell my wife that. She'll get a kick out of it." We pulled down an alley and passed a Hispanic guy about twenty. "That guy was stealing those tires that were down here."

"The kid's bike ones?"

"Yeah."

"Maybe."

"Um, sure. They were back there and they're not there no more."

"I don't know."

"They were there last night, pieces to a bicycle."

"Oh. Should we go get 'em?"

"No they've been there forever."

(b) We pulled out of the alley and were waiting to make a right hand turn. "I'm gonna stop that." I looked up and there was a white jeep without its lights on. We zoomed ahead and got behind the car. The car got in the turning lane as did we. After the light changed and we were proceeding through the intersection, Sam flipped on the lights. The jeep pulled into a gas station. . . . Sam walked up to the car and Alisha walked up and flashed her flashlight in the windows. She walked back and stood next to me. The people in the gas station all watched us. The girl (Caucasian) got out of her car, walked to the

back and looked at her taillights. Sam spoke to her and then walked back to
the car. We got in and Sam said that her headlights were on but not her
taillights. He let her off with a warning.

(c) We decided to go to 7–11 to get coffee. We walked in and the lady clerk
knew Sam and Alisha. She gave them these big cups and Sam went and filled
them with coffee. I walked over and didn't see any of the cups like they had
so I just grabbed the largest coffee cup they had and filled mine up. Alisha
was looking down the aisle with all the medicines. I told her she should get
Tums for her stomach. Sam came over and made some comment. Alisha replied that she had a tough stomach and she didn't need anything. Sam got a
Mounds candy bar. We each paid and then went back to the car and started
driving around again. As we were driving, Sam rolled down his window and
pretended to throw his candy wrapper out the window. "You didn't?" Alisha
asked. With a big smile on his face, Sam said, "no," and showed her the wrapper. Alisha went on to explain that she had a real thing for not littering, especially when they were working. "I think we need to be examples. What does
it look like if somebody sees a candy wrapper fly out the window of a cop
car?"

(d) As we were driving through a residential area we heard, "Crack! Crack!" I
immediately thought, fireworks? In retrospect that seems like such a dumb
thought, but having never heard gunshots except at a range, I guess I'm not
used to assuming something is gunshots. Sam said something about a car I
hadn't seen and it having only one taillight. He floored the car, the engine
raced and we flew down the street. Alisha threw her coffee out the window
and both she and Sam pulled their guns out. "Get ready to duck if I tell you"
she told me. She then called in that we would be out in the area on possible
gunshots. "That fucker split." We flew down the street. At one point we came
up on a car coming towards us and we met the car as it was driving through
a narrow spot with cars parked on each side of the road. Sam locked up the
brakes, the tires squealed and somehow we made it through. Sam floored it
once again and once again we were flying down the street. We hit a bump
and I flew out of my seat. I heard the things in the trunk bang on the top of
the trunk. "I want to find that car Alisha!"
    "Did you see the people in it?"
    "No. They were just hauling ass and it's got a fuckin' taillight that's out
and I don't even know what kind of car it is." We drove around for a while
and then gave up the search. "Damn. I want a felony tonight. We have to find
a felony tonight, Alisha. I want to point my gun at someone. Where are all
the felons? That was a pretty close call there."
    "Yeah. But I trust your driving Sam. I had to throw my coffee out though.
Maybe we should go see if it's still there." [Sam teases Alsiha for having to
throw her coffee out the window.]
    "How was I supposed to get my gun out and hold my coffee?"
    "I did it and I was driving."
    "That's because Sam, you're such a stud."

"I kept mine." I said jokingly and they laughed.

"So you're talking to me about not littering and you go and throw your coffee cup out the window."

"Correct me if I'm wrong, I did realize my mistake afterwards, and I requested that you go back so I could retrieve my coffee."

"No you said, 'Go back and get my COFFEE!' is what you said." We all laugh.

"But the coffee had to be in a cup in order for me to get it."

"Would you do some police work and run this plate?" (It was a little surprising how fast the atmosphere had transformed. From total intensity to carefree joking in minutes.)

(e) Sam began to follow an old beat up American car. He sped up and told Alisha to call it in for wants and warrants. As he pulled in closer, I saw that the registration said 1991 [it's now January 1993]. "Come on. Come back Code 36 Charles." Sam said, hoping the plate would come back with felony wants on it. The plate came back all clear, expired reg. The car made a left off of the main street and as we turned to follow, Sam flipped on the lights. The driver was a black male. Alsiha shined her flashlight in the back seat and Sam walked up to the driver's window. The driver handed Sam his license and registration. Sam spoke with the man for a minute and then walked back to the car. As he got in he said, "That's a responsible father. I'm not going to write up a responsible father. He had his kids' immunization records in his glove box. That's not our crack dealer."

"Just cause someone's a father doesn't mean he doesn't deal."

"That's not what I meant. Fathers can be drug dealers, but responsible fathers aren't drug dealers."

In this fieldnote tale, as two patrol officers drive around, they react to events observed outside the car and to topics raised in talk within the car. The episodes reveal their now-teasing, now-supportive work relationship. The tale also conveys the tenor of routine police patrol work—ongoing ordinary talk, endless driving, occasional breaks—punctuated by moments of excitement during a chase which, in turn, dissipate as the officers slip back into normal work activities. Clearly the quick shifts interest the writer, who comments in an aside how suddenly the officers turn from tense excitement to informal joking.

These actions clearly provide the material for a story or perhaps more accurately several possible stories. One story might be of a night's work for two patrol officers; another might be about the ethnographer riding along with two officers, his efforts to figure out what they do and why, and his hopes to gain some acceptance from them. But it is not at all clear that these were stories the ethnographer intended to tell at the moment of writing. Rather his concerns were to write up "what happened" as he remembered it. He does so by constructing a series of episodes.

Not all these episodes are closely connected. Obviously the writer links some actions in one episode to actions in subsequent episodes: for example, the coffees purchased at the 7–11 store in episode *c* play a key role in the subsequent chase episode *(d)*. But no explicit connections are apparent between other episodes. Even though the police stop two cars, there are no indications that the second car-stop was in any way connected to the first, although a reader might well be able to suggest connections (e.g., the black father in the second stop had to be let off with a warning since the white woman in the first stop also had been simply warned).

In writing this tale, the ethnographer advances the action through time by grouping actions into discrete episodes; in fact he has no need to use an explicit transition term (e.g., then, immediately, next) to mark the shift into a new episode. He also avoids using causal transitions such as "because" or "consequently" or "despite" to forward the action and more clearly establish links building to an outcome. Such interpretive transitions overly determine the reasons for actions; this fieldworker, for example, did not know why each person acted the way he or she did. To avoid such interpretation, he simply juxtaposed related actions to show how the interaction developed. In general, transitions should only orient a reader in time, place, and sequence, rather than imply causal connections between actions leading irrevocably to an outcome, especially when writing a loosely structured, episodic fieldnote tale.

Ethnographers, however, also write tighter, more cohesive narratives. In such fieldnote tales, all episodes are clearly connected and the account builds to an ending or outcome. Consider the following tale in which the fieldworker tracks a single incident handled by the high-school dean, Mr. Jones. The ethnographer composed this fieldnote as a sequence of episodes, which for purposes of discussion, we have labeled *a* through *i:*

(a) Back in his office, Mr. Jones starts going through some of the paper work on his desk. One whole pile is set aside for those students caught smoking. According to Mr. Jones, smoking is a major violation at the school. "The first time you're caught, you get written up and you get a record. The second time—it's state policy now—you get suspended." I expressed my astonishment. Mr. Jones also noted with a sigh that "all the kids caught smoking are absent today."

(b) As Mr. Jones went through his files, he talked about "tagging" as an another

indicator of delinquency. I was unfamiliar with the term so I asked him what it means. He explained that "tagging" is doing graffiti. . . . "Most of the time if we catch you, you go to jail. That's if it's on the scale that we can charge you for it, of course. For the second time, they either get transferred to another school or they have to do fifteen hours service for the school. Usually, what we have them do is scrape down all the walls" (that they painted with graffiti). I asked if many students get transferred to other schools. He replied that they do and that "we can send them anywhere in the district. The only limit is transportation. We send a lot of the kids out for gang involvement. Most of them go over to Southside. But then again, we receive a lot of the same type of students from uptown, too." I asked him, "So a lot of the problems are just being shifted back and forth between schools?" He replied, "Well, the idea is that once a student is in a new environment, he might be more inclined to change. So if we can't seem to do anything for him here, we ship him off somewhere else where he might be away from some of his bad influences."

(c) But, flipping through his files, he finds one that he was looking for and stops. "Here's one right here. Yep, second time caught smoking. That means suspended." He turns to me and says with a confidential air, "You know, it can really ruin a student's future to get suspended, because it can lead to not being admitted elsewhere. We try to let them know it's serious." The student's name is Sokoloff (or something very similar and distinctly Russian-sounding). He looks at the schedules to see where Sokoloff is during second period and we head up there.

(d) Walking into the room where Sokoloff was supposed to be, I see all the kids looking around at each other seriously. Mr. Jones asks the teacher, a middle-aged white man, if he knows if Sokoloff is here. The teacher had to ask the class if there was anyone there by that name. Many of the students look over to a short, white male with long hair and a heavy metal T-shirt. He stood up and acknowledged his name. Mr. Jones looks at him sternly and says, "Get your bags, you'll be needing 'em." We walk out of the room. (I was actually only in the doorway, trying to remain as inconspicuous as possible.)

(e) The kid has a Russian accent. He seems panicked once we are in the hallway. He is walking side by side with Mr. Jones and looking up at him. In a pleading voice, he asks him, "What did I do?" Mr. Jones responds, "You got caught smoking for the second time. That means we have to suspend you." The kid lets out an exasperated sigh of disbelief and whines, "But that was last semester. I don't even smoke [now]. Please do me a favor." Mr. Jones goes into explaining the state policy and tells him there's nothing he can do but suspend him. The kid starts talking about a Ms. Loges who ". . . told me it [rule] was going to change this semester. You can ask Julio [a classmate]." Mr. Jones seems to be getting frustrated and says, "I have enough trouble. Look! I'm activating school policy." With this, we walked into the attendance office.

(f) (A little uncertain about how I should position myself to be unobtrusive, I sit

down at the desk opposite Mr. Jones's and start acting like I'm looking at some of the papers on his desk. The kid is starting to take notice of me now and keeps looking at my notebook.) He keeps on pleading with Mr. Jones to do him a favor. Mr. Jones inquires, "Don't you read what smoking does to you?" He gets on the phone and tells him, "I'm calling your mother. Does she speak English?" The kid replies affirmatively. As he talks to a receptionist where the mother works, he retains his authoritarian tone in introducing himself: "This is Mr. Jones, Dean of Discipline at the High School. Is Mrs. S. there?" The mother is not at work yet.

(g) The kid pleads a little more calmly, "Do me a favor." Mr. Jones replies authoritatively, but with less vigor, "I'm not going to do you a favor. Not since I don't know what Ms. Loges said." The kid continues to plead, while Mr. Jones stays silent for awhile. The kid tells him, "My friend, Igor, got suspended on the third time." Finally, Mr. Jones says, "Well, it is a new policy this year, so I suppose Ms. Loges could have gotten some of her facts turned around."

(h) As he says this, a short, middle-aged Asian woman walks into the room and seems amused by what is going on. (She sees me sitting at the desk and immediately I get the impression that it is hers. I stand up quickly, looking back down at it and then back up at her.) She seems to know exactly what is going on with the student. She turns to him and starts saying, "You've been smoking, hah? Well, don't you know how bad that is for you?" She asks him, "Do your parents smoke?" He says, "Yes, and my cousins. My whole family." (He seems noticeably relieved and more than willing to talk about the acknowledged evils of smoking.) He says, "I have been trying to stop, and I have been doing pretty good. But it's hard, you know?" The Asian woman says, "Ah, you just have to put your mind to it. I used to smoke." Mr. Jones adds, "Me too. I used to smoke." He nods his head knowingly. In a softer voice, he says to her, "I told him I wouldn't suspend him this time because he got some wrong information. But next time, that's it."

(i) Then, the Dean dismisses him with a slight wave of his hand. The kid leaves the office.

In writing this tale, the ethnographer interconnected the separate episodes—the talk and doings—to show actions as unfolding and developing in a chronological order. The tale moves from an opening which initiates the action (dean examines pile of smoking infractions), through a middle which advances actions as they develop (finding a delinquent student, threatening him with punishment), climaxes in a turning point involving a change in action (offering student another chance), to an end which indicates an outcome or brings the actions to a resting point (student leaving).

But even though this tale, unlike the previous one, moves to a specific ending, the writer does not foreshadow this outcome by building it into his writing. In the last episodes (*h* and *i*), we learn only that the male dean and the female administrator work together, and that she discusses the smoking habit in greater detail with the student. She might have influenced the dean to change his mind, simply through her presence; for, he changes after she enters. But, we never get a clear sense of why the dean relents or appears to relent: he may, after all, have been intending all along to simply scare the youth rather than to actually suspend him. The ending merely writes a closing to the fieldnote tale and is almost anticlimactic: the student simply exits the scene. But a more definitive ending which made a point (about discipline or the dean's and student's actions) would have distorted the incident, attributing import that those involved did not, or hypothesizing consequences that might or might not occur. Remaining true to his observations, the writer squelched any inclination to craft a more emphatic ending.

Composing these tales often highlights a fundamental tension felt by many ethnographers as they write fieldnotes. The researcher wants to write the actions as she perceived them in the moment of observation and to include as many details as possible. However, writing is a way of seeing, of increasing understanding, and ultimately of *creating scenes*. Indeed, writing on a page is a process of ordering; the writer, perforce, selects this and not that, puts details in this order and not that one, and creates a pattern out of otherwise fragmented or haphazard details.

Narrating is a particularly structured way of seeing and ordering life and, consequently, may heighten the strain between trying to write "everything" and creating an intelligible slice of life on the page. The more unified and climactic the narrative he envisions writing, the more compelled the ethnographer feels to interconnect actions and to exclude any details which the building story line renders peripheral or irrelevant. For example, in the story about the dean disciplining the student, only episode *b* about graffiti does not bear directly on the story line about the smoking infraction. Had the ethnographer written down other details more extraneous to this story line, the tale would have been more episodic and less driven by an internal consistency. The tale might have included, for example, extraneous dialogue with a secretary who remarked after she got off the phone, "Your wife called to say you forgot your lunch," or incidental actions such as a student waiting at the office door holding a balloon in her hand. However, he did not include such irrelevant details; his tale has few gaps.

In telling a fieldnote tale, the ethnographer must juggle these contradictory impulses: to include even peripheral actions and to create an ordered progression telling the "something that happened." If she truly writes "everything," she likely will create mumbo-jumbo on the page; but if she overdetermines the connections in her story, she might close her mind to other possible interpretations. Faced with this dilemma, we suggest that the ethnographer aim to write the more loosely structured fieldnote tales. Such a tale tends to be episodic: it describes seemingly extraneous actions which happen during the incident recounted; it might have gaps between episodes with no apparent connections leading from one set of actions to the next; it often begins in the midst of action and closes without necessarily arriving at any consequences or resolution.

Such a fieldnote tale reflects the ethnographer's perceived experience at the moment of writing. It tells the story as he understands it that day. But every fieldnote tale is embedded not only within the day's entry but also within the context of ongoing fieldwork and note-taking. The researcher returns to the field the next day to further explore his hunches about the previous day's events. He sees a character in various situations over time and deepens his understanding of that person's relationships and patterns of action. Thus, as writing continues and fieldnotes accumulate, the ethnographer may begin to see earlier tales differently than when he wrote them. He may reexamine the implicit connections, the gaps he did not understand, and the endings he inferred, and consequently, he asks himself questions which stimulate a closer look when he returns to the field.[13]

The cohesion of fieldnote tales, then, is temporary and conditional: ethnographers' understandings of recounted events may change as fieldwork continues. In the light of further observation of related activities and reappearing characters, the ethnographer may reassess connections and disjunctions between episodes in a fieldnote tale. After observing the dean many times, for example, the writer of this tale might come to see the dean's talk about graffiti as an essential unit in what, after all, seems to be a rather cohesive story: the dean talks about graffiti as a serious infraction in order to highlight the minor nature of smoking violations. He would then come to understand the tale as following this common pattern: An authority threatens punishment for infraction; the student exhibits properly deferential behavior, offers an excuse, and promises to do better; the authority relents and lets the student off with a warning. In this version of the story, the student will not be suspended as long as he is cooperative.

In reviewing his tale, the ethnographer not only should reflect on the implicit connections he made but also reconsider the gaps between (and within) episodes. The apparent gap in the dean's story—between the suspension threat and the remission—might have various interpretations. The ethnographer, for example, could infer any one of the following: (a) that the dean lets smoking students off-the-hook if they are deferential; (b) that the dean generally defers to the opinions of the female, Asian administrator; (c) that the Asian administrator intervenes often for foreign students. To locate grounds for choosing between these possibilities, the ethnographer would further observe the dean as he disciplined students.

Finally, continuing fieldwork and note-writing may lead to revised understandings about the ending of a tale; for, there is an element of arbitrariness in both the beginnings and endings of stories. The writer begins the tale at the point she began observing an event, key characters, or an interesting situation. She ends her story either when that incident concludes (the dean dismisses the student) or when she shifts her attention to other characters, activities, or situations. Initially, the writer's experience and attention creates the parameters of the fieldnote tale. But as she rereads a tale and thinks about it, she might realize that this tale is inextricably linked to others about the same characters. The specific endings are mere resting points. For example, although this one police patrol tale ends, Sam and Alisha continued their patrolling for several more hours that evening and during other subsequent observations; the story continues through many more pages.[14] In this respect, fieldnote tales have temporary endings because the story about people's lives continues the next day and throughout the fieldnotes.

In sum, ethnographers write fieldnote tales which reflect daily experience, rather than craft artful, suspense-driven narratives. They draw on narrating conventions which order actions so that a reader can visualize them and which, nevertheless, remain true to their immediate sense of the incident. But the understanding a researcher has of any one event often fluctuates and develops as he continues to write and reread his notes. By considering alternate interpretations of a tale in the light of his ongoing research, the ethnographer opens up the tale to more incisive questions. Therefore, ethnographers commit themselves only tentatively to the version they write today, for the "something that happened" might well change. Thus, each fieldnote tale links to and comments on other episodes and tales within a set of fieldnotes. In that sense, each tale—as one version among many—remains open-ended.

IN-PROCESS ANALYTIC WRITING: ASIDES,
COMMENTARIES, AND MEMOS

As the field researcher participates in the field, she inevitably begins to reflect on and interpret what she has experienced and observed. As previously noted, writing fieldnotes heightens and focuses these interpretive and analytic processes; writing up the day's observations generates new appreciation and deeper understanding of witnessed scenes and events. In writing, a field researcher assimilates and thereby starts to understand an experience. She makes sense of the moment by intuitively selecting, highlighting, and ordering details and by beginning to appreciate linkages with or contrasts to previously observed and written-about experiences. Furthermore, she may begin to reflect on how she has presented and ordered events and actions in her notes, rereading selected episodes and tales with an eye to their structuring effects.

To capture these ruminations, reflections, and insights and make them available for further thought and analysis, field researchers pursue several kinds of analytical writing that stand in stark contrast to the descriptive writing we have emphasized to this point. As the result of such writings, the researcher can bring a more probing glance to further observations and descriptive writing and consequently become more selective and in-depth in her descriptions.

These interpretive and analytic forms of writing include asides, commentaries, and in-process memos. These analytic writing strategies move progressively further from the descriptive writing that produces the bulk of the researcher's fieldnotes. Asides and commentaries are analytic writings touched off while composing fieldnotes; the researcher might get an idea as she recalls and puts on paper the details of a specific observation or incident. In-process memos, however, are products of a more concentrated effort to identify and develop analytic themes while still actively in the field and writing fieldnotes. Such memos are not usually stimulated by writing up a specific event. Taking a more consistent analytic stance, the fieldworker produces in-process memos by reading recently completed pieces or sets of fieldnotes to identify and develop particular interpretations, questions, or themes.[15] Clearly, these distinctions are not absolute; the lines between asides, commentaries, and in-process memos are often blurred. We offer them as heuristic devices that may sensitize the fieldworker both to momentary and to more sustained concentration on analytic writing while actively producing fieldnotes.

Asides are brief, reflective bits of analytic writing that succinctly clarify, explain, interpret, or raise questions about some specific happening or process described in a fieldnote. The ethnographer dashes off asides in the midst of descriptive writing, taking a moment to react personally or theoretically to something she has just recounted on paper, and then immediately turns back to the work of description. These remarks may be inserted in the midst of descriptive paragraphs and set off by parentheses, as in the following examples. In the first, the writer pauses in an aside to explain his reaction:

As we're driving along I ask George how long he has been teaching and he tells me, "Well, it's going on my eighth year." I respond with a "Wow! (I didn't think he was as old as that.) He smiles as he looks at me and goes on to explain where he used to teach.

In the next excerpt, the ethnographer notes his uneasy feelings in an aside about someone watching him:

I turn around, away from the office, and face the woman with the blondish hair who is still smiling. (I can't shake the feeling that she's gazing at me.) "I'll see you Friday," I say to her as I walk by her and out the front door.

Fieldworkers often write somewhat more elaborate asides, several phrases in length, again triggered by some immediate piece of writing and closely tied to the events or scenes depicted in that writing. In the fieldnote below, the fieldworker describes a moment during her first day at a crisis drop-in center and then reacts to that experience in a more extended aside:

Walking up the stairs to the agency office, I noticed that almost every step creaked or moaned. At the top stands an old pine coat hanger, piled high with coats. Behind it is a bulletin board containing numerous flyers with information about organizations and services of various kinds. (Thinking about the scene as I climbed those stairs, I think that if I were an upset, distraught client, I would most probably find it difficult to find helpful information in that disorganized mass.)

In providing her own "lived sense" of the agency, the student incorporates in her description the meaning of physical space, while allowing for the possibility that others might perceive it differently. Asides may also be used to explain something that would otherwise not be apparent, or to offer some sort of personal reflection or interpretive remark on a matter just considered. Ethnographers frequently use asides, for example, to convey their explicit "feel" for or emotional reactions to events; putting these remarks in asides keeps them from intruding into the descriptive account. A *commentary* is a more elaborate reflection on some specific event or issue; it is contained in a separate paragraph and set off with parentheses. Commentaries involve a shift of attention from events in the field to outside audiences imagined as having an interest in something the fieldworker has observed and written up. Again, in contrast to descriptive fieldnotes, commentaries may explore problems of access or emotional reactions to events in the field, suggest ongoing probes into likely connections with other events, or offer tentative interpretations. Putting commentary in separate paragraphs helps avoid writing up details as evidence for preconceived categories or interpretations.[16]

Commentaries can be used to create a record of the ethnographer's own doings, experiences, and reactions during fieldwork, both in observing-participating and in writing up. A researcher/intern placed in a social service agency wrote the following commentary after describing an incident that she felt marked a turning point in her relationship with staff:

Entering the kitchen, where staff often go to socialize alone, I began to prepare my lunch. Soon, several staff had come in, and they began to talk among one another. I stood around awkwardly, not quite knowing what to do with myself. I exchanged small talk for awhile until D, the director, asked in her typically dramatic tone loud enough for everyone to hear: "Guess where A (a staff member who was also present) is going for her birthday?" There was silence in the room. Turning in her direction, I realized that she was speaking to me. "Where?" I asked, somewhat surprised that she was talking to me. "To Hershey Park!" she exclaimed. "No way!" I said, and feeling embarrassed, I started laughing. "Yeah," D exclaimed, "She's gonna dip her whole body in chocolate so R (lover) can eat her!" The room filled up with laughter, and I, too, could not restrain my giggles.

(With that, the group broke up, and as I walked back to my desk, I began to feel that for the first time, I had been an active participant in one of their kitchen get-togethers. This experience made me believe that I was being viewed as more than just an outsider. I have been trying to figure out what it takes to belong here, and one aspect undoubtedly is to partake in an occasional kitchen get-together and not to appear above such practices.)

In this commentary the researcher not only reports her increased feeling of acceptance in the scene but also reflects on the likely importance of these informal, sometimes ribald "get-togethers" for creating a general sense of belonging in the organization.

Finally, commentaries can raise issues of what terms and events mean to members, make initial connections between some current observation and prior fieldnotes, and suggest points or places for further observation, as in the following excerpt:

> M called over to Richard. He said, "C'm here lil' Homey." Richard came over to sit closer to M. He asked Richard about something Richard said earlier (I couldn't completely hear it) . . . something to do with weight lifting. Richard replied, "Oh, I could talk about it for hours. . . ." M asked Richard if there was a place where he could lift weights on campus. Richard said there was a weightroom, but only "hoops" could use it today. M then asked Richard what 'hoops' was. Richard answered that "hoops" was basketball.
>
> (Is the word *homey,* possibly derived from *homeboy,* somebody who is *down* or *cool* with another person? It seems to me that M, who apparently didn't know Richard, wanted to talk to him. In order to do that, he tried to let Richard know M thought he was a *cool* person? *Homey* appears to be applied regardless of ethnicity. . . . Their interaction appeared to be organized around interest in a common activity, weight lifting. Judging by the size of M's muscles, this was something he excelled in.)

This ethnographer has been noticing the ways blacks use the terms *cool* and *down* to refer to inclusion of non-blacks in their otherwise black groupings. In this commentary, he reflects on other terms which also seem to be inclusive.

In-process memos are products of more sustained analytic writing and require a more extended time-out from actively composing fieldnotes. Often they are written after completing the day's fieldnotes. Although perhaps touched off by thoughts generated by writing up a day's fieldnote entries, such memos address incidents across several sets of fieldnotes. In writing in-process memos, the fieldworker clearly envisions outside audiences and frames his thoughts and experiences in ways likely to interest them.

In-process memos can profitably address practical, methodological questions that include: Where should I observe next? What questions should I ask to follow up on this event? These questions help direct the ethnographer's attention, focusing and guiding future observations and analysis. Asking such questions helped a researcher in a battered women's shelter identify gaps in her understanding of how staff viewed and accomplished their work:

The goals staff have talked about so far of "conveying unconditional positive re-gard" for clients and "increasing their self-esteem" seem rather vague. How does the staff know when they have achieved unconditional positive regard? Is it based on their interaction with the client or by their refraining from being judgmental or critical of them during staff meetings? I will attempt to discover how they define and attempt to achieve the goal of "increasing a woman's self-esteem." It has been made clear that this goal is not only seen to be achieved when women leave their abusive relationships. If leaving their abusive partners were the primary indicator of achieving raised self-esteem, the organization would be largely unsuc-cessful, since most of these women go back to their abusive relationships. Yet, while I have learned what raising self-esteem is not, I have yet to learn what it is.

In this more extended series of comments and questions, the fieldworker identifies two matters that shelter staff members emphasize as goals in their relations with clients: "conveying unconditional positive regard" and increasing client "self-esteem." She then considers ways she might look to understand how these general policies/values are actually imple-mented and their success or failure practically assessed in interactions within the shelter.

In-process memos may elaborate new interpretations developed from subsequent incidents or understandings, as in the following:

Several weeks ago, I wrote about a client whom staff found to be quite aggravat-ing and "annoying" because she had been continually calling the crisis line at all hours of the morning. At the time I had been under the impression that staff perceived such calls as unnecessary unless they pertained to immediate threats of physical injury. Through a conversation that took place today [included in earlier notes], I realize that this was an accurate but oversimplified notion. Although the staff finds late night crisis calls quite aggravating, they also acknowledge the neces-sity of maintaining such an option to deal primarily with violence of an immedi-ate and physical nature. But even if the caller's situation does not fit into that category, she wouldn't necessarily be identified as a "nuisance" unless she had called repeatedly and had enough familiarity with the organization to know bet-ter. Each caller seems to be viewed as an individual case and is treated accordingly. It is only when their issues become too time consuming or chronic that are they identified as nuisance callers.

Here the student developed a more complex analysis by correcting and extending an earlier analytic claim. Writing helped her clarify her ideas and draw out subtle differences as she systematically examined new infor-mation in light of what she had previously understood.

As a general practice in writing commentaries and in-process memos, the field researcher should remain open-minded, avoiding conclusive analytic statements in favor of possibilities and alternatives. These writings are most helpful when offering probing reflections, tentative musings, and open questions. For example, phrases such as "possibly," "apparently," "appeared to be" reflect these qualities in the field researcher's commentaries on the term "homey."

The field researcher may experience uncertainty and strain in deciding when to concentrate on writing thoroughly descriptive fieldnotes and when to record and develop analytic insights. Writing analytic commentary and in-process memos can easily displace time and effort needed for writing core descriptive fieldnotes. Yet we have often found that new ideas, like the descriptive details that make vivid fieldnotes, are fleeting; if not written down immediately, they tend to "get lost" or remain underdeveloped. So the field researcher may constantly have to balance the impulse to write down ideas and insights when they occur against the compulsion to "get it all down" as quickly and completely as possible without interruption.

In sum, ongoing reflection and analysis, even as the fieldworker continues to observe in the field and to actively write fieldnotes, is crucial for ethnographic research. Writing analytic asides, commentary, and in-process memos helps the field researcher carry forward analysis contemporaneously with the collection of field data. Such reflective writing often incites the researcher to pay closer attention to what she sees and, thus, to write more detailed and vivid descriptions. In-process analytic writing in turn increases the possibility of making the kinds of observations needed to develop and support a specific analysis. The more explicitly analytic themes are identified, the better able the fieldworker is to "check out" different alternatives, making and recording observations that can confirm, modify, or reject different interpretations. Theoretical asides and commentary, as well as more elaborate theoretical memos, enhance these prospects.

REFLECTIONS: FIELDNOTES AS PRODUCTS OF WRITING CHOICES

In writing fieldnotes, ethnographers have as their primary goal description rather than analysis. A researcher writes notes with a specific purpose in mind: to record a slice of life on a page. But these contrasting terms—description and analysis—refer more to recognized kinds of writing than to separate cognitive activities. In that sense, writing fieldnotes is a process of "analysis-in-description." Indeed, all descriptions are selective, purposed, angled, voiced, because they are authored. To "write up life" in this way, an ethnographer uses language conventions to create an envisioned scene. Sketches and episodes present a still-life or tell a story; they paint portraits of settings, people, and actions rather than offer causal explanations or build an argument.

All writing, by definition, is an abstracting and ordering process: clear writing always has internal coherence, the product of the writer's attention to the subject as well as to the potential reader. Ethnographers construct their fieldnotes in a process more accurately captured by the expression "writing up" than "writing down" or "getting down" people's doings and sayings. Writers do more than inscribe the world. Just as the ethnographer-as-observer participates with members in constructing a social reality, so too the ethnographer-as-writer creates that world through language.

In this chapter, we have seen that even though restricted to actual observed details, an ethnographer always "creates" the described scene. Writing fieldnotes *processes* experience not only through a researcher's attention in the field but also through a writer's memory and compositional choices at the desk. An ethnographer perceives interactions and selects significant details; in writing she groups these details into a coherent whole according to conventional writing strategies.[17]

Awareness of writing conventions, however, is not meant to lead a writer to be more craftily inventive through the use of persuasive rhetorical skills. Rather it invites the ethnographer to make more conscious choices when creating fieldnote records that portray social worlds as experienced and perceived by others. Consider the effects of writing: not only does a writer's theoretical stance influence compositional choices, but the reverse also happens. Even by inadvertently imitating an "objective" social science style, for example, with its measured wording, omniscient viewpoint, and use of the passive voice, descriptions reflect an affinity—though ever so subtle—for that orientation. Certainly, a writing style tends to shape any writer's vision. How researchers see in the field, in part, results from what they find noteworthy and "writable" as a fieldnote. Consequently, students concerned about research integrity must develop a conscientious respect for how their writing choices influence both fieldwork and note-taking.

Whether carefully or haphazardly written, every fieldnote mirrors an author's choices: to include these details rather than those, to view actions either through this character's or that one's eyes, to sequence actions in this way or that way (or randomly), or to write with particular readers in mind. These authorial choices, if only subliminal, result in on-the-page descriptions with certain kinds of detail, a particular point of view, a tone and attitude toward the persons depicted, and a distinctive voice. These day-to-day renderings of scenes pile up, and writing choices assume a cumulative effect: the notes portray that world through this particular writer's lens. In making writing choices, therefore, *how* ethnographers write fieldnotes becomes as consequential for readers and those depicted as what they write. Whether as privately filed resources or as public excerpts in final documents, fieldnotes persuade.

chapter five

Pursuing Members' Meanings

At first glance, it might seem that the pursuit of members' meanings is fundamentally a matter not of writing but of what one does in the field—of asking questions and of positioning oneself to hear and observe others' concerns. Members' meanings, however, are not pristine objects that are simply "discovered." Rather, these meanings are interpretive constructions assembled and conveyed by the ethnographer. This process certainly begins with asking questions and paying attention what is relevant to people in some indigenous group. But the key to the process lies in sensitively representing in written texts what local people consider meaningful and then in making their concerns accessible to readers who are unfamiliar with their social world. Ultimately, members' concerns must be written down as fieldnotes and then incorporated into more comprehensive ethnographic accounts.

Given these complexities in capturing members' meanings, it is not surprising that field researchers' efforts to do so have been partial or inconsistent in two distinctive ways. First, some field researchers blunt appreciation of members' meanings by importing outside categories to describe local scenes and actions. This sort of imposition obscures indigenous meanings. Second, some researchers present static taxonomies of native terms. The ethnographer's task, however, is more complex: she must not only apprehend and convey members' categories, but she must also explain how members use terms in specific interactional situations and how involved parties differentially understand and evaluate them.

In this chapter we examine how ethnographic writing can become sensitive to and vividly represent member-recognized meanings. In writing fieldnotes, the ethnographer makes her initial and perhaps most fundamental choices about seeing and presenting members' meanings. But she must not lose that commitment to local views when she writes memos or later on when she composes her final ethnographic document—even though she may be tempted to transform members' meanings into analytic concepts more familiar to herself and to her readers. Indeed, to infer and present members' meanings is perhaps one of the greatest challenges in ethnographic writing, whether in the immediacy of detailed fieldnotes or in the more public, abstract writing of final texts. Thus, in this chapter we provide illustrations taken not only from students' original fieldnotes but also from working memos and final ethnographic papers. We begin the chapter by considering how accounts often obscure or suppress members' meanings by imposing outside understandings of events. We then examine ways of writing to convey the meanings of those studied. First, we suggest ways of writing about what is significant to members; we then explore the problems involved in conveying local meanings.

Imposing Exogenous Meanings

All too frequently ethnographic fieldnotes fail to attend consistently to members' meanings, instead importing outside or exogenous categories and meanings. Imposition of outside categories produces fieldnote descriptions that fail to *appreciate* local meanings and concerns (Matza 1969:15–40) and that tend to frame events as what they are *not* (that is, by reference to categories or standards that differ from those recognized and used by members). In general, field researchers concerned with members' meanings are leery of any classifications which do not refer to the categories that the people recognize and actually use among themselves.

Failures to appreciate members' classifications arise from several sources. First, lapsing into classic ethnocentrism, researchers may take a category, standard, or meaning from one culture or locale and use it to describe events in another context. For example, based on their own expectations, Westerners in an African cinema or theatre might describe as "disruptive" loud audience remarks to characters and thus fail to appreciate such participation as a locally appropriate way of expressing an evaluation of the performance. Or an observer may employ exogenous criteria to evaluate school classrooms as "noisy" or "chaotic," thereby ignoring teachers' and students' actual understandings of how classroom activities should be conducted. Both procedures caricature rather than describe behavior on its own terms.

Second, in a similar vein, ethnographers may use a term, category, or evaluation that is recognized, used, and honored by *one group* in a particular social world to describe features or behaviors of another group in that world. For example, psychiatric staff might interpret certain patients' behavior as "acting out" or "denial," even though the patients understand the actions as common, everyday behavior. Often a field researcher who comes across different local understandings of the same event has a tendency to accept one view as "true," thereby marginalizing competing versions. In one situation in Zambia, for example, a diviner-healer determined that an older man who suddenly could not walk had been bewitched and, after treating him for a year with medicines and massage, cured him. However, the medical doctor at the local hospital, on hearing the account and later meeting the man, concluded that he had had a stroke resulting in paralysis. In writing fieldnotes, a Western ethnographer might be tempted to privilege, though ever so subtly, the medical doctor's "scientific" account and then to describe the diviner's interpretation as "belief," thereby prioritizing one practitioner's explanations as more "accurate" and implicitly more efficacious.

Third, field researchers may adopt a dismissive attitude toward members' meanings, treating such meanings as flawed, hypocritical, contradictory, or fallacious. For example, a student ethnographer working in Los Angeles observed in weekly meetings of a study group devoted to the philosophy of Edgar Cayce. In the following fieldnote, she describes an incident recounted by a member to the group:

Dolores lost her purse and did not panic. She threw the white light around it and asked God to protect it. She also asked that no one be tempted to take her identification, credit cards, and money. The next day when she went to work, she asked the guard on duty if the purse had been turned in. Indeed it had and nothing had been displaced.

The student initially interpreted this story as indicating an extremely "passive" approach to the problems of daily life:

The moral of the story was to leave everything in God's hands. . . . To me visualizing the white light and talking to God are very passive ways of dealing with an emergency situation as opposed to going to the police or retracing one's steps.

This interpretation dismisses "casting the white light" and "talking to God" as ineffective nonactions at best and as pathological delusions at worst. It implicitly counters, and hence negates, the group member's claim that the purse had been turned in and nothing taken *because of* her prayerful actions. The result is to debunk the actual beliefs of this particular group about the efficacy of action in everyday life.[1]

Fourth, fieldnote descriptions and memos may be framed in terms of a standard of what is "supposed to be" that derives from official rules or understandings that are held to govern action in some specific setting. For example, noting a discrepancy between an elder's account of the traditional meaning and sequences of a ritual and the actual performance of that ritual, an ethnographer might describe this ritual as "in decline" rather than as subject to adaptation and variation.[2] Similarly, an ethnographer might describe and analyze police action on the streets in terms of official regulations for the use of force; how actual police officers evaluate specific street situations and decide when and what kinds of force to use is thereby ignored.[3] In both instances, ethnographers implicitly determine whether actions should count as conforming to or departing from the "traditional" version or "official" regulations and hence whether these actions are "in fact" "authentic" ritual behavior or a "legitimate" use of force.

Fifth, the researcher may invoke a priori theoretical categories, often those sacred to the core of a particular discipline, to characterize events and settings. For example, in studies of traditional narrating, past researchers relied heavily upon the analytic categories of "myth," "legend," and "folktale" even in explaining non–Western traditions. Since these categories often impose Eurocentric notions and thus misrepresent a people's storytelling traditions and practices, contemporary folklorists increasingly characterize storytelling with the indigenous terms and explanations of the group studied and describe how people use these terms in particular storytelling events.[4]

Indeed, a field researcher may implicitly impose such categories exactly in asking exogenous questions rooted in an a priori research agenda or theoretical framework. Not only might a researcher impose ideas when questioning an "informant," but she might also impose an inappropriate form of expression whose constraints distort responses. For example, a field researcher who asks for a list of ingredients in cures or discrete steps in a ritual may get arbitrary lists intended to please the researcher. Or, when asked questions imposing external analysis and itemization, people may offer "non-answers" such as "yes," "no," or "sometimes," especially if they usually describe these healing and ritual events by recounting the story of the experience.[5] In sound ethnographic research, in contrast, "both questions and answers must be discovered from informants" (Spradley 1979:84).[6]

Finally, describing local settings or actions in terms of dichotomized variables may involve an imposition of exogenous categories. For an ethnographer to describe those present in a bar as "regulars" and "non-regulars," for example, may ignore a range of other, more variegated distinctions bar patrons may draw between one another. In general, the reduction of ongoing social life to variables and to dichotomies tends to produce a radical decontextualizing and destruction of local meanings.

In all these ways, ethnographers tend to produce fieldnotes and in-process memos that ignore, marginalize, and obscure indigenous understandings. In the following sections, we suggest alternative procedures for writing fieldnotes that avoid such impositions and that help develop descriptions and analyses that are sensitive to local concerns, meanings, and categories.

REPRESENTING MEMBERS' MEANINGS

A number of distinct moments in group life highlight how members express, orient to, and create local meaning. Ethnographers begin to construct members' meanings by looking closely at *what members say and do* during such moments, paying particular attention to the words, phrases, and categories that members use in their everyday interactions.

Members' Terms of Address and Greetings

The way members address and greet each other is one of the most immediately noticeable and revealing kinds of talk. Ethnographers often begin by noting and learning the proper terms of address, especially when working in a foreign language and culture. In many communities, the way people address one another reflects their relative statuses; consider, for example, the difference between first-name familiarity and the deference marked by formal titles such as Dr. or Mr. and Ms. Furthermore, how people greet each other—both with words and body language—often indicates something about the closeness, respectfulness, deference, or hostility of that relationship.[7]

In Chokwe villages, for example, people address each other with kinship terms, such as *tata* (father), *mama* (mother), *yaya* (older sibling of the same sex as speaker), *mwakwethu* (younger sibling of the same sex as speaker), or *ndumbwami* (any sibling of the opposite sex of speaker) (Fretz 1987:58–65). Listening to other people call out to each other reveals their kinship relationship and helps the researcher learn local expectations for appropriate speech and behavior. For instance, Chokwe grandparents and their grandchildren may be publicly affectionate and joke together about sexual matters in ways deemed inappropriate for other relationships. In contrast, in-laws greet each other formally from a distance (the younger person must step off the path) and never eat together. Similarly in American society, terms of address and greetings can reveal distinctive features of social relations. It may be significant in classroom and psychiatric settings, for example, whether students and clients address teachers and staff by first or last name. In the same way, whether people exchange greetings, and how they do so, may provide indications of locally significant ethnic affiliation and disaffiliation (Anderson 1990:168–73).

Everyday Questions and Answers

An astute ethnographer notices the kinds of questions local people frequently ask and the kinds of answers ordinarily given. For example, in many African societies, people greet and ask each other the appropriate, basic questions many times a day. The Chokwe, for instance, inquire about each other's well-being, including the entire extended family (*"Kuci ku nzuwo?"* "How is it at home?"); they also ask about their own and the family's health (*"Unahindvuka, nyi?"* "Are you well?"). These questions can open to conversations about health, work, money problems, quarrels in the family, births, deaths, eating well or searching for food, or celebrations. Learning to appropriately ask and answer such questions can lead into conversations about issues which Chokwe consider vital to their everyday success or failure.[8]

Ethnographers sensitive to members' experiences and views not only listen to members' questions; they also ask questions that are intentionally open-ended, so as to allow members to use their own language and concepts in responding to them. In addition, they orient such questions to topics which members find meaningful, that is, interesting, relevant to everyday concerns, in keeping with the ways they act and talk. By orienting questions to mutually observed actions and overheard speech, an ethnographer is more likely to ask questions which make sense to members; he might ask a question about an incident they both witnessed, about the member's explanation of a term he just used, or about a comment someone else made during a conversation. Such questions allow people to answer with familiar forms of expression, embedding responses in a context which makes sense to them and thereby revealing their concepts—their *member's orientation* to the "information."

Naturally Occurring Members' Descriptions

Ethnographers pay close attention to how members themselves characterize and describe particular activities, events, and groups. Recognizing that an event has no single, necessary, or invariant meaning, the field researcher does not assume that she knows what significance members attribute to the incidents and objects that make up their world. Rather she listens closely to what members say in the course of their ordinary activities about what something "was about" or what import an occurrence has for them.[9]

Members frequently provide naturally occurring descriptions of their setting when they introduce or orient outsiders. Such descriptions may be explicitly framed to highlight qualities members consider special or unique. For example, in the following fieldnote, a HUD [Housing and Urban Development] caseworker describes his work to the researcher and points out the distinctive features of his agency.

"The larger a bureaucracy is, the less luxury a professional working within that bureaucracy has of making human contact. If I'm interviewing 20 or 25 people per day, I don't have time to break through. I have to do the job and I have to move on to the next. Sometimes, that's truly a case of numbers, why people in government jobs act the way they do. We're a small agency, we sometimes have that luxury. Other times we don't."

This caseworker expresses his concern about making personal contact with applicants for federally subsidized housing, but at the same time he signals that practical constraints sometimes make such contact an impossible "luxury." Thus, his description does more than orient the researcher to the place; it also reveals his views about his work.

Naturally occurring descriptions can also arise more informally in the course of ongoing talk about significant events in the setting. Here, for example, a field researcher may want to pay close attention to how any other newcomers are introduced to and taught "how things are done." Since newcomers are learning the ins and outs of what to do, they often ask questions and make mistakes that reveal, through their own ignorance of them, the implicit knowledge and skills that most long-time members take for granted.

For these very reasons, the ethnographer may want to record in detailed fieldnotes how she learns to make her way into and through a setting, since members often socialize and instruct researchers just as they do any other newcomer or their own children. Indeed, in many situations such socialization is unavoidable. For example, when first living in a Chokwe village, every move the fieldworker made as she learned to cook outdoors on a charcoal burner—down to exactly how to stir the pot—was subject to laughter, commentary, and correction by watching neighbor women. Since people regularly work together and freely tease each other about mistakes, they enjoyed the researcher's awkwardness and jokingly told her she seemed like a child. The fieldworker not only learned appropriate behavior but also was able to notice the kind of expressions—laughter, reprimand, correction—through which people socialize others.[10]

Special problems arise when a researcher has directly observed a particular event; it is very easy to assume that since one saw something happen, one knows what it means to others in the setting. Here the field researcher should try to supplement her own description by listening to how members talk about this event with others at some later time. Thus, the fieldworker who has observed a complaint-filing encounter between a district attorney and police detective may later record fieldnotes detailing how the former recounted "what happened" to a colleague over lunch.[11]

Similarly, the ethnographer should not assume that the local meaning and import of written documents are transparent and unproblematic. Instead, he should seek to understand how documents are read, understood, and interpreted by members. Thus, rather than simply treating a report as an objective record, a field researcher might look closely at how a staff person summarizes the "essence" or "gist" of that report and then include in fieldnotes both what was in the document and how the member responded to it.

Consider, for example, the following fieldnote describing a probation officer's interview with Tom, a sixteen-year-old, white surfer enrolled in a special probation school. Having looked at a "progress report" from the special school the youth was attending, the researcher wrote the following fieldnote:

Overall his progress report has improved a little. But there was one day when Tom was sent home. Shelly asked him about this.

Here the researcher uncritically asserts that the progress report "has improved a little"; or more likely, since the probation officer a little bit later characterized the report in these terms, the researcher has simply taken over this judgment as her own. This procedure ignores the processes of interpreting a progress report, of finding "improvement" or "lack of improvement" in it. It treats the report as a factual record of the youth's behavior rather than as an opaque document produced in one setting and now being used in another.[12] It obscures how the probation officer's characterization of "improved a little" may have been formulated specifically for this situation (e.g., to keep up the youth's morale). In general, through this approach the researcher has taken over a member's interpretation, treating it as a matter of fact rather than as a meaning constructed in a specific context for a particular reason.

Field researchers not only listen for naturally occurring descriptions; they can also elicit members' descriptions, carefully drawing out others to talk about what is significant to them.[13] Thus, the fieldworker might ask a probation officer to talk about what she makes of a particular report or what she finds significant in it.

Members' Stories

People may present extended descriptions of events they witnessed or directly experienced, or of the reported doings of others (e.g., "gossip"), organized by means of some narrative strategy into a personal story.[14]

Such members' stories may provide insight into the people and events they describe. However, such stories are always partial, being told for many different reasons and adjusted to fit different relationships and situations. In this sense they may provide insight into the teller's momentary concerns and circumstances. Consider, for example, this extended story told to a researcher by a probation officer:

> "You been missin' the action, man," Jim said to me. I replied, "What happened?"
>
> Jim walked over to the vending machine to get his staple snack. Then he started to tell me that parents of a twenty-one-year-old male called him today and they wanted their son arrested. The son had just gotten out of the "house" [jail] and had evidently not shown up for his first appointment for probation. His father said he was already back on crack and "binging hard." Doing nothing all day except for smoking crack, he would stay in bed . . . only getting up to eat and go to the bathroom. And the father said, in the phone conversation, that his son should not be given the choice of jail or rehabilitation because he would always choose prison. (By choosing jail, the convict can be back on the streets smoking crack again in only a month.)
>
> Jim continued to tell me that he went over there to arrest him because he was "crashing." . . . When he arrived, he had the parent sign all the legal papers. And, when he opened the door to arrest him, Jim noticed "he had a strawberry with him" (a whore who sells her body for drugs, not money). He said that the arrest went smoothly because the son "was so out of it"; he was "in the house right now."

While this story is *about* a young man on probation, it *reveals* the probation officer's ordinary work practices and concerns, and the distinctive perspectives and commitments which underlie them.[15] In this sense, ethnographers do not take a member's story as a factual account but rather as an expression of the speaker's experience and views at a particular moment in time, to a specific audience, in order to accomplish particular purposes. He values and documents these stories as revealing a member's experience and perspective.

Ethnographers should also look out for and record different stories told about the same events. These different versions might be grounded in some of the same details, but each account is likely to include details not present in the other, to order actions in slightly different ways, and to offer different interpretations of cause and responsibility. Thus, a teacher's account of a "disruptive" classroom fight told to a field researcher might sound very different from the version the teacher subsequently relates to his peers over lunch. In writing fieldnotes, the researcher should preserve these differences if she is fortunate enough to hear both versions.

Diverse versions provide insights into the ways different members construct and make meaning of the same event.[16] For example, in a study of personal experience stories about the Los Angeles riots that followed the acquittal of the police officers who beat Rodney King, an African-American student researcher highlighted the diverse voices of African-Americans talking about their similar experiences. In the following story, for example, the teller exults in the camaraderie between different races and the "sense of community" he felt with those helping each other "take the sh—, the stuff":

"I remember—hearing the verdicts were in, and—this was at school, and—uhmm also being in a state of disbelief, that, uhmm they came back not guilty, the cops.

"And, uhmm, I went home, and my friends were coming by and I didn't know that they were about to go out. So, I went with them and we went out into downtown, and—we started taking things.

"And I just remember that it was—like a unified effort and everyone was in the streets. And people who were gangbangers and everything else were, like, helping you take the sh—, the stuff. Like, 'Oh you want that man? Here, I'll get that for you.' And it was like I felt, a, a, sense of community there, with different races. I mean, these were Hispanics and everything else, and we were all throwin' up the power sign and goin' in taking what we wanted. And, uhmm—basically that's what went on after I had first heard."

Judy, a married, property-owning woman, talked about similar events and her own experiences in very different terms:

"I talked to a lot of the neighbors. And, I asked the, the Latinos, why is you stealin' all this stuff, you know. It's bad, you know, you know.

"And me and my husband, we went walkin'. We just went walkin', you know, we wasn't hurtin' nobody, 'cause you could easily walk up and down the streets and see what was goin' on.

"And, you know, the funniest thing, you know, one of the neighbors said, 'You know, my clothes is in the cleaners around there.' And so they started walkin' over there to see had they messed up the cleaners. And when they got around there—'they was at the cleaners.' And there was her clothes, one of the Mexican guys had them—And my husband told them to 'put that stuff back there.' And [the neighbor] said, 'You ain't gonna take my clothes. You ain't gonna take my clothes. You ain't gonna take my clothes.' Cause that was the main reason we went around the corner."

In the first story, the African-American narrator identifies himself as an active participant in "taking stuff," along with "gangbangers," "Hispanics," and everyone else. He narrates the experience as a bonding between people, as a "sense of community there, with different races." In contrast, from the very beginning of the second story, another African-American teller depicts the conflicting stances people took in the street activities: some are out walking around just to look, while others are actively "stealing." She begins telling about watching and rebuking the Latinos for "stealin' all the stuff." Then, she continues by recounting her neighbor's experience as a near-victim of such stealing: the teller, her husband, and the neighbor go to check on the local cleaners and find "one of the Mexican guys" taking the neighbor's clothes; they insist that the man "put that stuff back there." The two stories reveal the narrators' strikingly different alignments toward the rioters and, more implicitly, their different understandings of the nature and significance of the riot. In writing about these stories, the ethnographer—herself an African-American present during the riots—pointed out that this ethnic community did not respond as a homogeneous group but rather voiced a variety of views. In fact, though some called it a "riot," others referred to it as a "rebellion" to more emphatically express their political interpretation of the fires and looting. By carefully documenting multiple stories, this researcher was able to examine the different ways people make meaning of a community event.

Members' Terms, Types, and Typologies

Ethnographers give close attention to the terms or phrases that members regularly use to characterize people and events. Many ethnographers are less concerned with the formal, technical terms that reflect the demands of bureaucracy, public relations, and frontstage civility; they are drawn to everyday, colloquial, and often evocative terms, terms that may be graphic or earthy (e.g., "shit work" in Emerson and Pollner 1976; "assholes" in Van Maanen 1978) and that reflect and express practical, mundane concerns.

Consider some of the types recognized among those living in a residential facility for ex-mental patients (Shaw 1988:282–320). On the one hand, staff identified some residents as "together" or "movers," implying that they would benefit from therapy and eventually find a job and set up independent living situations. They contrasted this type with "losers"— chronic patients with minimal skills and resources who are deemed unlikely to ever get out of the system of mental health care. On the other hand, residents recognized distinctions based on whether one emphasized ties with some other residents or oriented toward developing ties and receiving favors from staff. The former included "gadflies," "therapists," "spiritualists," "nice guys," and those known to hang out with the "drug group." Residents called those peers who were oriented to staff and staff concerns "old powerhouse" and "top dogs." Clearly the differences between these various terms suggest important differences between the practical concerns of staff and different groupings of residents.

The ethnographer who hears such native terms should not assume that they have single, discrete meanings, but rather she should explore their various shades of meaning and differing import to members positioned differently within the setting. For example, a student ethnographer observing in a cottage for delinquent girls at the Reyes Reform School heard both staff and inmates talk about "buzzes"—personal letters written by one inmate to another that were officially banned by staff as an expression of gang affiliation. In the following incident recorded in her fieldnotes, she presents an inmate's concern about staff searches for "buzzes":

Then Kate started talking about how she was so excited that there wasn't a room search today because she remembered during 4th period that she had 7 illegal buzzes in her room.

But "buzzes" had very different significance for staff and inmates. Staff saw buzzes as a form of gang activity that might well escalate tensions between gang members. The girls described buzzes simply as "love letters" without implications for gang affiliations and activities. Consider, for example, these comments taken from an analytic memo written by the ethnographer:

Three girls in the cottage described buzzes in the following ways:
    Claudia: "It's like a regular letter . . . like a love letter we write to boys, or they write to us."
    Kate: "Illegal letters—not passed through POs and we get 24s" [24 hour seclusion in their room].
    Dani: "A small note that is passed to any other minor in the form of communication and if caught with one, you must suffer consequences, such as in a 24."

Not only do these descriptions lack any reference to gangs; they also convey that buzzes are significant to the girls exactly because they comprise the focal point of the staff's stringent searches and expose those caught to a standard house punishment ("24s").

REPRESENTING MEANINGS 121

To explore and convey broader meanings, it is useful to pay attention
to how a term's use compares with and differs from the uses of related
terms. For example, the Chokwe have terms for several different kinds
of "tellings."[17] They distinguish between these tellings by using various
cognitive categories, which are marked by distinctive terms, expressive
features such as diction and style, and social behaviors appropriate to
different situations.[18] For example, *kuta pande* refers to informal talking
and telling about recent personal experiences—usually in an exaggerated,
dramatized manner—as people visit together in the late afternoons and
evening. However, *kulweza sango* refers to telling about community news
or events which people know to have happened; people tell such news
often as a part of greetings or when visiting. In contrast, *kuta yishima* refers
to telling traditional stories (and sometimes proverbs), supposedly based
on real events the ancestors experienced and reported to others long ago.
People describe *kuta yishima* as "coming from the ancestors" and as "told
to make us wise," but they recognize that these tellings are a sort of fic-
tionalized truth often manipulated during the performances for persuasive purposes.

But these terms do not sufficiently indicate all the distinctions which
the Chokwe make. Although they do not use distinct terms for each, the
Chokwe do distinguish between two different kinds of *yishima*—short
sayings or proverbs and longer stories. People employ the shorter *yishima*
(proverbs) in informal and formal conversation (e.g., court sessions) to
make a point. In contrast, people tell the longer *yishima* only at night as
they sit around their fires visiting and entertaining themselves. In these
latter situations, narrators are inventive composers playing to the enthusi-
astic responses of listeners; thus, different narrators will tell different versions of the same story, and the same narrator's version of a story will vary
from telling to telling. If pressed to verbally distinguish between kinds of
yishima, people might say "the long ones" *(yishima yisuku)* for stories or
"the short ones" *(yishima yipinji)* for proverbs, but these distinctions are
not commonly made verbally. Furthermore, in specific instances people
do sometimes make further distinctions between kinds of stories, even
though they are all known as *yishima.* For example, when listeners want
to participate more fully in the performance by singing along, they might
request a *chishima-cha-miaso* (a story-with-a-song), in which the narrator
weaves a recurring song into the plot.

Indeed, ethnographers should attend to momentary and situational
distinctions between terms as well as to more pervasive ones. Though

these distinctions may not become evident in any one observation or interview, over time by writing fieldnotes and memos such distinctions become increasingly evident to the researcher. By noticing members' distinctions between related terms, an ethnographer is less likely to impose her own ethnocentric distinctions. A close attention to the situated use of terms often reveals additional distinctions within the cognitive categories the terms at first appear to indicate.

In some situations, ethnographers may come to focus on member-recognized *types*. People may refer to types with distinct terms or expressions. For example, social agencies routinely come to distinguish between different client types, as analyzed in a student ethnography of a community mental health clinic:

The chronic client is seen as having a low level of functioning, unsocial behavior, and residual "symptoms" (i.e., hearing voices and talking back to them). These people are viewed by staff as "hard to handle" and "in their own world." . . . In contrast, the client with "potential" is seen as having a favorable prognosis and exhibits occasional "symptoms" as contrasted with the ongoing "symptoms" of the "chronic." The staff usually use terms such as "cooperative," "intelligent," and "potential" in describing these clients. There clients are also seen as "trying more than the chronics," as having greater possibilities as well as capabilities. As Julian said of one such patient: "Even though Sam messes up sometimes, he's a good guy. He tries, you know what I mean?"

In identifying members' types, this ethnographer not only specified the terms used in referring to a type, such as "chronic client" and "client with potential," but also she incorporated members' descriptions of types into her ethnographic account: a chronic client has ongoing symptoms, whereas a client with potential is intelligent, cooperative, and "trying" to improve.

Indigenous Contrasts

While ethnographers seek to avoid describing events and settings in terms of what they are not (that is, by contrast with other, familiar settings and standards; see Gearing 1970), there are occasions when members themselves use such characterizations. These sorts of "indigenous contrasts"[19] may provide useful insights into members' perceptions and evaluations. For example, in talking to a student ethnographer, a probation officer compared the Reyes Reform School and its residents with several other juvenile halls and their residents:

Having worked previously in detention halls for juveniles, she was struck by the differences at Reyes. At Reyes they are less stringent than in the halls. "The big thing here is buzzes, which are like nothing to me." In the halls, pens and pencils aren't allowed, but they are in Reyes. Metal isn't allowed in either; she took a metal splint that she found in Kate's room for fear that it could be used as a weapon. . . .

She described Reyes as a "placement center" where the kids receive "treatment." "These kids aren't terribly sophisticated." The kids in the halls would hide things in Noxema or baby powder, but that wasn't as big a concern here. In the halls "potential danger's always present." Here the girls mostly just want to talk to the boys.

Here the researcher picks up and writes in her fieldnotes about the contrast that a staff member draws between this reform school and juvenile hall. This indigenous contrast highlights several differences between these two work settings that are relevant to this staff member: less staff concern with danger, more relaxed forms of surveillance, more effort to "help" the kids. On other occasions as well, local staff made similar comparisons between Reyes and juvenile hall, emphasizing the former's "leniency" relative to the latter.

Similarly, in police patrol work, officers frequently contrast those who "hustle a lot" with "burn outs" who are just "putting in their time." A student ethnographer elaborated this contrast in the following memo:

The term "hustling" is used by deputies to refer to an officer who is always looking for crime, for a "good shake," for someone to take to jail. A "good shake" refers to someone whose search by the police will lead to a "good arrest." A "good arrest" typically refers to most felony arrests and some misdemeanor arrests (i.e., possession of a concealed weapon). One deputy described some recent good arrests: "The rapist I got yesterday was pretty fun. A couple of weeks ago, I got a biker with a 45 automatic. He also had a bulletproof vest and some drugs. That was a pretty good arrest." . . .

[In contrast], hustlers characterize burn-outs as making "bullshit" arrests; that is, he arrests people for crimes not considered to be serious by hustlers, but merely for the sake of "stats." "Stats" are a monthly record of which deputies at the station are making the most arrests. Burn-outs are thought to be concerned merely with the quantity, not the quality, of their arrests. One deputy remarked that he didn't want to work with another deputy, Al, because he feels Al arrests people for "petty shit"—drunkenness and traffic warrants.

The one-sidedness of the contrast drawn here is particularly striking. Those who identify themselves as "hustlers" characterize as "burn-outs" those to whom they attribute an alternative work style. The contrast, moreover, is extremely value-laden; "hustlers" make "good shakes" while "burn-outs" arrest for "petty shit" simply to satisfy administrative pressures. As a result, there is no way of telling whether those designated as "burn-outs" would identify themselves as sharing a distinctive approach to patrol work. Nor is there any appreciation of the alternative perspective toward police work that might be articulated by those who so identify; they might explain that their work style reflects the experience and maturity lacking in the violence-prone, "gung-ho" attitude of younger, more aggressive officers. In this light, indigenous contrasts may not always prove useful as ways of characterizing a setting as a whole; rather, such contrasts might alert the ethnographer to what specific groups within a setting identify as crucial or significant differences.

Members' Explanations and Theories

An ethnographer should look for and seek to convey members' more complex *explanations* for when, why, or how particular things happen. In effect, the ethnographer puts aside his own inclinations to explain when and why particular events occur in order to highlight members' accounts of them. In this way the ethnographer seeks to elicit or distill members' theories of the *causes* of particular happenings.

By way of illustration, consider a study of the door-to-door canvassing activities of the local chapter of a feminist political action committee. The committee sought contributions and signatures on petitions supporting state legislation on behalf of women. Canvassers were assigned to territories or "turfs" in crews of 4 to 14 persons under the supervision of a field manager, and they were paid a percentage of the contributions they brought in above a preset minimum. Canvassers varied widely in the contributions they collected: some worked a full shift and brought in little or nothing, while others working the same turf collected hundreds of dollars in an evening.

These variations might well have tempted the researcher to come up with her own explanation for why canvassers differed so drastically in collecting contributions. Instead she attempted to understand what issues were of most concern to those involved in the campaign. In asking this question, she noted that participants in the fund-raising effort were themselves deeply and practically interested in differences in canvasser performance, and that the explanations offered varied depending upon one's position in the organization. *Canvassers* emphasized distinctions between "good turf" and "bad turf," contending that no one could raise significant amounts of money when going door-to-door in neighborhoods where most people were predisposed against their message. The researcher wrote of one incident:

It had been a hard week canvassing in Beach City and no one was making any money. The crew was vocally complaining, and wanted to leave immediately because it was "bad" turf and was upset at management's unresponsiveness to their plight.

Supervisors supported different explanations, generally honing in some failure in the canvasser's technique. For example, the researcher quoted one supervisor's comments on how to get canvassers to focus on improving a weak "money rap":

"People want to attack and blame the turf because it is the most varying condition. This is the most natural reaction. But, we need to make them realize that there are other factors going on while one is canvassing that they can control. If a person has a lot of signatures and talked to a lot of people but got small contributions, then they are connecting with people, and it's just a matter of working on the money rap."

Supervisors and front-line canvassers came into recurrent conflict over exactly which theory was most accurate and hence what could be done to alleviate the problem. Management strategies for training supervisors, for example, emphasized practices that would prevent canvassers from "blaming the turf":

A consultant advised a prospective field manager: "When someone has done shitty, get them away from blaming the turf even when they are emotional. Act as an emotional lightning rod but hold firm."

The officer manager urged her field managers: "When you pick all the canvassers up at night, you should do what are called 'trunk talks.' When you pull up to a person's pickup spot, pull a few feet away from them and hop out to debrief them. If they did well, ask them what was going good for them that made the evening successful. If they did poorly, take a moment to look at their turf sheet and do a quick analysis of what went on out there. This trains them to analyze the evening instead of automatically blaming the turf."

In this instance, then, the ethnographer proceeded exactly by tracing out different "members' theories." As she made the differing nature and location of these working theories her analytic focus, she went on to explore their practical, interactional, and organizational uses.

Finally, the field researcher should realize that people may offer more than one explanation for an occurrence and, indeed, may express what appear to the researcher as "contradictory explanations." Particularly in multicultural and multilingual communities, people frequently shift between languages, cultural expectations, and differing frameworks for perceiving and assessing behavior. In contemporary Africa, this flexibility is not uncommon. For example, in Northwest Province of Zambia, the Lunda, Luvale, Chokwe, Luchazi, and Mbunda peoples intermingle and intermarry. In addition, many younger people have completed grammar school taught in the official national language, English. In this multilingual context, people regularly invoke contrasting cultural frameworks. For example, when talking about illnesses and deaths caused by *wanga* (sorcery/witchcraft), young people often shift between traditionally-based views and biomedical explanations learned in school. Talking in Ki-Chokwe with the ethnographer and several other neighbors, a man reflected on a young woman friend's untimely death, concurring with the local diviner's claim that she had died from *wanga*. Later on, explaining details of her life to the ethnographer and one of his brothers in English, he talked about her long-term symptoms as characteristic of "TB" and "AIDS." Since he did not see these explanations as mutually exclusive, in foregrounding one he did not negate the other one: *wanga* was the cause of death, though TB or AIDS was the disease. Recognizing that, as their social identity, situation, or language shifts, human beings readily adjust their explanations, an ethnographer should carefully document in fieldnotes when, how, and to whom people explain their crises.[20]

MEMBERS' CATEGORIES IN USE: PROCESSES AND PROBLEMS

Members' descriptions, stories, types, and theories, no matter how rich and evocative, provide only a starting point for ethnographic fieldnotes. Deeper, fuller memos and analyses in a final ethnography require examining not simply what terms members use, but when, where, and how they use them and how they *actually* categorize or classify events and objects in specific situations.

By way of illustration, consider the following fieldnote provided by a student ethnographer with extensive gymnastic experience, in which he identifies terms for those attending an "open gym night" at a local university campus:

At open gym nights there are different classes and subclasses of people attending. The major classes include the regulars, the visitors, and the walk-ins. Of these there are many subclasses too. In the regulars class, there are the novice, the ex-gymnasts (old-timers), and the advanced amateur. The novices are people that have never taken gymnastics, classes or lessons, and are people that just walked in one day due to interest. The advanced amateurs are people who were never on any gymnastics teams, but have taken classes or lessons, or used to be walk-ins. Finally, the old-timers are those who competed at either the high school or college level. . . . Walk-ins are students who have had a long term interest in gymnastics and would like to learn from the old-timers.

This description provides a typology of those coming to the gym: "Regulars" (subtyped into three further classes—"novices," "advanced amateurs," and "old-timers"), "visitors," and "walk-ins." But as it stands, this typology identifies only categories recognized by the ethnographer; it is not clear that people in this setting actually apply these categories to others (and themselves), and, if they were to do so, when, where, and under what circumstances. Thus, the problem with this typology is two-fold: we do not know whether or not members recognize and use terms such as "regular" and "walk-in"; and more fundamentally, we do not know, if they do use these terms, exactly how, when, and for what purposes.

In insisting on considering members' actual situated use of specific terms or categories, the issue is not the "validity" or "reality" of these categories in a conventional sense. Rather, any object or event can be categorized in multiple ways; and the fact that some objects/events *might be* classed in one way or another (e.g., on the basis of having this or that trait or attribute in common) is not adequate grounds for recommending a particular classification, since we can always invoke or imagine other traits that would produce very different sorts of classifications.[21] Gym participants might indeed, *at some times for some purposes,* recognize "regulars," "visitors," and "walk-ins" as meaningful categories. But we cannot tell from this description, since no effort is made to look at how members actually talk about and identify others on specific occasions; that is, the types are presented without interactional context, as always and everywhere relevant. Since multiple classifications are always possible (Heritage 1984:144–50), the ethnographer should not impose classifications, even when starting with indigenous categories. Rather the ethnographer, alerted to possibly relevant local categories, should look closely at *how members actually classify events* on particular occasions for particular purposes.

Ethnographic fieldnotes, then, should not simply report any indigenous terms discoverable in a setting. Fieldnotes should more fundamentally detail members' actual, situated uses of such terms. The following pages provide two extended examples of how field researchers' notes and other writings can be made more sensitive to the interactional uses of member-recognized categories.

"Storytelling" as "Doing"

Stories are told for specific purposes. Indeed, people may tell a story to convey and support a particular interpretation of past events or to define current relations in order to shape future actions. Thus, what stories are "about" must consider the kind of speech, to whom the teller is speaking, the stated or implicit purposes, as well as other contextual influences.[22]

Consider the following incident that occurred in Zambia as Rachel Fretz was preparing to leave a Chokwe village in which she and a local assistant, Mwatushi, had been working for several weeks (Fretz n.d.). Mwatushi's father called his wife, son, and the ethnographer into his house for a farewell discussion and well-wishes for travel:

> We greeted each other and then chatted about our leaving. . . . He [the father and host] said that he was very pleased that I had come to stay here and that they did not know until yesterday that we were leaving today. Otherwise they could have sent something with us. Now they only have sweet potatoes to send, and maybe when I come the next time, they can send something good, like a chicken, with me.
>
> Then he started to narrate. His voice shifted into the rhythms of storytelling and speeded up. . . .
>
> "There was a *chindele* (foreigner/white person) who had two servants, and when he went back to his country to get married, he left his house and all his things with his servants to watch over them until he came back. Now the *chindele* stayed longer than they expected, and so the one servant said, 'Let's leave, he's not coming back.' But the other servant said, 'No, he told us to stay here until he came.' The one servant left, and when the master came back, only one servant was there—"
>
> He paused: "Ah no, I made a mistake. Both servants stayed until the *chindele* came. He came with his wife and he said, 'I am very pleased that you stayed here until I came, and because of that, I will give you each a small present. It is only a

small present for you to take back to your village, to your wives. It is small because I used all my money to get my wife, but please take these small bundles of grass as presents.' Then he gave each one a very small bundle of grass.

"Then the one servant said, 'Why should we take these very small bundles of grass to our homes, because we have much grass in our own villages.' 'But no,' the other man said, 'he gave us the bundles and said to take them to our village.' And so they left.

"Halfway home, the one man said, 'Ah we have much grass at home and here I am carrying this small bundle. No, I will not carry it. I'll throw it away.' But the other man said, 'No, I am carrying mine to the village.' So they went.

"When they arrived in their village, the one man gave his wife the bundle of grass and said, 'It is a small present from the *chindele* because I stayed until he came back. Here, put it in the house.' So she saved it. Then later that day it began to rain, and it came through the holes in the roof, so the man took his grass and repaired his roof. That night they slept well.

"In the morning, the other man—the one who threw his grass away—got up and looked out his window. He called his wife and said, 'Come see the house of our relative, the one who repaired his roof with the *chindele*'s grass.'

"They saw a large house with a tin roof and windows and many rooms. In the yard they saw two vehicles, one for the man and one for the woman, who just then came out wearing good clothes.

"Then the man who threw his grass away said, 'Wife, let's go back on the road to where I threw the grass away so that we can bring the grass and have a fine house, too.' But when they got to the place where he had thrown the grass, they found that the bundle was scattered and all the grass broken."

The father (narrator) continued, "Thus even though we do not have much to give you—we have no chicken to send with you—we give you these small words to keep and not throw away: May God bless you and carry you well on your journey. May He keep you where you are (live)."

I said, "*Twasakwila* (thank you). I have already received very much from you. I have received much help with my work, which your son and I will study when we go back [to my village]. And I thank you for these words which I will carry with me." . . .

Then he said, "It is good that you are taking our son with you. He should do everything you tell him. If you call him to come with you, he will come. If you tell him to stay, he will stay. Whatever you tell him, he should do."

[After more talk Mwatushi's mother also offered an apology for not sending a chicken.] Then she said, "So please receive this small gift," and she gave me a 500 kwasha bill [which, as the price of two chickens, did not seem small to me]. . . . We said, "Goodnight and sleep well," and left.

This story is a gift, presented to the ethnographer in lieu of a chicken, and it offers a blessing for the return trip to another village where she lives. The father implies that this seemingly small gift of a blessing and money, like the grass in the story, may turn out to be of exceptional value.

Our gift, he suggests, may be a great benefit to you, if you have the sense to receive it properly.

Furthermore, the story is a *misende* (parable) through which people address each other indirectly (Fretz 1994) and which here provides a context within which to hear the subsequent conversation. The father uses the parable to introduce a conversation about reciprocal relations. He continues by establishing that Mwatushi, his son, will not only work very well for the researcher and follow her directions exactly, but also that the ethnographer must become his family in the distant village where she lives:

"So it is for you to keep him. . . . It is for you to advise him so that he lives well. Because he is alone over there [without relatives in the village where the researcher lives and works], you are now his mother, his father, you are his grandmother and his grandfather. You are his brother and his sister. It is for you to keep him."

The parable provides connotations for the word "servant," suggesting that someone who stays with the *chindele* will (and should) be rewarded like the servant in the story who exactly followed the directions of the master. But in the subsequent conversation, the father suggests that Mwatushi as "family" will be even more closely allied and loyal to the researcher than a "servant" would be; for, the father continues by further discussing Mwatushi's work for the ethnographer—suggesting that perhaps he would travel a great distance with her. Having established these relationships, the father then asks for a gift which the ethnographer might bring in the future should she return from America to Zambia. According to the Chokwe, people in a close relationship not only give each other gifts, but they respectfully ask each other for gifts and favors in order to establish and solidify a good relationship. As a respectful form of speech, the parable graciously created an opening for his comments and requests.

In sum, the parable—heard in context—subtly reinforces and extends through connotation the father's courteous remarks and questions about reciprocal relationships. His story is not only an immediate gift and blessing for the road, but also connotes an ongoing relationship. The father's creation of family ties with the ethnographer would indeed have long-term benefits to her. But only by recognizing the storytelling as a *misende* through which the father addressed her indirectly, could this ethnographer truly hear what he was saying.

Members' Terms in Everyday Interactions

Through experience in commission sales, student ethnographers have found that salespersons who regularly or blatantly "steal customers" are termed "snakes" or "sharks" by coworkers and are generally subject to a variety of pressures, rebukes, and sanctions for their behavior. It is tempting for a field researcher to simply accept these definitions of particular salespersons as "snakes" and to then contrast how they work the floor or deal with customers with those not categorized as "snakes." But ethnographers who proceed in this way will produce truncated rather than complex and nuanced descriptions and analyses of relations among workers in these settings. Specifically, they will fail to fully appreciate and document the micro-political, interactional processes through which some workers determine that others are "snakes" and attempt to convince coworkers that this is indeed the case. And they will fail to fully trace out the intricate *local knowledge* (Geertz 1983) which underlines any competent use of members' terms in specific situations.

To illustrate the depth and complexity that can be added by looking closely at the problematics of how members actually use indigenous categories, consider the following fieldnote written by a salesperson/ researcher who worked as a saleswoman in an expensive, high fashion women's clothing store and who herself played a major role in the workplace dispute she describes:

I was helping a woman who was shopping with her husband, and I had taken her to the back dressing room where she was trying on a lot of clothes. Whenever a customer is trying on a lot of clothes, all the salesgirls notice the customer and who is helping her. While I was fitting her in the dressing room, the husband obviously had to wait outside the dressing room. As it turned out, he asked Ellen at the counter about a pretty sweater hanging above the cash drawer. It was a $710 Iceberg sweater with a beaded picture of Tweety and Sylvester on it. He quickly told Ellen that he wanted to buy it as a present for his wife and to wrap it before she came out of the dressing room. As soon as I came out I saw Ellen writing up this sale. I was furious. I was helping the wife and they were a unit. If I am helping her, then I am helping him also. Ellen said that she didn't know that I was helping his wife in the back when I asked her why she didn't get me to help him. I didn't believe her. The sale was too big and easy for her to pass up. So when the wife came out with about $500 worth of clothes to buy, Pat and Jane, watching over the counter, gave me eyes like they can't believe what Ellen had just done. . . . Ellen had snaked my customer and we all knew it.

I confronted Ellen and said that what she did was wrong, implying that she was a snake. She became very defensive. She said, "Hear me out and then I'll listen to you." After I heard her out, I started to talk but she cut me off in the middle of my sentence and said, "Let's see Sammie" [the manager]. Meanwhile, Pat and Jane both told me that I should have the whole sale. I went upstairs to speak to Sammie alone first, and she asked me if I wanted the whole sale or half of the sale. I said that I believe I deserve the whole sale, but I will split it if she understands what she did wrong. Sammie then told Ellen that she must split the sale with me. When I went up to Ellen to say that it was not fair that she cut me off earlier, she cut me off again saying, "It's over!"

Initially, note the explicit one-sidedness of this fieldnote account; its author does not take the stance of a neutral, uninvolved party but clearly presents herself as one of the story's two major protagonists. The account is explicitly political in that it is "making the case" that Ellen "snaked my customer." The accusation appears at least partially contested by Ellen, who is indirectly quoted as saying she did not know "I was helping his wife in the back" and who clearly refused to relinquish her claim to the commission.[23] The author ignores these possibilities in laying out specific grounds for her claim: any competent salesperson should "know" that husband and wife are a "unit" and would notice a promising customer trying on a lot of clothes; other parties in the setting interpreted the event in the same way as the author; and the local authority figure actually settled the conflict in a way that confirmed the author's version.

The circumstances described in this fieldnote account also direct attention toward the interactional work that took place to get this incident defined and treated as "snaking." While this incident ends up being treated interactionally by others in the setting as an instance of "stealing a customer," this result is not predictable in advance but emerges as the interaction unfolds, as the various parties advance their respective claims and accounts and appeal to and elicit support from co-workers. In general it is important for ethnographers to look beyond simple use of such members' terms to appreciate the underlying micro-political character of these processes. In the case of "snaking," this author, as a careful ethnographer, pushed beyond the mere claim that another "stole a customer" to look at *how* salespeople establish claims to specific customers, when and how such claims are ignored or bypassed, how they reassert and sustain these claims, and how conflicting claims and interpretations are presented and resolved.

Furthermore, this account points the way toward appreciating the extensive local knowledge required to make convincing accusations of "snaking." Specifically, the claim that another salesperson "stole my customer" presumes knowledge of a whole set of local practices for "claiming customers." Elsewhere the student researcher began to sketch these practices in the following terms:

Having asked a customer if she would like any help, you stand nearby; if any other salesgirl makes a move towards the customer, then we can say that person's name out loud. When she looks over, we can point to the customer, signaling that we have already asked them if they would like any help and implying that they are "my" customer. This is how we preserve our claim to the average customer who walks in off the street.

"Stealing a customer" thus assumes that a salesperson specifically ignored this sort of asserted claim. Indeed, the account of the Iceberg sweater incident underlines how the accused culprit "must have known" that the customer had been tagged: "Whenever a customer is trying on a lot of clothes, all the salesgirls notice the customer and who is helping her." In this sense, a members' term presupposes and encodes specific local knowledge and practice that the ethnographer wants to identify and describe.

As ethnographers pay close attention to members' meanings, they begin to appreciate how much interactional and political "work" it takes for people to create their meanings. In so doing, the careful ethnographer learns to explore the knowledge which undergirds the implicit claims which people make about events. These often unstated purposes and claims make it clear, however, that field researchers cannot fully determine members' meanings through interviews or informal questioning. Ethnographers must discern local knowledge not simply on the basis of people's talk but rather through their "talk-in-interaction," that is, they must notice what people do in relation to others in order to produce specific, situated meanings.

RACE, GENDER, CLASS, AND MEMBERS' MEANINGS

Because they are committed to members' meanings and experience, ethnographers treat the relevance of gender, race, or class for everyday life in ways that differ significantly from common theoretical approaches which set forth a priori assumptions and definitions. Even though, like such theorists, the ethnographer may assume from the start that these are significant matters that should always be attended to in understanding social life, she places priority on how people themselves deal with gender, ethnicity, and class within the dynamics of specific instances and situations.

This ethnographic stance toward issues of gender, ethnicity, and class has been criticized on several counts. One line of criticism insists that ethnographic research is uninformed by theories which might enable the fieldworker to transcend the limited view of specific events and allow her to write about more generalizable social forces. Another line of criticism holds that ethnographic treatments of gender, ethnicity, or class are narrowly restricted to empirical observations: that is, that ethnographies describe specific locales and situations as isolated from the broader social structures and forces that critically determine specific events and individual lives.

Certainly, both criticisms highlight areas in which an ethnographic approach to gender, ethnicity, and class differs from more encompassing theoretical approaches. Committed to members' meanings and experience, ethnographers are more attracted by what Geertz (1976) termed "experience-near" as opposed to "experience-far" concepts; thus, they generally give priority to these meanings over a priori, received theories. Valuing the local and the specific, field researchers look in a focused way at daily life rather than in a broad and sweeping manner at general patterns. Ethnographers certainly prefer to see the direct influence of social structures, rather than to assume their relevance and effects at the outset. At first glace, this "experience-near" approach seems to create tensions between ethnography and theories about the effects of broader social structures. However, some of these apparent tensions lessen, perhaps even disappear, by looking closely at several ways that ethnographers can and should bridge their commitment to members' meanings with their concern for gender, ethnicity, and class.

At the most basic level, the ethnographer with strong interests in gender, ethnicity, and/or class should carefully select a site for field research where he expects one or more of these processes to be particularly salient. In choosing a site, the researcher should look for a setting where gender, ethnic, or class diversity not only seems clearly highlighted but also where these issues concern the members. Examples would include police forces with increasing numbers of women or ethnic recruits, or schools with ethnically diverse student populations. In addition, a researcher might choose to study events through which members directly address these issues. For example, an ethnographer interested in gender issues might research occasions in which elders teach the next generation. In many societies, initiation ceremonies explicitly focus on instructing youth about gender roles and responsibilities. Among the Chokwe in Zambia, such rituals as *mwadi* for girls after they begin menstruating and *mukanda* when boys are circumcised are central village events which provide explicit information about gender construction.

Indeed, an ethnographer not only can select a setting and events which focus directly on gender, ethnicity, or class, but she might also design a field research project exactly for its relevance to a theoretical issue derived from these concerns. Those researchers concerned with the reproduction of class distinctions in schooling, for example, might want to follow the progress of a group of working-class youth over time in one particular school (Willis 1977). Or, they might look specifically at the differential decision-making by school counselors in tracking working- and middle-class youth (Cicourel and Kitsuse 1963).

Once in a setting, the ethnographer's first concern should lie in exploring the significance of gender, ethnicity, or class matters for those studied. A first step in this direction requires paying close attention to any occasion upon which people *explicitly* talk about and/or act toward each other on the basis of race, gender, and/or class. For example, rather than assuming that ethnicity is invariably a causal factor producing a behavior or event, the ethnographer seeks to describe in detail any interaction in which ethnic identification becomes a matter of attention. In the following fieldnote, a student ethnographer describes what happened when an African-American high school teacher opened a discussion of white-black relations in an African-American history class:

Ms. B picked Dapo next. Dapo said that he had just moved to the Valley, Southland Hills. This comment drew a couple of "woo's." Dapo grinned. He said the area he moved to is a "white neighborhood." One time he was walking down the street by his house and passed a white child playing there. The child's parents saw Dapo and grabbed the kid and dragged it inside. Dapo was kind of laughing as he said this. He said he wanted to tell the people, "I'm Black, but I'm not going to kill you." Some classmates burst into laughter and talked among themselves. Dapo continued, "My parents are Creole. . . . They're all (lowers voice to an aside) 'you're not really Black.' My cousins have blue eyes and blonde hair and all that . . . ." He continues, his voice firming up, "I'm Black. I'm a Black person. . . . I'm proud to be Black."

This account conveys a number of dimensions and contradicitons of ethnic identity that are meaningful to a high school student. For example, we see the complex tensions that exist between who his parents tell him he is ("You're not really Black") and who he is to those in this neighborhood and for this class ("I'm Black").

However, the significance people attribute to gender, race, or class may be difficult for ethnographers to document because people do not always directly reference them. On some occasions, an ethnographer may feel that people regularly act toward one another in "classed" or "gendered" ways; yet, they may not be able to pinpoint how this is so or to record specific scenes or actions in which these features are explicitly alluded to. It may thus be extremely difficult to identify and tease out these matters in writing fieldnotes. In other situations, a researcher might expect gender, race, or class to be important but find that members fail to acknowledge these factors. In such instances, the ethnographer must push beyond explicit use of relevant terms to make more systematic observations to identify patterns of activities that reflect the relevance of gender, ethnicity, or class.

For example, in her study of storytelling in a Chokwe village, Fretz was consistently told that "anyone may tell *yishima*." And, indeed, in most villages, men and women, adults and children told stories around the family firesides. But in her own research in the village of the highest chief, after one initial evening in which a woman narrated in the *chota* (the chief's pavilion), she could not get any woman to tell a story. With continued observation and reflection, she eventually realized that not only did the chief consistently dominate the storytelling, but he requested that all storytelling take place in his pavilion, a locale where men meet to talk and where women, if invited, participate by responding and singing. Thus, questions about women's roles in storytelling did not reveal the status and gender impact of "storytelling rights" in the pavilion because the answers to these questions were not linked to storytelling but to other relational and situational factors. Only repeated observation and comparison between similar situations finally led to an understanding of the complex web of situational, gender, and status influences working in this context.[24]

On other occasions, specific talk by members will provide a useful starting place for further inquiry to trace out the relevance of ethnicity, gender, or class in wider realms of local life. For example, one group of students set out to study relations between students in an ethnically diverse school. One of the group came back with the following talk about different "groups" on campus:

Around the lunch table today, a bunch of guys who hang around together were talking. I thought they could help me understand the different groups at Central. They used a lot of terms I'd heard before to describe the kids. One guy talked about "trendy people," and how I could recognize a trendy person if I saw one. Someone else said there's "ballers," which are people who play basketball, and then there's "footballers," people who play football and then people who "kick" [hang around with] all the groups. And then there's "posses." They said a posse is a group of students who hang around together, kick it together, and they do it because it gives them a sense of belonging. One Black guy goes, "It's just a coincidence that all the people in my posse are Black." We were all laughing so hard. He goes, "No, no, we all come from the same neighborhood. Some of them are interracial." Then there's the "swim team," those are the druggies because they use so many drugs that their eyes are always bloodshot so it's like they were swimming. Then there's the "GCP," the Green Card Posse, they go, "Oh, the Wetbacks." A "cool" person wears nice clothes. I asked, What if you don't have money for nice clothes, does that mean you're not cool? They said, If you have a good personality. But if your personality is the same way you dress, then forget it. "This place is a fashion show."

Here we see that students invoke a range of local categories in distinguishing and categorizing one another. Some of these categories make direct and explicit reference to ethnicity, e.g., "the Green Card Posse." Ethnicity is also directly mentioned with reference to "posses," but specifically how it is relevant appears more open: one speaker identified his posse as all black; another claimed that some posses are "interracial." In contrast, another speaker minimizes ethnicity as the basis for group formation. Finally, most of the categories are not explicitly identified with any particular ethnicity, e.g., "ballers," "druggies," "cool" people. An ethnographer in this setting would want to follow up and seek to establish the ethnicities of students identified as belonging to each of these various categories. This inquiry would be primarily a matter of observing the ethnic status of students identified with each category, then perhaps talking to students about observed ethnic patterns.

An ethnographer could also use this incident as a starting place for tracing out connections between these student categories and gender or class. It appears that this talk about groupings occurs among and is about boys; but the field researcher would want to find out specifically if any of these categories include girls and to ask further questions about similar or different groupings among girl students at the school. Here in particular the ethnographer should trace out gendered patterns of segregation and difference, as well as of integration and overlap, among students and their activities.

Handling issues of social class is more complex. Compared to gender and ethnicity, class is an "experience-far" rather than an "experience-near" concept (Geertz 1976). As a result, ethnographers rarely encounter members explicitly talking about "class" per se. But people employ a number of terms that refer to elements or components of the concept of social class. This instance, for example, directly involves a kind of naturally occurring "ranking" of persons that mirrors one concern of the social class concept. Furthermore, these students discuss "money," "nice clothes," and the school as a "fashion show," suggesting that parental income and conspicuous consumption might bear on how one is categorized within the school. Thus the field researcher might further question and observe these matters in order to describe what students consider "nice clothes," the care they take to display them, and where these clothes and the money needed to purchase them come from.

LOCAL EVENTS AND SOCIAL FORCES

Finally, field researchers can employ a number of different strategies to try to link local events and specific outcomes to more distant social settings and more remote consequences. Initially, the ethnographer can look for specific connections within the setting to outside social influences. The ethnographer should attend foremost to how the people involved talk about and understand their connections with these outside entities and forces, but he would not be limited to these member-recognized understandings. Field research on the homeless, for example, might well begin by examining how people living on the street understand and cope with the conditions of their daily existence on a day-to-day basis, including how they see their relation to the wider society (e.g., Snow and Anderson 1993). But the researcher would also observe the various persons, agents, and institutions that have recurrent contact with the homeless: for example, missions, hotels, and other places that provide occasional residence; regular feeding lines and informal arrangements with restaurants as sources of food; relations with police patrol officers and jailers; caretaker agencies and welfare/relief workers.[25] And then a researcher (or other researchers) might move out to examine these institutions and agents and their conditions of existence. Ethnography can also explore links to broader social processes by observing people and settings as they change *over time*. Long-term, continuous field research is necessary, for example, in order to understand how working-class youth react to and are affected by their contacts with schools. Introducing a longitudinal component to field research, while practically difficult, allows the researcher to describe different life chances and to understand how these chances are shaped and determined. Field researchers, for example, often examine particular "institutional careers" (Goffman 1961) and the factors that shape them, whether these involve moving through schools to different final outcomes or through processing by the police or courts to different fates. The limited "breadth" of many ethnographies can be attributed directly to a lack of concern with change over longer time spans, to an assumption that one can look atemporally at one piece of life without considering changes over time.

REFLECTIONS: USING FIELDNOTES TO DISCOVER/CREATE
MEMBERS' MEANINGS

In this chapter we have proposed strategies for writing ethnographic fieldnotes that collect and represent members' meanings in a rigorous, grounded manner. These strategies require the ethnographer to bracket preconceptions about what is important in order to attend to people's indigenous ways of ordering and interpreting their worlds. In so doing ethnographers assume that members' meanings are *consequential,* that how people act is based on their understandings of their local social worlds.

In pursuing members' meanings, ethnographers begin by looking at how members describe and categorize people and events; they try to discern *their* terms, phrasings, classifications, and theories. But indigenous categories provide only a starting point; the ethnographer's task is not simply to identify member-recognized terms and categories but also to *specify the conditions under which people actually invoke and apply such terms in interaction with others.* For no term or category is self-applying to actual situations; its relevance to specific circumstances cannot be determined in advance. Hence the ethnographer should not describe social scenes by applying member-recognized terms and categories to situations independently of members' actual applications. Indigenous terms and categories must be indigenously invoked and fitted to specific situations. In writing about those in the open gymnastics session discussed previously, the ethnographer who identifies someone as a "regular" in his fieldnotes independently of actual (interactional) treatment by members of that setting has appropriated the power of fitting categories to specific situations.

Several implications flow from recognizing that the ethnographer who writes fieldnotes about indigenous meanings should specify the conditions under which members' meanings are invoked and applied. First, such fieldnotes must incorporate not words and phrases abstracted out of context but the actual interactional occasions in which these members' terms are used. Fieldnotes useful to appreciating members' meanings, then, will be interactionally rather than cognitively focused; they will document not how members talk about various social objects, in general and out of context, but how members *construct meaning* through interactions with other members of the group, how they actually interpret and organize their own and others' actions.

Some methodological implications follow. Many ethnographers seem to assume that the pursuit of members' meanings is equivalent to interviewing people about what is important to them. But ethnographers collect materials relevant to members' meanings by focusing not on members' decontextualized talk but on naturally occurring, situated interaction in which local meanings are created and sustained. Writing ethnographic fieldnotes that are sensitive to members' meanings is primarily a matter not of asking but of inferring what people are concerned with from the specific ways in which they talk and act in a variety of natural settings. Thus, interviewing, especially asking members directly what terms mean to them or what is important or significant to them, is not the primary tool for getting at members' meanings. Rather, the distinctive procedure is to observe and record naturally occurring talk and interaction. It may indeed be useful or essential to interview members about the use and meaning of specific local terms and phrases, but the researcher's deeper concern lies in the actual, situated use of those terms in ordinary interaction.[26]

Finally, focusing on interactionally situated uses of indigenous terms heightens the ethnographer's sensitivity to the intricate processes of situated judgment and skilled interpretation that characterize members' use of local categories. Members' categorizations are not invariant and transcendent but are tied to specific situations for varying purposes. Extensive local knowledge and judgment-making skill are necessarily involved in their use. In the gym, for example, those about to undertake a particular gymnastic routine requiring a "spotter" may have a practical interest in recognizing and distinguishing between the experience and skill level of others present. Indeed, experienced gymnasts can see at a glance how much training another has had, on the basis of her performance and actions. In general, a deeper appreciation of indigenous meanings requires learning when and how members actually make such assessments and what knowledge they rely on in so doing.

chapter six

Processing Fieldnotes: Coding and Memoing

At some point—after weeks or perhaps months of writing notes—the ethnographer needs to draw back from the field, to cease actively writing notes. He must shift gears and turn to the written record he has produced with an eye to transforming this collection of materials into writings that speak to wider, outside audiences. Efforts to analyze now become intense, concentrated, and comprehensive: the fieldworker begins to sift systematically through the many pages of fieldnote accounts of discrete and often loosely related incidents and happenings, looking to identify threads that can be woven together to tell a story (or a number of stories) about the observed social world. The ultimate goal is to produce a coherent, focused analysis of some aspect of the social life that has been observed and recorded, an analysis that is comprehensible to readers who are not directly acquainted with the social world at issue.

The prospect of creating coherent, focused analyses from a mass of fieldnote data, which by now can easily number several hundred pages, overwhelms many students—even those who have been writing analytic commentaries all along. But fieldworkers have found that the task can be handled effectively by recognizing several distinct practices involved in carrying out analysis.

Initially, writing fieldnotes gives way to *reading* them: the ethnographer reads through all fieldnotes as a complete corpus, taking in the entire record of the field experience as it has evolved over time. He begins to elaborate and refine earlier insights and hunches by subjecting this broader collection of fieldnotes to close, intensive reflection and analysis.

Second, the researcher combines this close reading with procedures for *analytically coding* fieldnotes on an ongoing basis. Ethnographic coding involves line-by-line categorization of specific notes. In this process, the researcher's stance toward the notes changes: the notes, and the persons and events they recount, become textual objects (although linked to personal memories and intuitions) to be considered and examined with a series of analytic and presentational possibilities in mind.

Qualitative analytic coding usually proceeds in two different phases. In *open coding* the ethnographer reads fieldnotes line-by-line to identify and formulate any and all ideas, themes, or issues they suggest, no matter how varied and disparate. In *focused coding* the fieldworker subjects fieldnotes to fine-grained, line-by-line analysis on the basis of topics that have been identified as of particular interest. Here, the ethnographer uses a smaller set of promising ideas and categories to provide the major topic and themes for the final ethnography.

Reading through and coding fieldnotes on a line-by-line basis inundates the ethnographer with a mass of ideas, insights, and connections. While continuing to code, she elaborates these insights by writing theoretical *memos*. Early on in the process of analyzing data, fieldworkers write *initial memos* on a series of discrete phenomena, topics, or categories. Later, as the fieldworker develops a clearer sense of the ideas or themes she wants to pursue, memos take on a more focused character; they relate or integrate what were previously separate pieces of data and analytic points. These *integrative memos* seek to clarify and link analytic themes and categories.

The analytic practices that we present in this chapter draw heavily from methods developed by sociologists taking the "grounded theory" approach to analyzing qualitative data.[1] Grounded theorists give priority to developing rather than to verifying analytic propositions. They maintain that if the researcher minimizes commitment to received and preconceived theory, he is more likely to "discover" original theories in his data. By making frequent comparisons across the data, the researcher can develop, modify, and extend theoretical propositions so that they fit the data. At the actual working level, the researcher begins by coding data in close, systematic ways so that he can generate analytic categories. He further elaborates, extends, and integrates these categories by writing theoretical memos.

The grounded theory approach depicts analysis as a clearcut, almost autonomous activity. In emphasizing "discovering" theory in fieldnotes and other qualitative data, practitioners of grounded theory treat sets of already collected fieldnote data as unproblematic starting points; they implicitly assume that such fieldnotes can be analyzed independently of the analytic processes and theoretical commitments of the ethnographer who wrote them. In contrst, we insist that data do not stand alone; rather analysis pervades all phases of the research enterprise—as the researcher makes observations, records them in fieldnotes, codes these notes in analytic categories, and finally develops explicit theoretical propositions. Viewed in this way, analysis is at once inductive and deductive, like someone who is simultaneously creating and solving a puzzle, or like a carpenter alternately changing the shape of a door and then the shape of the door frame to obtain a better fit.

In this chapter, we develop an approach to analyzing fieldnotes based on these ideas. Initially we suggest ways to begin the analysis of fieldnotes: close reading, open coding, and writing initial memos. We then consider procedures helpful in carrying out more specific, fine-grained analyses: focused coding and writing integrative memos. While we discuss reading, coding, and memoing as discrete steps in analytically processing fieldnotes, we want to emphasize that the researcher is not rigidly confined to one procedure at a time or to undertaking them in any particular order. Rather, she moves from a general reading to a close coding to writing intensive analyses and then back again. Said another way, from reading comes coding and written memos which direct and redirect attention to issues and possibilities that require further reading of the same or additional fieldnotes.

READING FIELDNOTES AS A DATA SET

The ethnographer begins concentrated analysis and writing by reading her fieldnotes in a new manner, looking closely and systematically at what has been observed and recorded. In so doing, she treats the fieldnotes as a data set, reviewing, reexperiencing, and reexamining everything that has been written down, while self-consciously seeking to identify themes, patterns, and variations within this record.

We strongly recommend reading line-by-line through as many pages of fieldnotes as possible, at least until coding seems to generate no new ideas, themes, or issues. Reading notes as a whole and in the order they were written confers a number of benefits. First, the fieldworker can perceive changes in her relations with those in the field over time. The gradual movement from distance to rapport, for example, may only become apparent when reading in a matter of hours a record of events which took place over weeks and months. Second, the ethnographer gains fresh insights as she changes in her own understanding and interpretation of people and events by reviewing the completed set of notes. Based upon what has subsequently been learned, initial interpretations and commentaries now reencountered may seem naive or erroneous. This contrast between initial and later understanding is often striking when working in a totally unfamiliar culture and language. The fieldworker begins to reinterpret the import and significance of events and actions in novel ways. She may feel that foreign concepts and terms have no equivalent in English. And patterns and tendencies recognized when reading all of the notes may suggest alternative interpretations of actions or talk previously understood in another way. Finally, working with the complete set of fieldnotes allows the ethnographer to take in for the first time, in a relatively concentrated time stretch, everything that she has been able to observe and record. Reading notes as a whole encourages recognizing patterns and making comparisons. She begins to notice how an incident is like others in previously reviewed notes. Conversely, she also begins to note important differences between incidents previously seen as similar.

To undertake an analytically motivated reading of one's fieldnotes requires the ethnographer to approach her notes as if they had been written by a stranger. Indeed, many fieldworkers find it difficult to achieve the sort of emotional distance required to subject to analysis those with whom she has been deeply immersed. Some fieldworkers report discomfort at "examining under a microscope" the lives of people with whom they have become deeply involved and in many cases care about. For some, analysis comes close to an act of betrayal; many fieldworkers report having taken several weeks or months after they stopped writing fieldnotes before they could begin their analyses. Indeed, a number of ethnographers find that relations with those in the setting have become primary. In that case the ethnographer may set the project aside for years or even abandon it altogether. Some researchers resolve this internal conflict by working collaboratively with people in the setting, even occasionally coauthoring their writing with a local assistant.

Although the deliberate and self-conscious analysis ethnography entails may contribute to feelings of estrangement, it may be helpful to remember that making sense of "what's going on" is an activity that members of the setting engage in and that it is one of the usual and expected activities of social life. And it is also sometimes helpful to remember that while our analysis of patterns of social life in the field site is ordinarily for audiences and purposes outside of it, we seek to convey an appreciative understanding of the world and lives of persons under study.

ASKING QUESTIONS OF FIELDNOTES

Coding begins with the ethnographer mentally asking questions of specific pieces of fieldnote data. In asking such questions, the ethnographer draws on a wide variety of resources, including direct experience of life and events in the setting; sensitivity toward the concerns and orientations of members; memory of other specific incidents described elsewhere in one's notes; one's own prior experience and insights gained in other settings; and the concepts and orientation provided by one's own profession or discipline. Nothing is out of bounds!

But the secret of coding lies in turning the answers to these questions into a distinctive kind of writing—a word or short phrase that captures and signals what is going on in a piece of data in a way that links it to some more general analytic issue. Such writing is integrally linked to the processes of thinking and interpreting whereby the ethnographer "comes up with" a code to write down. In turn, writing down codes—putting an idea or intuition into a concrete, relatively concise word or phrase— helps stimulate, shape, and constrain the fieldworker's thinking and re- flection. This mutually necessary relationship between reflection and writing is expressed in John Forester's (n.d.) apt phrase, "thinking with your fingers."

We have found the following sorts of questions useful in beginning to examine specific fieldnotes:

- What are people doing? What are they trying to accomplish?
- How, exactly, do they do this? What specific means and/or strategies do they use?
- How do members talk about, characterize, and understand what is going on?
- What assumptions are they making?
- What do I see going on here? What did I learn from these notes?
- Why did I include them?

Such questions reflect and advance several specific concerns linked to our approach to ethnography and writing fieldnotes. First, these questions give priority to *processes* rather than to "causes" or internal psychological "motives." Specifically, this priority means asking questions that identify what is occurring and in what order, rather than "why" questions that ask what is causing or producing some outcomes. In this sense, we view open coding as a means for developing interpretations or analytic themes rather than causal explanations.

Second, these questions reflect a sensitivity to the *practical* concerns, conditions, and constraints that actors confront and deal with in their everyday lives and actions. This concern with the practical or the pragmatic requires paying attention to the mundane, ordinary, and taken-for-granted rather than looking only or primarily at the dramatic or exceptional action or event.

Finally, these questions can help specify the meanings and points of view of those under study. We try to frame questions that get at how members see and experience events, at what they view as important and significant, at how they describe, classify, analyze, and evaluate their own and others' situations and activities. Yet, to get at these matters, it is initially crucial to clarify what the ethnographer felt was significant about what occurred by asking: "Why did I include this item in my fieldnotes?" It is then important to ask whether or not and on what basis members seem to attribute this same significance to events or incidents. These procedures keep the ethnographer aware of the complexities involved in pursuing members' meanings; in other words, they remind the ethnographer that there is no "pure" way to capture what is important to members, their meanings or points of view. Rather, the ethnographer always writes her *interpretation* of what she feels is meaningful and important to them.

Such questions will lead to codes which the ethnographer writes in the margins of his fieldnotes. The following example, from a student whose ethnography examined her work as an usher, illustrates this process:

customer types: late arrivals	Dance audiences do tend to come right at curtain, so we have to hold many out. Tonight was no dif-
holding out audience members	ferent. I'd say we had about 50 people waiting in the lobby through the first number. . . . One man
waiters: irate	we held out was irate. He had already been in but had come out for some reason. When we closed the door, he began yelling at the door attendant. He said
latecomer claims exception	he was already in—not like these other people who were "LATE." He was not late and shouldn't be
mgr intervenes	treated like them! The house manager came over and smiled and told him in a quiet voice why he
passing the buck	was being held out—that it was requested by the

calming latecomers
keeping occupied
distracting

smiling
minimizing the wait

dancers. He calmed down but was still angry. He waited without another word, except when I came around. I went around giving out programs so they could read something and so the ushers wouldn't have to waste time doing that when these people charged their doors. I also asked people if I could tell them which aisle to go to so as to alleviate confusion for the door attendant. When I got to this man and asked him if he wanted me to tell him which door to enter through, he said in a huff that he had already been in and knew where to go. Other people were just as irritated. I just smiled and told them it would just be a few minutes. I think that calmed them a little, because the exasperated look left their faces.

This student ethnographer focused on the practical situation of ushers, implicitly asking how ushers understood and made sense of behavior and events and how they interacted with one another and with customers. Specifically, in the code "late arrivals" she identified the practical work consequences of the inevitable tendency for some ticket holders to come late. Furthermore, the codes "holding out audience members" and "calming latecomers" identify specific processes for dealing with and managing latecomers as practical work problems. The ethnographer then asked herself *how* these activities were actually done by ushers, which led to a series of more specific codes for "calming," e.g., "keeping occupied," "distracting," "smiling," "minimizing the wait."

These codes begin to identify and elaborate a variety of analytic distinctions. For example, the code "late arrivals" names a particular "type of customer"; in framing "late arrivals" as a "type," she asserts that coming late is a normal, routine event in this setting and that "late arrivals" are one among a range of customer types. In identifying one customer type, this code raises the possibility that other customer types exist and hence opens the question of just what these other "customer types" might be. That is, the process here is a dialectical one that consists of asking, "Of what more general category is this an instance?" In answering this question, the field researcher may draw upon a wide variety of experiences and different sorts of knowledge: her own experience as an usher, her awareness that dealing with people who come late is a practical matter that ushers must routinely confront, her experiences as someone who has come late to a performance, and her familiarity with sociological thinking about waiting as a key to power differences (e.g., Schwartz 1975).

But while latecomers are expected at dance performances, the code "irate waiters" distinguishes an audience type, a latecomer who is a source of trouble and special concern. The code "latecomer claims exception" identifies both the responses with which ushers have to deal and the categories and distinctions advanced by this particular latecomer. The next codes—"mgr intervenes," "passing the buck," "keeping occupied," and "distracting"—identify additional forms of "backup" responses. These responses include the manager's efforts to placate the disgruntled patron, and the writer's attempts to take waiting audience members' minds off the delay.

Codes, then, take a specific event, incident, or feature and relate it to other events, incidents, or features, implicitly distinguishing this one from others. By comparing this event with "like" others, one can begin to identify more general analytic *dimensions* or categories. One can do this by asking what more general category this event belongs to, or by thinking about specific *contrasts* to the current event. For example, the response of "holding out" customers would stimulate a concern with the reverse situation (e.g., "taking latecomers in during a performance") and, hence, would suggest looking for observations describing how this would have to be managed.

While many of the codes used here involve members' concerns and specific terms, we also see attention to members' meanings in the code "latecomer claims exemption." This code tries to capture the actual distinction that this audience member advances in trying to get back in to see the performance—that some people arrived after the show had begun, but he had arrived before, was now trying to reenter and, therefore, was "not late" and should be treated differently than those in the first category. In the staff response, we see the practical irrelevance of this distinction; to the staff, what presumably matters are not considerations of justice and fairness (such that "real latecomers" should be treated differently from those who had to leave momentarily and hence were returning) but the disruption that would be caused by anyone entering at this time.

Through an initial line-by-line reading of her fieldnotes, this student began to clarify the socially ordered work activities of an usher for dance audiences. As she continues through her notes, asking the question, "What are the processes by which the ushers accomplish their work?" she will generate more codes; some will be further instances or elaborations of earlier codes, while others will suggest entirely different themes and lines of analysis. Having identified, for example, "latecomers" as one group of dance audience members, she will proceed through her notes looking for other member types or categories. Similarly, having a code, "waiters: irate," implying that getting irate is only one response in the general category of audience responses, she could go on to look for others. She could also wonder: this goes on here, but does it always to on? What are the conditions under which it occurs?

Similarly, the student may identify an order or natural sequence of events or stages that make up the larger activity. She can further develop themes along these lines by continuing to look for expected or routine events that are problematic at each stage and the kinds of skills and practices used to respond to them. For example, the strategies noted in the codes—"keeping [customers] occupied," "distracting," and "smiling"— suggest that she look for further instances to illustrate the general issue of ways that ushers manage, respond, control, or cope with different types of audience members.

In creating codes, the fieldworker is engaged in an analytic process; she seeks to move beyond the particular event or situation in the fieldnotes to capture some more general theoretical dimension or issue. While it is often useful to begin coding by focusing on a term in the notes—whether the fieldworker's or a member's—the fieldworker must transform that term so that it references a more general category. Yet, at the other extreme, it is not useful to use very general categories as codes. For example, it would not be helpful to code as "social control" staff procedures for searching residents' rooms for "buzzes" and other contraband in a reform school. This category is too general and without specific connection to the events described in the notes. But, a code like "staff control—room searches" would categorize these staff activities as a specific kind of control and perhaps stimulate the field researcher to think about and identify other forms of "staff control."

OPEN CODING

While subjecting fieldnotes to this careful, minute reading, the ethnographer begins to sift through and categorize small segments of the fieldnote record by writing words and phrases that identify and name specific analytic dimensions and categories, as these are suggested by the recorded

observations. Such codings can be written in the margin next to the pertinent fieldnote, on a separate sheet of paper (with some marking of the
location of the relevant fieldnote), or in a "comment" field in some word
processing programs or a keyword field in a text database. In such line-
by-line coding, the ethnographer entertains all analytic possibilities; he
attempts to capture as many ideas and themes as time allows but always
stays close to what has been written down in the fieldnote. He does so
without regard for how or whether ideas and categories will ultimately
be used, whether other relevant observations have been made, or how
they will fit together.

Coding fieldnotes in this way differs fundamentally from coding in
quantitative research. In quantitative coding, the researcher proceeds deductively by constructing questionnaires with categories derived from
theory. He fits peoples' responses to the questionnaire into the already
established categories in order to determine the frequencies of events
within those categories. Qualitative research proceeds inductively by
writing fieldnotes that reflect the significance of events and experiences
to those in the setting.[2] Qualitative coding is a way of opening up avenues
of inquiry: the researcher identifies and develops concepts and analytic
insights through close examination of and reflection on fieldnote data.
Such coding is not fundamentally directed at putting labels on bits and
pieces of data so that what "goes together" can be collected in a single
category; the ethnographer is indeed interested in categories, but less as
a way to sort data than as a way to name, distinguish, and identify the
conceptual import and significance of particular observations. In contrast
to quantitative coding, then, in qualitative coding we identify, elaborate,
and refine analytic insights from and for the interpretation of data.[3]

This view of qualitative coding implies that the same set of fieldnotes
could be coded differently by ethnographers with different theoretical
sensitivities and commitments. Disciplinary background and interests in
particular will exert a deep influence on analytic coding: anthropologists
working with the concept of culture, for example, might formulate
different analytic categories than folklorists interested in performance and
the dynamics of performer–audience interaction. Theoretical differences
within a discipline may produce almost as marked variations in coding.
For example, two sociological field researchers studying households
might well write and code their fieldnotes quite differently (even, we
would argue, were they to carry out their studies in the same setting);
one might focus her coding on the consequences of economic policy on

household relations and the division of labor, the other on women's invisible work in families. In sum, there is no single, correct way to code fieldnotes inasmuch as ethnographers ultimately decide which among a number of possible patterns and ideas, including member concerns and interests, to choose as a focus.

In open coding, the ethnographer should not use preestablished categories to read fieldnotes; rather he should read with an eye toward identifying events described in the notes that could themselves become the basis of categorization. Nor should code categories be avoided because they do not fit with the fieldworker's initial "focus"; this focus will change as the researcher moves through the notes. Rather, the ethnographer should seek to generate as many codes as possible, at least initially, without considering possible relevance either to established concepts in one's discipline or to a primary theoretical focus for analyzing and organizing this ethnography. All ideas and concepts that can be linked to or generated from specific fieldnotes should be treated as of possible interest and should be framed and expressed as clearly and explicitly as possible. Hence, any particular code category need not necessarily connect with other codings or with other field data; integrating categories can come later, and one should not ignore or disregard codings because they suggest no obvious prospects for integration within a major focus or with other emerging categories.

By way of illustration, consider the following open coding of an incident from a support group for those taking care of family members afflicted with Alzheimer's disease:

trouble: memory loss; *bad driving* *dr does not "help"* *asks advice*	Lucie says her husband is in good health, but his symptoms include memory loss and poor and dangerous driving. The doctor does nothing to stop him from driving. She asks, "What does everyone else think?" Some other members say, "Change
fam pressures dr *med test → no results*	doctors." Lucie explains the doctor is a friend of the family. Her son has stressed to the doctor that his father's driving is dangerous and they could be legally involved. The doctor has done a catscan but there is no direction from that.
don't rely on dr *cger to DMV*	Pat, the group leader, recommends, "Take it into your own hands." She suggests that Lucie go to the DMV. Lou says she thinks there is a new law that states anyone with a mental deficiency, including Alzheimer's disease, is not supposed to drive. Lucie

no med dx

advice: coalition w/dr

practical remedy: deception

proposed remedy will not work

"talking to"

says, "But I don't have a name on it—that's what hinders action. I am so frustrated."

Vie says, "Isn't it important for the doctor to tell him not to drive?" Lucie says, "Why won't he do that? Maybe he's too close and he doesn't want to get involved." Lou: "What about Nicholson? He's a geriatric psychiatrist." Others suggest that she hide the car keys. Joey says, "You need to lie to him." Lucie says, "I must say I have been doing that." Joey says, "We all have." . . . Lucie says in terms of the car keys, he knows there is a second set. Another woman says she talked with her husband and he doesn't drive anymore. "I've done this. It is not working." Someone says, "You need a good diagnosis from a medical doctor." Lucie: "That's what I think." Others in the group agree.

Through these marginal codes the fieldworker has identified a variety of loosely related (or even unrelated) issues:

- driving by Alzheimer's patients may be dangerous; family caregivers may have to actively manage those who insist on continuing to drive;
- medical diagnoses may play a critical role in caregivers' efforts to manage patient activities;
- caregivers may experience frustration with doctors who fail to be sensitive to and support family concerns;
- support group members may suggest ways of getting around obstacles presented by doctors;
- support group members may recommend various practical remedies that will prevent the person with Alzheimer's from driving.

Some of these codes reflect issues that the field researcher was interested in from the start: practical "troubles" and how people respond to or "remedy" such troubles (see Emerson and Messinger 1977). But many of these codes elaborate or specify a prior concept in original and unanticipated ways, e.g., "hiding the keys" as a practical remedy for dangerous driving. Other codes identify issues that are entirely unexpected; for example, doctors as both barriers and possible allies in handling unfit drivers.

By the time the ethnographer finishes reading the complete set of fieldnotes, her categories and themes will have fundamentally changed. And many of those categories will be dropped, in turn, as the researcher becomes more focused and aware of other, more interesting and recurrent issues. Furthermore, the process of generating codes may help clarify the meaning or import of previous as well as upcoming notes, for coding shapes and may alter the fieldworker's sense of what the notes "contained" in the first place. As one student commented: "You feel you know your notes because you wrote them, but the thing is, you wrote them so long ago that it doesn't click."

Many students report that the evolving, seemingly unending character of coding initially proved discouraging and upsetting:

> The coding process, it happened once and then it happened again. I ended up coding again and again and again. . . . I had to get over the fact that I would do it the wrong way, or I wouldn't really find any good categories or things wouldn't relate to one another. I had to get over the fear of thinking that there was nothing there.

Coding is indeed uncertain, since it is a matter not simply of "discovering" what is in the data but more creatively of linking up specific events and observations to more general analytic categories and issues. Though researchers inevitably draw on concepts from their particular disciplines to develop linkages, coding keeps them focused on and anchored in their data. Often the researcher is already familiar with the key concepts and interests of her discipline and quickly sees how a given piece of data is relevant to them; but at other times the researcher may have to turn to specific writings that she has not previously read to find pertinent concepts. With time, practice, and wider exposure within a discipline, the researcher gains confidence that she can make analytic connections, and coding becomes less threatening and uncertain.

This open-ended approach can lead to anxiety on several different levels: some students fear they may never come up with a specific focus for a paper. Others, finding line-by-line coding time consuming and tedious, want to focus on a smaller number of themes in order to move ahead quickly, without a lot of "wasted" effort. Still others express concern over a procedure that, in seeking to generate so many different codes, contradicts what they have been taught about "logical" (i.e., carefully planned in advance) thinking and writing. Consider the comments of two students:

> I didn't have any categories before I began. I just was looking at the notes and jotting down codes, but it didn't seem that I was going about it in a very logical way.

I went through two or three sets of notes and there were so many random, recurring themes and not anything that was organized.

But the fact that fieldnotes seem unwieldy, with codings leading in many different directions, is actually a good thing at this stage; such codings will suggest a myriad of possible issues and directions. Especially early on in the process of open coding, we recommend resisting these inclinations to focus on specific themes and topics while continuing to go through the fieldnote record and generating additional codes.

Yet, we have also found that continuous open coding can generate a great deal of frustration as ideas begin to coalesce; continuous open coding may actually discourage developing a specific focus when it would be possible and useful to do so. A strategy of *selective* open coding, in which the fieldworker uses these procedures at different times and with discrete sets of fieldnotes, may therefore be advisable. For example, one may begin with systematic open coding, but then after going through a significant portion, code remaining notes and recode previously coded notes selectively, focusing on "key," "rich," or "revealing" incidents.

WRITING INITIAL MEMOS

Inspired by reading and coding fieldnotes, the fieldworker begins to entertain a wide variety of ideas and insights about what is going on in the data. He can preserve and elaborate these ideas by writing initial theoretical memos. We encourage writing memos about as many ideas, issues, and leads as possible. While some of these ideas reflect concerns and insights the fieldworker brings to the reading, others grow out of reengaging the scenes and events described in the fieldnotes.

Memos written while coding fieldnotes are generally more analytic than in-process commentaries. At times, it is helpful to take a specific, "rich" fieldnote and explore its theoretical implications. The ethnographer studying family members caring for persons with Alzheimer's disease composed the following memo as a series of "observations" on a single, brief but "suggestive," fieldnote excerpt:

Fieldnote: During the support group Fumiko comments on her husband's behavior: "Once in a while he is a pussycat" (laughter), "but he was a raging bull when the VNA came to give him a bath." She adds that recently he has fought her shaving him, but "this morning he let me do it."

Memo: Note how this description suggests that caregivers recognize that *coopera-tion* can vary independently of ability or condition for the person with Alzhei-mer's. Thus, it is one issue whether or not the person with Alzheimer's can feed or bathe him/herself, shave himself, etc.; the stance the person with Alzheimer's takes toward these helping/caring for activities is another matter.

Note also how *unpredictable* these matters may be for the caregiver; bathing and shaving go smoothly on some occasions, but produce major hassles on others. And the caregiver does not seem able to find a reason or explanation for when and why one outcome rather than another occurs.

Furthermore, it may well be uncooperativeness or *resistance* in caregiving mat-ters, rather than the amount or kind of help per se, that generates critical problems and burdens for caregivers. In this respect, the core of a caregiving management regime may rest in those devices and practices that inhibit, overcome, or sidestep resistance. With someone with Alzheimer's who is cooperative (or nonresis-tant)—in most matters—the caregiver can say: "I can still guide him." Similarly, a person with Alzheimer's who is cooperative is one who can be "talked to," i.e. convinced to make changes in his/her daily life, more or less "voluntarily."

In this memo the fieldworker identifies two initial, somewhat unrelated issues in the fieldnote: some caregivers report that patient cooperation can vary independently of physical condition and that cooperation may wax or wane unpredictably. In the final paragraph, she speculates on the possible relevance of one of these issues—cooperation (and its counter-part, resistance)—in shaping the broader pattern and course of family caregiving for persons with Alzheimer's disease.

At other times, the ethnographer can use an initial memo to try to name and specify a particular analytic issue that cuts across a number of particular incidents. Here, for example, one might try to identify and explore a general pattern or theme, drawing upon and attempting to link a number of disparate incidents or events. Along these lines, consider the following memo from a study of support and interaction among court-room personnel (clerks, recorder, bailiff), which explores patterns of "sus-taining community and insideness" in courtroom proceedings:

Examples of "sustaining community and insideness" tend to occur during dead time (recess), on easy days with little business and also after session ends for the day. . . . For example, after today's session, all of the participants except the judge, who always leaves, were actively looking for interactions. Their methods included making eye contact with each other, walking toward each other, making jokes, and interrupting conversations. In this way, information could be shared and opinions could be aired.

This category can be distinguished from idle chatter during recess by the involvement of the participants in the events. High involvement equals community and insideness; low involvement, which is evidenced by briefness of interaction and lack of emotion and eye contact, equals idle chatter.

Here the field researcher identifies a regular pattern of more intense, animated talk and action between courtroom workers which she contrasts with other occasions of less engaging interaction ("idle chatter"). In writing she offers some initial observations on *when* this pattern of relating occurs (during recesses, on slow court days, etc.), as well as on *what* it involves (actively seeking out others, joking, etc.).

In sum, initial coding and memoing require the ethnographer to step back from the field setting to identify, develop, and modify broader analytic themes and arguments. Early on, these efforts should remain flexible and open, as the ethnographer reads, codes, and analyzes fieldnotes to foster a wide range of new ideas, linkages, and connections. Eventually, however, the ethnographer will move beyond these open, inclusive procedures to pursue more focused, analytic themes more intensively. Initially, this narrowing and focusing process involves selecting a small number of core themes which the researcher will subsequently pursue through focused coding and integrative memoing.

SELECTING THEMES

Through initial coding and memoing the ethnographer identifies many more ideas and themes than she will actually be able to pursue in one paper or monograph. Hence she must decide which ideas to explore further and which to put on the back burner, at least for the moment.

Field researchers have different ways of selecting core themes. One consideration is to give priority to topics on which a substantial amount of data has been collected and which reflect recurrent or underlying patterns of activities in the setting under study. Fieldworkers may also give priority to what seems significant to members, whether it is what they think is key, what looks to be practically important, or what engages a lot of their time and energy. For example, one student who wrote fieldnotes while an intern at a county probation office described the following process:

I was going through [the notes] and kept thinking of things like we have all this paper work to do, and people have to sign this and that and I started to get the sense of this larger issue—how is the department dealing with so much paper work? And as I went through it, I found, "Oh, well, a lot of times we help each other out." One probation officer will say I saw your client yesterday on the Commons; that will count as a collateral contact [a kind of contact that must be noted in the paperwork] for you because I saw him. There are shortcuts that way. There are summary reports called "quarterlies" that summarize basically three or four months' worth of work into one sheet. So three or four things like that are subtopics of this larger issue.

This student, in going through her notes, began to notice the different tasks that probation officers must accomplish with a sensitivity to the conditions and constraints that accompany the work. Looking at what probation officers actually did amid the practical constraints and opportunities offered by other agencies—police, clinics, etc.—provided a frame for drawing together what had initially seemed like discrete tasks. Discovering additional themes of this sort provided a guide to reading and coding the rest of her notes.

The fieldworker must also consider how a selected theme can be related to other apparent themes. A theme that allows the researcher to make linkages to other issues noted in the data is particularly promising. Finding new ways of linking themes together allows for the possibility that some of the themes that might have been seen as unrelated and possibly dropped can in fact be reincorporated as "subthemes."

In the process of identifying promising themes and trying to work out possible linkages, the fieldworker may lose for the moment a sense of focus and have to rework ideas until she can reclarify matters. A student who studied the band at a public high school started coding with a good sense of what her paper would be about only to find her direction changed. She reflected on these processes in an interview:

I first thought I would explain how, in the face of budget cuts, somebody could keep a program, an extracurricular program like this going. And then in listing the ways that the teacher does that, I came across the idea that he has to do things to get all of these kids to be friends together. And then I thought, wait a minute, that could be a whole topic of its own. There's so many things going on. How do I explain in my paper the different social cliques with 110 kids; there's so many social cliques? And then I just started looking at the relationships that students have with each other inside band and outside. It was just the weirdest thing—I lost my paper! The more I coded, the more I lost my paper.

Eventually, this student shifted her focus from the many differences between social cliques to how the teacher kept the program going both in the face of budgetary cuts and the divisive tendencies of these different cliques. What was reported negatively as "having lost her paper" really indicates an openness to new meanings and ways of putting things together.

Students engaged in this process often talk about a particular theme "jumping out at them" or, alternatively, of the "focus" for the ethnography "disappearing." This experience is so strong and pervasive that it is important to recall two closely related issues that were touched on previously. First, while the ethnographer's experience is often one of "something going on in the notes," neither the fieldnotes nor their meanings are something "out there" to be engaged after they are written. Rather, as creator of the notes in the first place, the ethnographer has been creating and discovering the meaning of and in the notes all along. Particular sensitivities led to writing about some topics rather than others; these sensitivities may derive from personal commitments and feelings as well as from insights gained from one's discipline and its literature and/or the course instructor. Second, when an ethnographer thinks he has "a substantial amount of data" on a topic, it is not so much because of something inherent in the data; rather it is because the ethnographer has interpreted, organized, and brought the data to bear on the topic.

Once the ethnographer has identified a set of core themes for further analysis, he may find it useful to sort fieldnotes on the basis of these themes. Here, the fieldworker breaks down the corpus of fieldnotes into smaller, more manageable sets, collecting together, in one place, all those pieces that bear on each core issue. This sorting or retrieving procedure involves physically grouping segments of the data on a theme in order to more easily explore their meanings. Sorting into one place or pile facilitates analysis by concentrating fieldnotes relevant to an emerging issue.[4]

In sorting fieldnotes, it is advisable to use themes that are inclusive, allowing for notes that may have been identified with different but related codes to be grouped together. In the study of family caregiving for persons with Alzheimer's disease, for example, after extensive open coding the researcher decided upon "management practices" as one core theme. Management practices were to include any actions caregivers took to manage and control the patient's circumstances and behavior. This category was intentionally inclusive, and it allowed the researcher to incorporate fieldnotes given widely varying codes; thus, under the rubric "management practices," she collected incidents including: incessant monitoring of the patient; warning or "talking to" the patient; and deliberately deceiving the patient in order to manage troublesome behavior. The analysis at this stage is still preliminary, and the meaning and significance of any fieldnote is open to further specification and even fundamental reinterpretation. For this reason, the ethnographer should feel free to include any particular fieldnote excerpt in multiple categories.

Sorting requires physical movement of the data in ways that alter the narrative sequence of the fieldnotes. In the past, fieldworkers often cut up a copy of their fieldnotes and sorted the pieces into piles which would then be repeatedly rearranged as analysis proceeded. A variety of computer programs can now perform the sort function very quickly and efficiently, although some fieldworkers still prefer the flexibility that an overview of fieldnotes spread out on a table or the floor affords.[5] We strongly recommend that those who use this later method keep either a computer copy (with a backup) or a hard copy of the original notes intact for later reference.

Focused Coding

Having decided on core themes and perhaps having sorted the fieldnotes accordingly, the ethnographer next turns to a fine-grained, line-by-line analysis of the notes in focused coding. This involves building up and elaborating analytically interesting themes, both by connecting data that initially may not have appeared to go together and by delineating subthemes and subtopics that distinguish differences and variations within the broader topic.

As an example, the fieldworker whose research focused on caregivers looking after family members with Alzheimer's disease became aware of the *stigma* frequently attached to the latter's condition and behavior. Sorting all fieldnotes on stigma (broadly conceived) into one long document, she then reread and recoded all these materials, in the process developing a series of subthemes of stigma. For example, she came to distinguish "passing"—efforts to prevent the stigma from becoming publicly visible—from "covering"—efforts to cover up, normalize, or distract attention from visible stigmatizing behavior. She also recognized and coded for situations in which the caregiver cooperated with the person with Alzheimer's to manage stigma and for situations in which the caregiver entered into some kind of "collusion" with others to apologize for or manage the stigmatizing incident and its social effects.[6] In focused coding, the researcher constantly makes comparisons between incidents, identifying examples that are comparable on one dimension or that differ on some dimension and hence constitute contrasting cases or variations. When the ethnographer identifies such variation, he asks how the instance differs and attempts to identify the conditions under which these variations occur.

By breaking down fieldnotes even more finely into *subcodes,* the ethnographer discovers new themes and topics and new relationships between them. The same openness to new ways to understand and fit pieces of data together that we encouraged earlier applies to focused coding as well. In some cases, this process generates new issues or opens up new topics that carry the analysis in an entirely different direction and may even require a rethinking and regrouping of the fieldnotes. One student ethnographer reported:

You're both discovering and creating the pattern as you create the pieces—the initial codes—and these begin to structure and frame what the other pieces are going to be and how they will fit together. You have one note and you say to yourself, "Oh, this note seems to fit and be similar to the first note, but it's slightly different and that's what I mean by variation. But somehow they seem to follow one another." Then you continue and read and maybe 15 pages later there's something that seems like it follows or fits. You begin to find pieces that fit together in some kind of way. Don't worry how they all fit in the total paper, just keep fitting them together even if you don't have the connections between them. The aim is to identify what is going on irrespective of whether you will use it later on.

Another student, initially overwhelmed by the number of preliminary codes, said: "I felt that there were so many codes that it wasn't very logical." But she persevered until she could begin to see that there was more to discover in the notes: "I did see that within the more general codes I could see how that once I cut them up I could separate them out into smaller subgroups. What I need to do is do them again." Through the process of focused coding, the ethnographer begins to recognize a pattern in what initially looks like a mass of confusing data. With focused coding, the ethnographer may also begin to envision possible ways of making an argument or telling a story.

Students often express concern when they have only one example of a particular kind of incident or issue. They are concerned that writing about just one instance may distort their analysis if it reflects the response of only a few of those in the setting. Finding only one example would be a problem if the field researcher's purpose were to make claims about frequency or representativeness. But frequency is only one dimension for analysis. While the researcher delights in numerous examples of a theme or topic, the goal in ethnographic analysis is not representativeness. Rather, the ethnographer seeks to identify patterns and variations in relationships and in the ways that members understand and respond to conditions and contingencies in the social setting. That there is "only one case" often does not matter.[7] When the ethnographer is fortunate enough to find more than one instance, it is important to note how they are the same and how they vary. Useful questions to keep in mind at this point include: How is this example the same and different? What were the conditions under which differences and variations occurred?

INTEGRATIVE MEMOS

As the ethnographer turns increasingly from data-gathering to the analysis of fieldnotes, writing integrating memos which elaborate ideas and begin to link or tie codes and bits of data together becomes absolutely critical. In writing integrating memos, the ethnographer seeks to explore relationships between coded fieldnotes and to provide a more sustained examination of a theme or issue by linking together a variety of discrete observations. At this point, many ethnographers continue to write primarily for themselves, focusing on putting the flow of their thoughts on paper and maintaining the loose, "note this" and "observe that" style characteristic of several of the memos we have considered to this point. Others, however, find it useful to begin to write with future audiences explicitly in mind. For these researchers, integrating memos provide a first occasion to begin to explicate contextual and background information that a reader unfamiliar with the setting would need to know in order to follow the key ideas and claims. Imagining this future readership within a particular discipline spurs the ethnographer to write in a more public voice, that is, to word ideas in concepts and language that approximate the analytic writing in a final text. It is a first attempt to formulate a cohesive idea in ways that would organize a section of the final ethnography (see the discussion in chapter 7). Thus, such memos sound more polished.

Substantively, integrative memos may move through a series of fieldnote incidents, linking these incidents by connecting sentences. We examine the following extended memo on "remedial covering" by family members caring for persons with Alzheimer's disease to illustrate these processes:

Remedial covering involves attempts to correct the troublesome behavior once it has occurred. Caregivers take it upon themselves to watch over the family member and attempt to "smooth over things" in a variety of public places. For example, Laura explains what she does in the presence of friends:

> He may take the cup off the saucer and just put it somewhere else on the table. And I'll say, "I think you'd probably get that cup back over here because it'll get tipped over, and it's easier if you have it close to you like that." . . . I try to smooth over these things.

In a similar case, Carol recounts how Ned embarrasses her by removing his dentures in a restaurant and how she handles this:

> I got up real quick and stood in front of him and said, "Get your teeth in your mouth." Then she explains to me, "I felt I had to protect him. What if the waitress came?"

In this first segment, the ethnographer links two separate incidents occurring in restaurants through the themes of "watching over" and "smoothing over things." In doing so, differences between the incidents—for example, in the first instance, that something untoward is prevented from happening, while in the second the untoward action has occurred but is literally "covered" and then corrected—are subordinated to these commonalities.

The researcher then takes up a further dimension of remedial covering, specifying the contrast between covering that relies upon the cooperation of the person with Alzheimer's and covering that is carried out directly by the caregiver:

Remedial covering involves having to negotiate the individual's cooperation when he or she is capable of doing so. For example, Laura describes her husband in a local restaurant, how she instructs and physically maneuvers him through various eating tasks ("puppeteering," Pollner and McDonald-Wikler 1985) and how he responds. Her description of their interaction gives a real flavor of the minute detail to which the caregiver must attend:

> I'll say, "Now turn around some more so that your legs are under the table and then move over so that you're in front of the placemat." . . . Then he would set the beer out very perilously near the edge, and I'd move it back. . . . And then I'd have to arrange things . . . he picked up the tortilla, and it wasn't appropriate. And if anybody were watching, they'd say, "Tsk tsk."

While Laura suggests remedial practices to William in the above example, Tess in her situation takes over and attempts to remedy the situation on her own. She describes going to a buffet restaurant with some of her co-workers, where she tries to cover her father's mistakes so the co-workers are less likely to notice:

> Him and I go to buffets all the time . . . and I watch him. I make him go ahead of me so I can fix everything he screws up. He like takes the spoon, puts some cheese on his salad, puts the spoon on his plate. . . . And I grab the spoon and put it back . . . all the employees that I work with are behind me. . . .

Here the ethnographer sets up a contrast between two different responses to the problematic acts of a person with Alzheimer's. First, she notes Laura's handling of her husband by means of orders; in so doing she sees and marks a parallel with the concept of "puppeteering" developed in an article she is familiar with. Second, she examines Tess's ways of managing her father by directly "taking over." She then continues by considering the conditions under which one or the other form of remedial covering is likely:

As the person with Alzheimer's is less and less able to cooperate with the caregiver in these covering practices, the caregiver is forced to take more control of the situation. For example, Carol states, "I'm more ready to be the ultimate authority. . . . This is the way it's going to be done. In other words, take total control."

In composing this memo, then, the writer outlines a progression from milder to more active and restrictive forms of remedial covering likely to occur as the disease progresses. She ends by arguing that this progression fundamentally involves increasing control over the behavior of the person with Alzheimer's disease; she quotes a caregiver who talks openly of her need to now "take total control."

In writing analytic, integrative memos of this sort, the central task is to develop theoretical connections between fieldnote excerpts. In so doing, the ethnographer confronts difficult analytic choices. One major issue is deciding which theme to make the primary focus, which to include as subthemes, and which to exclude entirely. To return to the dilemma of the student who "lost her paper" while focusing and sorting her notes: one strategy was to divide the paper up into different sections, such that the issues of the teacher's strategies for managing the band and of the students' grouping themselves into cliques would be analyzed as a topics unto themselves. A second possibility was to see these strategies as different aspects of the more general theme. Here, the paper would focus on how the teacher managed to keep an extracurricular program going in the face of overwhelming odds—declining resources and a large and heterogeneous group of students. Specific subtopics would include how he tried to motivate kids to spend extra time on weekends or extra time during the week, and how he managed the tensions and different interests between the various student cliques.

Deciding how to frame an analysis often requires taking a step back from the particulars of the analysis in order to answer the question: What is the larger, more encompassing question(s) I am responding to? One student who studied an alternative school, for example, was able, once she clarified the story she wanted to tell, to incorporate themes from the following incident involving negotiations over the use of a chair at an all-school meeting:

> The chair was just sitting there, and I was sitting behind a group of guys who were saving chairs, and this girl took this chair and started to put her feet on it, and the guy says, "Hey, someone's sitting there." She said, "Well, can't I just use it until he comes back?" Then a student teacher comes along, and you can see him eyeing the chair, and he says, "Can I use your foot rest?" She said, "Someone's sitting there." He said, "Well, I'll just use it until he comes back," and then he sits down. But the first guy says, "Excuse me, someone is sitting there." He says, "Well, I'll give it back when he gets back." The student [whose chair it is] comes back and the teacher just got up and left.

The student ethnographer saw in this fieldnote ways the students at the school negotiated with one another and with a student teacher over seating. But while she found the incident and several like it of interest with regard to relations between students and between students and teachers, she struggled with how to link such incidents to a variety of other themes. She decided at this point to step back and attempt to relate the incident more broadly to what she knew and found interesting about the school. She thought, for example, about the pride that both students and teachers at the alternative public school took in the ethic of "democratic decision making" and "shared power." She contrasted this with many more traditional schools where teachers readily exert authority. With the more general issue of this contrast in mind, the student saw that, on some occasions, teachers in the alternative school may not hold or choose to exercise authority but rather negotiate or defer to student claims to space. This led the student to see that she could tie negotiating for space to a range of other incidents that were decided in nonauthoritarian ways. She also began to look for contrasts in this theme and specifically for examples of matters that were closed to negotiation. By pursuing this line of analysis, the student saw that what initially might have seemed an isolated, mundane incident was related to larger questions of power and authority. More fundamentally, finding a frame for this incident helped her not to take teacher and student claims to "democracy" and "power sharing" at face value or as givens but rather as achievements that were variously honored in the setting.

Again, there is no single, correct way to organize themes and subthemes. Part of the decision about which course to take depends on the kind of data that has been recorded. In the study of the high school band, very rich and detailed notes on types of students in the school would allow focusing on student cliques. But if such observations are lacking, cliques must move from the center of the picture and become part of the context or background with something else in the foreground. It is usual for ethnographers to try on, modify, discard, and reconsider several possibilities before deciding which tells the best story. As was the case when writing fieldnotes in the first place, organizational decisions will be influenced by factors that range from how inclusive an organizational scheme is to how well it highlights particular theoretical and substantive interests and preferences.

REFLECTIONS: CREATING THEORY FROM FIELDNOTES

Analysis of ethnographic data begins with concepts that are grounded in and reflect intimate familiarity with the setting or events under study. From close, systematic attention to the fieldnotes as data, the ethnographer seeks to generate as many ideas, issues, topics and themes as possible. This is an inductive process.

Ethnographers differ from other social scientists who proceed deductively with a theory that explains phenomena and attempt to find instances in the data that illustrate or disprove it. While fieldnotes may privilege certain kinds of events—those of significance to members or that illustrate social processes, for example—the ethnographer proceeds in a more open-ended way, seeking to identify issues and ideas by a careful sifting through and piecing together of fieldnotes. The ethnographer remains open to other possibilities and gives serious consideration to processes and issues that become apparent as she reviews the data.

This should not be understood to mean that the fieldworker completely ignores existing theory and has no theoretical commitments prior to reading through the notes. It does suggest, however, that for the ethnographer, theory does not simply await refinement as analysts test concepts one by one against events in the social world; nor do data stand apart as independent measures of theoretical adequacy. Rather, the ethnographer's assumptions, interests, and theoretical commitments enter into every phase of writing an ethnography and influence decisions that range from selecting which events to write about to those that entail emphasizing one member's perspective on an event over those of others. The process is thus one of reflexive or dialectical interplay between theory and data whereby theory enters in at every point, shaping not only analysis but how social events come to be perceived and written up as data in the first place.

The goal in fieldwork, then, is to generate theory that grows out of or is directly relevant to activities occurring in the setting under study. This contrasts not only with those who practice deduction from received theory but with proponents of grounded theory (Glaser and Strauss 1967). As suggested earlier, grounded theorists focus on the "discovery" and modification of theory through the close examination of qualitative data. But such an approach dichotomizes data and theory as two separate and distinct entities; it avoids seeing theory as inherent in the notion of data in the first place. But as we have emphasized, data are never pure; they are ripe with meanings and always products of prior interpretive and conceptual decisions. Grounded theory slights the processes whereby data are assembled, processes that build concepts into the data from the start in the very process of *writing* fieldnotes.

In this respect, it is something of a distortion to talk about "discovering theory," as we often are tempted to do. For while reading our fieldnotes carefully and reflectively, we frequently feel that we "discover theory" in the data contained in those notes. But theory only *seems* to jump out of the data and hit the researcher in the face; this flash of insight occurs only because of the researcher's prior analytic commitments built into the notes, the theoretical concerns and commitments she brings to the reading, and the connections made with other "similar events" observed and written about. Thus, it is more accurate to say that the ethnographer creates rather than discovers theory. She does so not simply in the culminating moment of reading and reflecting on what she has seen and written about previously, but also throughout that prior process of seeing as she writes fieldnotes.

In fieldwork, then, events and actions become meaningful in light of an emerging meaningful whole. The analysis of fieldnotes is not just a matter of finding what the data contain. Rather, the ethnographer selects out some incidents and events, gives them priority, and comes to understand them in relationship to others. Grasping the continuously analytic character of fieldwork often entails a shift in the ways we often think of the ethnographer's relationship both to the fieldnotes and to analysis of them. One student describes the process of finding her "ethnographic voice":

At first, I wanted the paper to emerge through the notes in the sense that it had its own story, and I was supposed to tell its story. But I had to make the shift from just wanting to talk about what was in the notes to making something solid out of them—my ideas, instead of thinking that it's hidden somewhere in the notes.

Rather than simply tracing out what the data tell, the fieldworker renders the data meaningful. Analysis is less a matter of something emerging from the data, of simply finding what is there; it is more fundamentally a process of creating what is there by constantly thinking about the import of previously recorded events and meanings.

chapter seven

Writing an Ethnography

In moving from fieldnotes to writing ethnographic texts, the ethnographer turns away from local scenes and their participants, from relations formed and personal debts incurred in the field. Now an author working at her desk, she reviews her recordings of members' everyday experiences and reorients to her fieldnotes as texts to be analyzed, interpreted, and selected for inclusion in a document intended for wider audiences. Thus, the dual awareness of members and outside audiences, inherent but often muted in the participant-observer role in the field, becomes overt and insistent in writing a polished ethnographic text.

While field researchers may envision different outside audiences, most write for other scholars.[1] Having been trained in a particular discipline (such as sociology, anthropology, or folklore), the field researcher draws upon and develops ideas which make sense within the conceptual language of that discipline. While disciplinary concerns will already have shaped many fieldnote entries, in actually composing ethnographic texts the researcher self-consciously makes his observations and experiences of particular local scenes speak to the concepts and traditions of a scholarly discipline. The ethnographer as author must *represent* the particular world he has studied (or some slice or quality of it) for readers who lack direct acquaintance with it. To do so, he moves back and forth between specific events recounted in his fieldnotes and more general concepts of interest to his discipline. An overconcern for a scholarly framework and concepts would distort and obscure the nuances of everyday life; but to simply present members' categories exclusively in their terms would produce texts devoid of relevance and interest to scholarly audiences.

In this chapter we present an approach to writing finished ethnographies that seeks to use and balance this tension between analytic propositions and local meanings. Rather than composing a tightly organized analytic argument in which each idea leads logically and exclusively to the next, we advocate writing ethnographies as narrative "tales" (Van Maanen 1988; Richardson 1990). Ethnographies are tales or stories not in the sense that they are fictional but in that the writer uses standard literary conventions (Atkinson 1990) to "construct" from fieldnotes a narrative that will interest an outside audience. Such tales weave specific analyses of discrete pieces of fieldnote data into an overall story. This story is analytically thematized, but often in relatively loose ways; it is also fieldnote-centered, that is, constructed out of a series of thematically organized units of fieldnote excerpts and analytic commentary.

We begin the chapter by examining the distinctive sort of ethnographic story we seek to produce—what we call a "thematic narrative." Thematic narratives incorporate several analytic themes or concepts linked by a common topic.[2] We then discuss a series of steps that move progressively toward creating a thematic narrative that is fieldnote-centered. These steps include writing out initial statements of analytic themes, then selecting, explicating, sequencing, and editing fieldnote excerpts in order to build up a series of thematically organized units of excerpts and analytic commentary. Finally, we discuss the writing of introductions and conclusions necessary to produce the completed ethnographic manuscript.[3]

Developing a Thematic Narrative

In coding and memo-writing, the ethnographer has started to create and elaborate analytic themes. In writing an ethnographic text, the writer organizes some of these themes into a coherent "story" about life and events in the setting studied. Such a narrative requires selecting only some small portion of the total set of fieldnotes and then linking them into a coherent text representing some aspect or slice of the world studied.

Writing a thematic narrative differs fundamentally from writing an analytic argument, both in the process of putting that text together and in the structure of the final text. Structurally, in a text which presents a logical argument, the author sets forth a formal thesis or proposition in the introduction as a stance to be argued, then develops each analytic point with evidence logically following from and clearly supporting the propositional thesis.[4] In contrast, an ethnographic story proceeds through an intellectual examination of evidence to eventually reach its contributing central idea. While a thematic narrative begins by stating a main idea or thesis, it progresses toward fuller elaboration of this idea throughout the paper. Indeed, the more precise, fuller statement of the thesis is often most effectively presented at the end of the story, in a conclusion to the paper.

In addition, the structure of an ethnographic story results from an ordered progression of fieldnote excerpts. The details in the fieldnotes stand as the essential kernels of the story. That is, thematic narratives use fieldnotes not as illustrations and examples of points that have already been made, but as building blocks for constructing and telling the story in the first place. In this sense, the main idea grows out of the process of coding and selecting excerpts, rather than prefiguring the choice of fieldnotes to include. The excerpts in an ethnographic story are not so much evidence for analytic points as they are the core of the story.

In terms of writing processes, developing a thematic narrative requires constant movement back and forth between specific fieldnote incidents and progressively more focused and precise analysis. To facilitate this process, we do not recommend beginning with a tentative thesis or working hypothesis. Instead, we urge the writer to hold off formulating an explicit thesis until the paper is finished, so that even in the process of writing, she will make discoveries about data and continue to balance her analytic insights with the demands of sticking close to indigenous views. We suggest that the ethnographer begin developing a thematic narrative by writing out a statement of a general *topic* or *question*. A topic ties a broad analytic concern or sensitivity to the events that occurred in the setting. For example, "ethnicity as social construction in a high school" and "parental involvement in juvenile court hearings" provide such topic statements.[5] At this early stage, topic statements point to a concern or phenomenon, but they do not pose a specific problem or question, nor propose a formal thesis or explanation. Rather, a topic or question identifies a more general focus and helps the author to begin tying fieldnotes together into a coherent whole.

In general, the topic of the ethnographic story will incorporate several more specific analytic themes, i.e., claims about key patterns, processes, or regularities within the setting. Hence one way to develop a topic is to review the earlier codings and memos, identifying a number of the more interesting or relevant themes in one's fieldnotes. At this point we advise that one write out phrases stating possible themes clearly and explicitly. Initially, the researcher need not be concerned with deciding how these themes relate to one another or how they might be tied together; the writing is intended simply to clarify and specify themes of possible interest. But once several promising themes have been identified, the ethnographer looks for ways of relating some of these themes to one topic and then decides to drop those themes which cannot be tied to this topic.

Alternatively, the ethnographer may come away from his coding and memo-writing with a clear sense of an interesting and unifying general topic. He should then write out this topic as explicitly as possible and then attempt to specify more particular themes that might develop that topic by reviewing his codings, memos, and perhaps even original fieldnotes. For example, having written the phrase, "I will show that parents become involved in court decisions," the student ethnographer studying juvenile court then asked in what different ways parents might become involved in these hearings. On reviewing his codings, he found two distinct patterns, one in which the judge used parents as a source of information about youth, the other in which the judge sought to help parents control their children. He then wrote out these two more specific themes: "The judge sometimes uses parental information against the minor in order to sentence him" and "the judge also might support the parents in disciplining the minor and therefore threaten punishment."

In either case, the ethnographer will move back and forth between topic and themes, writing an overview statement that relates themes to a topic and to one another, and/or developing explicit phrasings for each identified topic. The relations between themes need not be tight and closely reasoned; in "thematic narratives" the themes can be loosely integrated. Relating and ordering themes will usually require changes in wording and conceptualization. Clearly, some themes may not "fit" with others, even on these terms, and may have to be dropped. In fact, even after developing an overall plan for a first draft, it is quite common to revise both the specific thematic statements and their interconnections a number of times as work progresses and the ethnographic story begins to take shape.

Consider how one student began to develop a thematic narrative around the general topic "ethnicity as social construction" in a public high school. First, he wrote out an elaboration of his topic: "Through people's interactions 'ethnicity' is constantly being recreated and modified within a situation." Then, he wrote out a number of specific themes or issues that he wanted to deal with. Finally, to present these themes, he worked out the following order for five specific sections of the text— each centered on one theme:

1. I provide an overview of some different ways ethnicity is used in schools.
2. I demonstrate that students refer to and recognize different social and ethnic groups, but that the composition of the group varies.
3. I examine the use of black ethnicity and the ways black social groups maintain ethnic boundaries.
4. I discuss people who use ethnic aesthetics of other people (whites' use of black styles), in terms of boundary definitions.
5. I analyze ethnic conflict as a process of generating cultural distinctions.

In developing these themes, the ethnographer does more than name different situations; more fundamentally, he points out distinctions and interconnections between related phenomena. For example, the theme of how students talk about and identify "different social and ethnic groups" not only considers a range of ethnic (and social) groups but also deals with the ethnic identities assigned to others; in contrast, the theme addressing how "black social groups maintain ethnic boundaries" will involve examining how group members establish their own ethnic identity. Yet he also suggests important linkages between these phenomena; for example, exploring "whites' uses of black styles" suggests a concern with the blurring and crossing of ethnic boundaries that will elaborate and extend his interest in the maintenance of black ethnic boundaries.

To pick a topic and specific themes, the ethnographer must make choices. Fieldworkers regularly find that they have many more themes than they are able to include in any particular manuscript. The process of developing a story is essentially one of selecting some themes that resonate with personal or disciplinary concerns and that recur in a number of specific fieldnotes. In selecting these themes and the data they make relevant, the ethnographer inevitably ignores other themes and data, at least for this particular manuscript.

In developing a topic and then assembling themes into a story, the ethnographer should make every effort to incorporate multiple voices and perspectives. To do so often requires giving special attention to selecting and framing the topic and subsequent, interrelated themes, for how a topic or theme is named and developed can implicitly privilege some voices and perspectives and exclude others. For example, one student studying the relations between domestic workers and their employers initially identified "hiring" as one topic in her ethnography. But "hiring" frames events from the point of view of the employer, highlighting and privileging her concerns with finding a worker who is "reliable" and "trustworthy." "Hiring" implicitly neglects the domestic worker and her practices for "getting hired" or "finding work." A more relational framing—e.g., "the hiring situation"—would incorporate the perspectives of both employer and domestic worker.

In the following sections, we present ways of turning fieldnotes into ethnographic texts. While recognizing that the initial commitment to a general topic and several initial themes informs this process, we emphasize how the ethnographer elaborates, specifies, and excerpts fieldnotes— which may be only loosely associated with a common theme—in order to develop a finished ethnographic story.

TRANSPOSING FIELDNOTES INTO ETHNOGRAPHIC TEXT

Atkinson (1990:103) argues that the "persuasive force" of an ethnographic text derives from the "interplay of concrete exemplification and discursive commentary." We are explicitly concerned with producing such *fieldnote-centered texts*—stories that stay close to and are highly saturated with bits and pieces of fieldnotes. To create such a text, the ethnographer must conceptualize the relevance of local happenings so that they relate to analytic issues; but simultaneously, the ethnographer must remain sensitive to how these reframings might distort the meaning of member categories.

To begin this process, the fieldworker must return to the fieldnotes that inspired the story to look for potential excerpts that could develop a story line. The ethnographer first identifies pieces of fieldnote data and then writes interpretive commentary about these excerpts; she also edits each excerpt-and-commentary unit so that the analysis elaborates and highlights the fieldnotes which are the kernels of the story. Finally, the researcher must organize these excerpt-commentary segments into coherent sections of the ethnography; that is, she orders them in a sequence which creates a compelling story line which leads readers to an ever fuller understanding of the people and issues addressed.

Selecting Fieldnote Excerpts

With a topic involving a number of themes in mind, the field researcher can return to the set of coded fieldnotes to identify the particular ones most relevant to key issues. He returns to these sorted notes, creating fieldnote *excerpts* that will comprise the building blocks of the emerging ethnographic story. We suggest several guidelines for deciding which fieldnotes to excerpt.

Selecting fieldnote excerpts is not a simple matter of "picking the most interesting examples." Rather, the ethnographer has a variety of reasons for deciding which fieldnotes to include in the final text. In introducing a setting, for example, a field researcher may select fieldnotes because they aptly illustrate recurring patterns of behavior or typical situations in that setting. Similarly, a field researcher may choose fieldnotes recounting commonplace happenings or concerns. These excerpts may introduce more specific analytic themes or identify significant variations from what is usual.

The ethnographer also selects fieldnotes for their evocative and persuasive qualities. An excerpt may appeal because it portrays a rare or moving moment—someone expressing deep anguish or two people in a poignant exchange. Or a fieldnote description may seem likely to engage and persuade readers by enabling them to envision scenes, hear voices, and identify momentarily with the ethnographer's perspective on the action. In general, excerpts that contain close-up, vivid descriptions that portray actions and voices will situate readers in the scene; such excerpts will often enable readers to imagine and vicariously experience what the researcher observed. In contrast, a "skimpy" excerpt lacking vivid details fails to persuade because it relies more on the author's interpretation than on sights and sounds readers can visualize or hear. In addition, excerpts that report naturally occurring dialogue often persuasively reveal members' concerns. Through hearing people respond to each other in a conversation, readers can infer their interpretations of each other's words. Through such a dialogue excerpt, an ethnographer presents the negotiated quality of interactions—hence revealing a process rather than just an outcome. A perceptive author, therefore, looks for excerpts—especially with talk and actions—which reveal members' different views and concerns.

In selecting evocative excerpts, the ethnographer does not need to have a precise analytic idea in mind. But in most cases she will come to discern analytic significance in such excerpts. An ethnographer trusts her own intuitive sense that a particular written account is revealing even if, at the moment, she cannot clearly articulate why this might be so. Continuing reflection on how and why an excerpt is evocative, moving, or telling may ultimately lead to a new appreciation and a deeper, more insightful story.

When constructing a thematic narrative, the ethnographer also specifically seeks excerpts that illustrate concepts and suggest ways of elaborating or specifying these concepts. Finding and selecting excerpts clarifies and gives content to the emerging story. As ethnographers find and review new excerpts, they further clarify ideas, and, in turn, consider additional excerpts they had initially ignored. Often these insights happen spontaneously: as they clarify a theme or concept, a related instance recorded elsewhere in the fieldnotes comes to mind ("I remember another instance of that!") because it ties in analytically. And on finding and reviewing that piece of data, the ethnographer may further modify the core idea. He looks again in his fieldnotes and early memos for other excerpts that he may now see as relevant.[6]

A critical starting place, then, may lie in those fieldnote bits that touched off particular codings and memo-writing on themes of current interest. It is important to return to these previously thematized fieldnote accounts (and to related coding and memos), to review them, and to excerpt those that are relevant. For example, a research project on women applying for domestic violence restraining orders focused on the role of a friend or supporter in facilitating this process. The following fieldnote played a pivotal role in helping the ethnographer to recognize key dimensions in this process:

> Julie Peters was my fifth client. She was a 24-year-old Caucasian, married to a Caucasian cop. He had never hit her, but held a gun to her face and strangled her at one point and constantly abused her verbally. Julie had brought in her friend Tina who did most of the talking for her. I could tell that Julie was very quiet and preoccupied. Tina said that Julie was really "messed up" and was losing her hair, literally.
>
>> Julie: I just don't want my husband to lose his job. He's a cop, you know.
>> Interviewer: I know you're worried about him, but let's worry about him later. First, let's take care of you.
>> Julie: I know, you're right.
>> Tina: It took a lot for her to come in. I had to drag her in. She called me this morning, crying, and I said, 'That's it, we're going in.'

This friend's account of getting the wife to come in for a restraining order against her husband typified a process whereby a supporter pushed a "victim" to seek legal remedy. Having previously seen fieldnotes related to friends' active participation in the application for the restraining order, this fieldnote crystallized an appreciation of "third person support" in legal and other bureaucratic encounters.

In general, an excerpt may jog the memory, suggesting other "similar" instances or events, and, hence, provide a starting place for collecting a body of excerpts bearing on a common theme. Or, the ethnographer may begin to systematically review codings and fieldnotes, looking for excerpts of that "same thing." One might then note a common pattern or regularity captured in the mass of fieldnote data. In a study of probation progress hearings in juvenile court, for example, a field researcher observed that judges regularly solicited parents' views about their children's behavior, as in the following instance:

> Judge Smith answers [the minor] with a quiet but sharp tone: "I told you to get good grades. . . . You haven't been getting good grades. . . . I also told you to be obedient to your mother." He then asks the mother: "Has he been obedient or disobedient?" "Disobedient. He doesn't go to school when I tell him to go . . ." she answers while looking at her son.

By collecting a number of such instances, the ethnographer can see nuances within a theme and refine his interpretations of particular excerpts.

To do so, an ethnographer may begin to address issues of the *differences* between instances she has observed and written about. In the first place, she can look for *variations within the theme or pattern* seen in different fieldnotes. For example, in studying the role of friends and supporters in interviews applying for a domestic violence restraining order, one might look for instances, first, in which the supporter becomes actively involved in the interview and, second, in which the supporter says little and plays a secondary role. Similarly, one might look for excerpts showing differences in how parents respond to judges' questions about their children's misconduct. Thus, the ethnographer could juxtapose the excerpt in which the youth's mother reported that her son had been "disobedient" to the following one in which the mother supports her daughter—at least to some degree—by minimizing reports of misconduct:

> A young girl sits down to the left of her attorney. The mother sits down in the back of the room in a chair closest to the entrance. Judge Smith asks the mother

directly how the girl is doing. She comments that she has no problem at home "with her" but that school is "a problem."

Considering variations within a context of similarity helps the field researcher pursue further comparisons and thus make additional excerpts relevant.

In the second place, the ethnographer can select additional excerpts that involve more profound differences. Here, he looks for instances that *contrast with the previously discovered pattern.* In juvenile court probation hearings, for example, an ethnographer might select an excerpt in which the judge does *not* ask the parent for her view of her offspring's misconduct. Such excerpts begin to reveal the circumstances which shape and limit the pattern of interaction in the first place. In the juvenile court setting, this may occur in cases in which the parent has been discredited in some way or when incarcerating the youth is a foregone conclusion.

In this process, the ethnographer should actually write out all of the key dimensions, patterns, or distinctions. While the phrase or word which coded an excerpt implies an idea, an author's thinking often remains fuzzy until she actually writes it out in a sentence. In writing out ideas, she continues mulling over her interpretations. Ultimately, she will hone tentative ideas into more clearly articulated propositions in a final paper. But at this stage she aims for textured richness and flow, rather than logical tightness, and leaves precise formulations and wordings to be worked out later. She tries to fully explore variations in and exceptions to the theme she is investigating.

Throughout this process, an ethnographer continually refines her overall sense of the emerging ethnographic paper. Often a main idea for the ethnography becomes clear to her quite early—while determining a topic or identifying themes during coding. Other ethnographers clarify the main ideas while selecting excerpts. And for some authors, it is only with the start of writing commentaries on the selected excerpts that the central idea comes into focus. However, only when writing an introduction do many ethnographers finally settle on the exact focus and wording of a thesis statement. In the meantime, by writing out a tentative statement of the central idea, the ethnographer begins to shape the paper's overall focus and sense of what this ethnographic story will tell. But this tentative, central idea—not yet a controlling thesis statement—often changes during the process of explicating fieldnotes and revising sections of the paper.

Options for Explicating Fieldnotes

With a story in mind and a series of fieldnote excerpts and initial memos in hand, the ethnographer next begins composing more elaborated analytic commentaries that explicate each excerpt and link it to others. Proceeding in this manner—producing a series of written segments combining analytic interpretation with fieldnote excerpt—builds up piece by piece a coherent, fieldnote-centered story.

Ethnographers use two different textual strategies for creating and presenting units of fieldnote excerpts and interpretive commentary. An *integrative strategy* weaves together interpretation and excerpt; it produces a text with minimal spatial markings—such as indentation or single spacing—to indicate where the fieldnote ends and interpretation begins. As an example, consider the following account of one way in which amateur pyrotechnists—people who illegally construct and set off homemade fireworks and related devices—acquire their working materials:

> A second category of high-yield explosives that are obtained primarily by the core pyrotechnist includes such things as dynamite and various liquid and plastic explosives used for both military and industrial purposes. In certain areas, dynamite is reportedly very simple to acquire. I was informed that in a neighboring state anyone over eighteen years of age with a "respectable purpose" could make an over-the-counter purchase of dynamite. During the study, Arnold, Russell and Hank made an excursion to that state to buy, among other things, eight sticks of the explosive. As Arnold remarked: "We just said we had a mine south of —— that we were working, and the only purpose we had in mind was to set it [the dynamite] off, just like anyone who uses firecrackers—just for the entertainment of it." He further reported that he and the others proceeded to detonate the dynamite in a remote spot to avoid the risk of transporting the explosive across state lines back to their home state.

Here the ethnographer employs fieldnotes as illustrations or "exemplars" (Atkinson 1990) of a claimed pattern, selecting and reworking them to explicate and document those claims. As a result, fieldnotes and ideas are merged into a single, flowing text written in a single voice. The writer does not mark differences between fieldnotes recorded in the past and present interpretations through textual devices but, rather, indicates this shift through such transitional phrases as "for example" or "a telling episode."

In contrast, an *excerpt strategy* visually marks fieldnote extracts off from accompanying commentary and interpretation, usually by indenting and/

or italicizing. Consider the following paragraph from an ethnographic section on "the difficulties which autistic clients experience as they attempt to integrate into the community around them." The author begins the paragraph with the analytic point that neighbors frequently treat them in a "stigmatizing manner." Then she provides an excerpt:

> At times people in the community respond more inclusively to clients, although in a stigmatizing manner. At a local bowling alley, a bartender attempted to accommodate John but patronized him instead:
>
>> I went with John to the bowling alley to get his coffee. John asked the man behind the bar if he could have a "very large coffee." The man gave him a cup of coffee and then, when John went to pay for it, the man handed back the dollar bill and said, "I forgot your birthday last year, Happy Birthday." John put the dollar back into his pocket and said, "Thank you," to the man. When we got back into the car, John said, "It's just my birthday. I'm going to get some things to open up." John continued to repeat these phrases (to "perseverate") until another situation redirected him.

Although the bartender gives John positive social reinforcement, he too treats him in a discriminatory way. John in trying to "fit in" in his community receives a response showing that he remains locked out. The bartender's "special treatment" of John reveals that he views him as "special"—different—deserving of or in need of a break. In the bartender's attempt to do a good deed, he further stigmatizes a person who already has to work hard to attain the minimal entrance he receives into his own community.

Here, the particularized instance clarifies the more analytic statement the author sets forth as the topic sentence. The fieldnote description inclines the reader to be persuaded by her analysis. Then, through analytic commentary following the excerpt, this ethnographer extends her initial point by considering several features of the interaction: John's trying to fit in, the bartender's positive reinforcement, and the subtly stigmatizing effect of special treatment.

The fieldnote is easily recognized as an excerpt, since it is indented. This visual layout enhances the discursive contrast between descriptive and analytic writing. It also produces distinctly dialogic text, since the ethnographer speaks in two different voices—as fieldworker describing the experience depicted in the excerpt and as author now explaining those events to readers.

Furthermore, by visually separating excerpts from commentary, this mode of presentation frames fieldnote excerpts as accounts composed in the past, close to events in the field. In this sense, excerpting shapes up fieldnote bits as "evidence," as what was "originally recorded," standing in contrast to subsequent interpretation. Indeed, through clear-cut excerpts, the ethnographer adopts a stance toward the reader which says, "Here is what I heard and observed, and here is the sense that I *now* make of it."

Many ethnographers develop a preference for one or the other option and employ it consistently throughout a given text.[7] But it is also possible to use both integrative and excerpt strategies at different places for different writing purposes. The integrative style promotes a smoother, more thematically focused presentation of field data. It allows the author to convey many ideas in a concise, focused manner, since the writer heavily edits portions of the original fieldnotes that are not germane to the issue or argument at hand. Moreover, an integrative style is particularly suited for presenting longer, continuous fieldnotes: extended episodes with complicated background circumstances can be recounted as one continuing story.[8] For this reason, this strategy facilitates consistent use of the first person and hence encourages more flexible and reflective narrative accounts. Finally, the integrative strategy is also useful for bringing together observations and occurrences scattered in different places in the fieldnote record to create a coherent overview of an issue or pattern.

In contrast, the excerpt strategy preserves earlier descriptions and details without extensive editing, in some sense letting readers see for themselves the "grounds" for analytic and interpretive claims. By textually distinguishing fieldnote and analysis, the excerpt style invites the reader to assess the underpinnings, construction, and authenticity of the interpretations offered. Clearly, this strategy relies heavily upon the rhetorical impact of presenting fieldnote excerpts as "evidence" collected prior to and perhaps independently of the eventual interpretation. Finally, the excerpt strategy allows for maximum presentation of unexplicated details and qualities of events observed in the field. For ethnographers need not, and in practice do not, explicate every aspect of the fieldnote excerpts they incorporate into the text. Rather, they often allow the scenes to speak for themselves. Containing more than the ethnographer chooses to discuss and analyze, such excerpts give depth and texture to ethnographic texts. In fact, these unexamined qualities or details contribute to readers' tacit understanding of the scenes or events being described and analyzed. In this strategy, the excerpts evoke as well as convince and, thus, stand out as striking, central, key writing in the ethnographic story.

Despite stylistic and other differences, integrative and excerpt textual strategies share the common goal of interweaving portions of fieldnotes with analytic commentary. In this sense, both involve writing coherent units combining analysis with fieldnote data. We now want to address the specific writing processes involved in creating such excerpt-commentary units.

Creating Excerpt-Commentary Units

To maximize the interplay between analytic idea and excerpt, a fieldnote-centered analytic commentary does a number of things. It focuses attention through an *analytic point;* illustrates and persuades through a *descriptive excerpt* introduced by relevant *orienting information;* and explores and develops ideas through *commentary grounded in the details of the excerpt.* We use the term *excerpt-commentary unit* to characterize this basic component of ethnographic writing. While in some instances all these components can be combined into a single paragraph built around a particular piece of fieldnote data, in others full explication of the excerpt may require a number of paragraphs. We examine how ethnographers write such units using an excerpt strategy; we point out, however, that the integrative strategy generally involves only minor variations in the procedure.

Consider the following complete excerpt-commentary unit from an ethnography of a store-front continuation high school for gay and lesbian students. Following a paragraph introducing the theme of the section—students subtly undermine teachers' power and role by "sexualizing" exchanges—the author has presented and interpreted a typical incident of "sexualizing." He then moves to this unit:

analytic point	Furthermore, students sometimes position themselves as more powerful than the staff members by sexualizing the staff members' instructional comments. The
orienting information	following excerpt is between Michael, the tutor, and Mark, a student:
excerpt	Soon after Michael had left the room, after his exchange with Chris, he came back and looked at Mark and said, "Come with me, Mark." Mark, who at this point was putting some of his belongings in his back pack, had his back turned to Michael and said, "I don't want to come with you." While he said this, he looked up slightly towards Chris and smiled. The others [all students] laughed.

analytic commentary There are several aspects of this excerpt which are of particular importance. First is the sequence in which the comments occur. The teacher's command, "Come with me," is a function of his authority as a staff member, and Mark's subsequent sexualization is a challenge to this authority. Second, Mark not only refuses his authority command but also, by treating Michael's comment as a sexual proposition which he then turns down, further enhances his status. In essence, Mark had positioned himself as the more powerful of the two "potential partners" by refusing the staff member's "advance." Finally, the fact that this was done in front of the other students greatly affects the consequences of the interaction. When the other students laugh at Mark's comment, they are acknowledging the sexual component of his remark to the point that Michael cannot simply overlook the sexual aspect as he could if they were alone. In other words, the students' laughter makes the sexual component of Mark's comment real and consequential for Michael's role as staff member.

The author begins the segment with his *analytic point*—that students may sexualize staff orders as a way of redefining and resisting them. This statement not only links back to ideas in preceding paragraphs, thus contributing to the theme of the section and to the overall story of the ethnography; it also "instructs" the reader in how the writer intends him to read and interpret that excerpt by directing attention to certain of its features.

Following the analytic point, the author provides orienting information by writing a short sentence that acts as a bridge to the excerpt. This information identifies the major characters in the scene by name and role. Since the author has already described the physical structure and daily routines of this small school, he can assume that the reader understands that the action takes place in a classroom. He also assumes that the reader can understand the significance of the events that are about to transpire without knowing exactly when during the day this incident occurred or exactly what was involved in the unspecified encounter between the tutor and another student, Chris. In many circumstances, however, the author needs to orient readers explicitly to the context and previous actions of about-to-be-recounted events. Following this orienting sentence, the author presents his *excerpt* in indented form.

Finally, the ethnographer discusses the interaction described in the excerpt in more extended *analytic commentary,* raising three issues relevant to his theme: first, that Mark's remark represented a challenge to the teacher's authority; second, that Mark pulled off this challenge by interactionally reframing the instructor's command as a sexual proposition, playfully transforming their respective roles; and, finally, that other students made up an audience to this exchange, their laughing response confirming and dramatizing the sexualized meaning Mark had offered and making this incident a consequential challenge to Michael's authority.

In analytic commentaries, ethnographers further tell readers what they want them to see in the fieldnote. It is generally helpful when writing analytic commentaries to consider such questions as: What are the implications of the events or talk recounted in the excerpt? What nuances can be teased out and explored? What import does this scene have for the analytic issues addressed in the paper? Indeed, ethnographic writers often develop such commentary by exploring the tension set up between the focused idea and the more textured and less explicit fieldnote. Rather than just considering outcomes, for example, they might examine the negotiated quality of the interactions (e.g., transforming an order into a sexual proposition; examining the role of other students as audience).

As in the case in this segment, ethnographers often write the excerpt in the past tense but develop their analytic points in the "ethnographic present." This convention portrays the incident recounted in the excerpt as temporal and historical, whereas it presents the analytic commentary as ahistorical and generalizable.[9] Indeed, analysis inevitably generalizes specific individuals, unique interactions, and local events—at least to some extent. But these abstractions never veer too far when commentary stays grounded in fieldnote excerpts. The specificity and interactional dynamics, so vividly clear in the excerpt, temper the abstract insights.

In writing an excerpt-commentary unit, the ethnographer must closely examine his writing strategies to check whether idea and description reinforce each other. In a fieldnote-centered ethnography, a creative tension exists between analytic points and illustrative excerpts; the ethnographer tells the story through both excerpt and commentary and thus ideas and descriptive details must support each other. An excerpt should not only further a theme or concept; it should also *convince* the reader that the ethnographer's specific interpretation and more general story are justified. Conversely, the ethnographer should also ensure that the analytic point highlights the details of the excerpt. Often in checking the fit of fieldnote and commentary, the ethnographer must revise the latter to bring it closer to the excerpt. In some instances, this revision so changes the analytic commentary that it becomes irrelevant to the theme of the section; consequently, the entire excerpt-commentary unit may have to be deleted—at least for the moment—until its relevance becomes clear in another section.

A discrepancy between idea and descriptive detail might also arise from tensions between the implicit point of view in the excerpt and that implied by the analytic claim. To be convincing, the perspectives of the analy-tic point and the description must conform. For example, a student-ethnographer studying a juvenile detention hall wished to focus his ethnographic story on juveniles' responses to staff authority. Yet, consider the following excerpt and the perspective it presents:

The boys sitting in the dayroom had expressionless faces. One Hispanic boy rested his feet on one of the plastic chairs, and L told him to take his feet off. He took his feet off of the chair, and then L walked down the hallway. When she came back to the control room a few minutes later, she noticed that the boy's feet were back on the chair and she called him to the control room. He walked in with a grin on his face. She asked why he put his feet back on the chair, and he shrugged and looked at the ground. She then told him that when she tells him what to do, he had better do it. She told him to go and sit down in the dayroom.

Despite an initial focus on "the boys sitting in the dayroom," this excerpt quickly shifts from the point of view of an anonymous observer of the boys' activities to that of the adult probation officer charged with maintaining control in this setting. This staff point of view conflicts with an analytic focus on the activities of the boys and their responses to adult authority.[10]

The fit between fieldnote excerpt and analytic point should be seen as part of the progression of the whole ethnographic story. The author should think not only about writing an analytic point which develops the theme of this section but also about how this excerpt and accompanying commentary will convince through the interplay of fieldnote details and ideas and, therefore, move the story along. In writing excerpt-commentary units, the analytic point does not so much govern the excerpt as highlight its features; the excerpt itself—as previously constructed—constrains what analytic points the author can now make and how to angle them. In a sense, a thematic narrative progresses through incremental repetition. Each unit both repeats the theme but also through small increments adds some further ideas and glimpses of people. The repeated look at the section theme from different angles deepens the reader's understanding.

Finally, the ethnographer should consider the implications of excerpt-commentaries already included in the ethnographic story for any additional such units that might be developed. Indeed, Katz (1988:142) argues that well-crafted ethnographies possess a "weblike character," allowing readers to use data offered in support of one idea to confirm or disconfirm other ideas. The ethnographic author, aware of these confirming and disconfirming possibilities, should be sensitive to the import of unexamined features of other fieldnote excerpts and analytic commentaries for current theoretical claims.

Because selecting and writing moves dialectically between excerpts and by stating analytic points—rather than by stating a point and hunting for a good illustration—the author more likely maintains a commitment to members' views. A preexisting theory or thesis should not overly determine what the excerpts might reveal. Rather the ethnographer works back and forth between coding, potential excerpts, and analytic points so that together they move the story along. That process implants a creative tension between excerpts and analysis which enhances the story and deepens the reader's understanding of the world it represents.

Editing Excerpts

In writing an excerpt-commentary unit, the ethnographer reconstructs the relevant excerpt. The researcher has begun by reviewing the original fieldnote to decide which portions to block out and move to create a working excerpt. This decision involves making an initial determination about exactly where to start and where to end that excerpt. Generally, leaving in, rather than cutting, a longer fieldnote segment is a prudent policy in making these first cuts, since the author can later eliminate portions which prove extraneous.

The ethnographer continues to review and edit these initial excerpts as she elaborates an interpretive commentary. Indeed, we recommend thoroughly editing an excerpt as part of the process of writing an excerpt-commentary unit. Since the author is immersed in the details of the excerpt and its various analytic possibilities, this moment is an opportune time for assessing which portions of the fieldnote are pertinent to these issues and which are irrelevant. Such close reflection concerning the excerpt may push the researcher to new insights and analytic refinements. In building a complete excerpt-commentary unit, the author often decides to modify his decision about the point at which the excerpt begins and ends. The ethnographer may also decide to make his point more economically by shortening the excerpt and providing background details as orienting information in the prior text.

These editing decisions depend both upon the purposes for including an excerpt (e.g., providing vivid detail) and upon the issues pursued in the analytic commentary. But in editing excerpts, ethnographers also consider a number of more general criteria, including *length, relevance, readability, comprehensibility,* and *anonymity of informants.*

An excerpt should be held to an *appropriate length.* An excerpt should not ramble on endlessly just because the description or talk might be interesting; readers find it difficult to sustain attention and interest through long stretches—that is, pages—of unbroken fieldnotes. If deleting material is not advisable, the ethnographer can break up the initial excerpt into a series of smaller, separate units, and write interpretive commentary for each one.

Relevance provides a primary concern in editing fieldnote excerpts. In deciding relevance, the field worker must weigh both what qualities are vital to the descriptions provided and what qualities contribute to the theme of the section or analytic point of the unit. Thus, an ethnographer begins by marking those features which are core to the interaction and which reveal the point made. Then, she can review the intervening material and reflect on which portions can be deleted and which need to be retained to provide narrative continuity or to evoke a sense of scene and context. Following the editing conventions for elisions in a quotation, she then replaces the deleted portions with ellipses. Ethnographers should take special care in editing interview dialogue not to delete their own questions. Since these questions shape the answers given, they should be preserved as context for the responses of the person interviewed.

Consider the decisions Rachel Fretz made in excerpting and editing fieldnotes to include in a paper on Chokwe telling historical accounts *(kulweza sango)* in Northwest Province of Zambia. She was interested in the ways in which conventions common in narrating traditional stories were also employed in telling historical accounts about events that occurred in the recent past.[11] She focused on one instance of Chokwe storytelling about an aspiring political figure, Mushala, who, failing to win legitimate power, became an outlaw leading a band of soldiers who terrorized the community. Eventually, the government soldiers came to the area to search for Mushala and to free the community from his raids. Several listeners had witnessed these events and others had heard many reports of them; they occasionally offered their remarks and insights during the narration. The fieldworker tape-recorded the narration and audience comments; in her fieldnotes, she wrote primarily about the circumstances of the storytelling, the family members present, and what their reactions were afterwards that evening and the next day. She began to work on her analysis by listening to the tape and by rereading the following extended fieldnote:

We asked Uncle John if he knew anything about the events connected with Mushala. He paused and answered, "Yes, I know it very well." He began talking slowly, in serious tone of voice. He narrated about the way Mushala hunted and chased the Chokwe and Lunda peoples of this area: about the burning of villages, the slaughter of farm animals, about the villagers escaping into the bush to live there. He narrated for about one hour and a half. During the entire time, the family sat there very still. Uncle Don joined the group, but sat to the side with his own charcoal burner: Jerald, his nephew, went over to join him. Only occasionally did someone comment. [Listen to tape.] I noticed that it was a very traditional scene there by the fireside: a grandfather, two maternal uncles, and their nephews. Except for Joe's wife, Kianze, a young girl traveling with me, and myself, it was all men. [Most of the women were sitting by a fire in the kitchen house nearby and were also listening attentively.]

Before the evening was over the women, Nyalona and Kalombo, went home across the road. And Nyakalombo, the grandmother, went inside to sleep. Mwatavumbi (grandfather) was dozing and when he woke up, he went to bed too. And still Uncle John narrated: as I sat there, I noticed that he used the dramatic effects and dialogue conventions of storytelling and built his plot to peak and end with the killing of Mushala.

When he ended, everyone sat still for a while. I said, "Thank you," and then they started talking—Frank, Chester, and Uncle Don talked, each adding their personal knowledge of events. Don asked his brother John a question and he narrated more: his own father had known Mushala. He also talked about Chilombo, a neighbor, who was involved in these events. (Chilombo is the well-dressed man—in suit and tie who came by one day to talk in KiChokwe to me near the *chisambwe* [the pavilion where the men and guests sit]. He asked me if I would come to his village because he had stories to tell. I said I would come some time. Now today, Jerald said that he met him in town and that he asked him why I had not come and that I had promised. Jerald said that he—Chilombo—had waited for me. Next time!)

At the end of taping the narration, Mwatushi asked everyone to say his or her name. Even after the recorder was off, people just sat there and talked a while longer, rather spellbound by the shocking events. **As we crossed the road to**

return to our village, Mwatushi, Uncle John, Chester, Jerald, Kianze, and I kept talking about it. They told me (and demonstrated) how the villagers would cross the road backwards, so that their footprints would seem to be going in the opposite direction so as to confuse the soldiers. It took me a long time to fall asleep—in my mind, I kept hearing the song, *"Kanda uliya mwana, kanda uliya. Kaakwiza akuloze."* ["Don't cry my child, don't cry; they'll come to shoot you." It's a song composed by contemporary Chokwe who crossed the river to escape from the war in Angola—our earlier topic of conversation that evening.] I felt as though there were people hiding in the bush from the soldiers. We all slept a long time the next morning.

Today at lunch, Mwatushi said that it was Mushala's wife who betrayed him to the soldiers because she saw that eventually he would kill her family and her whole village. When she was near childbirth, they called a midwife to come stay with her in the bush. After the birth, one day when Mushala was away, she decided to leave with the midwife and then they ran into four soldiers. **She told them who she was and that she would tell them where he was hiding. She also told them his charms and that they would be protected against them if they were naked, but they were ashamed, so she took off all her clothes and they all walked naked on the path. Then they came to a pool of water, and she said you must wash here so that he cannot see you coming. Then they heard Mushala coming, and they stepped back into the bush. He came carrying his gun on his shoulder. He passed the first soldier who was shaking with fear and could not move. He passed the second soldier who also was shaking with fear and could not move. Then the third soldier shot him right in the eye and then in the chest. Mushala tried to walk on, but could not. He fell down. Then they all came and hit him with their bayonets. And that is how he died.** Thus, Mwatushi told the story of those events.

In reflecting on this extended fieldnote, the author came to see analytic issues in the two highlighted passages. The first suggested the possibility that, as part of their response to storytelling, people might reenact certain actions; such associations are most likely when a detail in the present landscape reminds them of traumatic events that had occurred there in the past.[12] The story of Mushala had evoked in listeners the memory of the abandoned villages, the surrounding bush where they hid, and the road which people had to cross as they sneaked back to their village occasionally to get supplies. To develop an excerpt-commentary unit, the author selected out and edited this brief account of the reenactment of walking backwards to trick Mushala's soldiers:

As we crossed the road to return to our village, . . . [we] kept on talking about it. They told me (and demonstrated) how the villagers would cross the road backwards, so that their footprints would seem to be going to the opposite direction so as to confuse [Mushala's] soldiers.

She introduced the excerpt by saying that people were going home in the evening after hearing the tale: thus she did not need to include that information in the excerpt. She also deleted specific names of speakers but kept the real name of Mushala, because he was a public figure—a common convention in excerpted fieldnotes; she also clarified in a bracket that it was Mushala soldiers, not the government soldiers, who were persecuting the people and from whom they were hiding their comings and goings.

The second passage suggested the idea that people recount and shape events to fit conventional story patterns. In the more casual conversation the next day, Mwatushi drew on familiar narrating conventions to recount how Mushala died: the use of charms to make oneself invisible (and invulnerable) and the repetition of three attempts to kill the villain with only the last effort succeeding.

> She told them [the government soldiers] about his [Mushala's] charms and that they would be protected against them if they were naked, but they were ashamed, so she took off all her clothes and they all walked naked on the path. Then they came to a pool of water, and she said you must wash here so that he cannot see you coming. Then they heard Mushala coming, and they stepped back into the bush. He came carrying his gun on his shoulder. He passed the first soldier who was shaking with fear and could not move. He passed the second soldier who also was shaking with fear and could not move. Then the third soldier shot him right in the eye and then in the chest. Mushala tried to walk on, but could not. He fell down. Then they all came and hit him with their bayonets. And that is how he died.

In editing this passage, the author did not include the wife's reasons for betraying Mushala, since they were not directly relevant to a discussion of these narrative conventions. She also avoided making any editorial changes in the wording of this account; she wanted to maintain as much of the sequence and details of Mwatushi's retelling as she could, even though it is not verbatim dialogue. She added clarification in brackets and determined what background information she could most efficiently provide in sentences leading into the excerpts.

When preparing the fieldnote for a final text, the ethnographer usually must do more than simply leave out portions of a longer fieldnote; rather, she must refocus and sharpen details in her editing. Consider the decisions that Linda Shaw (1988) made when describing borrowing and lending patterns among residents of a psychiatric board-and-care home. Her original fieldnote is not only longer but is also more detailed than the edited fieldnote.

Original fieldnote:

I went into the dining room to see what the snacks were and came upon Marie angrily talking to Michelle about the fact that Michelle told Reid not to lend her money. Michelle replied that she didn't tell Reid not to lend Marie money, but that he shouldn't lend anyone money, that he should keep his money for himself. Marie wanted to know who Michelle thought she was telling people not to lend to her, that she wasn't bumming but always paid her friends back. The argument went on this way for a little while, seeming to escalate as Marie charged Michelle with trying to cause her trouble and Michelle defending herself saying that she hadn't done anything to Marie. Then Mic, the only other member sitting at the table, said something—can't exactly remember what—that seemed intended to lighten the conversation, but had the effect of getting Marie off onto talking about Patsey being Mic's girlfriend and how could he have such a fat girl friend. Mic defended himself, saying Patsey wasn't so fat, and they had only dated anyway.

In the midst of this diversion, Michelle got up and left the dining room. Marie then turned to me and asked if everyone at Vista didn't bum money. I agreed that it was done by quite a lot of people. She said that Michelle was new, had only been there a month, what right did she have going around telling people not to loan to her when that's what everyone here does. She said again, "Michelle is new. Just wait until she is here for a while. She'll be doing it too." Marie went on to say that she helps her friends out when they need it. She spoke about having given Earl and Kara her entire rebate check last month because they were out of money and she felt sorry for them.

Edited fieldnote:

In the dining room after dinner I came upon Marie angrily accusing Michelle, a new resident, of having told Reid, another resident, not to lend her money. Michelle insisted she had urged Reid to keep his money for himself and not to lend *anyone* money, never mentioning Marie. Marie demanded to know just who Michelle thought she was, telling people not to lend to her; she wasn't bumming but always paid her friends back. Eventually Michelle got up and left the dining room. Marie then turned to me, asking if everyone at Vista didn't borrow. I agreed. She noted that Michelle was new, having only been at Vista a month; what right did she have going around telling people not to loan to her when that's what everyone here does? She continued, "Michelle is new. Just wait until she is here for a while. She'll be doing it, too." She added that she always helps her friends out when they need it; she gave Earl and Kara her entire rebate check last month because they were out of money and she felt sorry for them.

The author included this fieldnote in a section of her ethnography devoted to the broad theme of interdependence and cooperation among those living in the home. The fieldnote was chosen specifically to illustrate the point that because residents have little money and few sources of support, they count on being able to ask others at the home for small amounts of money and other needed items when they run short. In this excerpt, we see how intensely those in the home may feel when these sources are threatened. In editing this excerpt, the author preserved indirect speech in the original form and in the same order. She retained those parts of the fieldnote that revealed the grounds for participating in the system of exchange and edited out sentences and phrases describing actions that were unrelated to these issues (Mic and his girlfriend). She included aspects of Marie's talk that described those aspects of her participation that, in her view, demonstrated that she had entered into the exchange system (giving to others) in ways that entitled her to ask of them in return. Finally, she included Marie's explanation that only an outsider who had not fully experienced the need to call upon others would have questioned participation in the system of exchange. Hence, the author edited the fieldnote, dropping some of the description but preserving those sentences and phrases that bore most directly on that point. In the end, editing involves the delicate balance between efforts to preserve the essence of what members say and do, while focusing the reader's attention on those bits of talk that most clearly and economically support the story the ethnographer is attempting to tell.

There is always the risk in any condensation or selective quotation that the author will leave out details which might present people and their actions more convincingly. The process of editing is not a straightforward, simple task. On the one hand, shortening and editing for clarity forwards the smooth flow of the overall ethnographic story: too long excerpts bog the reader down in extraneous details. On the other hand, one always loses some of the vividness and complexity of the original fieldnotes in the editing process.

At times, field workers encounter problems because an excerpt is especially "rich," containing materials that bear on several different themes. Simply duplicating the fieldnote in several sections of the final text does not work. Because readers quickly tire of unnecessary repetitions, ethnographers avoid using the same fieldnote excerpt more than one time. Rather, the solution lies in clearly identifying the different analytic themes in the excerpt and then using these themes either to split the excerpt into two independent units or, if that is not possible, to discuss the various aspects of the excerpt sequentially. Consider an example from a study of domestic workers and their employers in which the following excerpt was initially used to illustrate workers' moral evaluations of their employers' own housekeeping practices:

"She never cleans her bathroom, and I couldn't get the scum off the—she had one of these tiled showers? And we used a good product, but I told her, 'you leave that on overnight.' 'Cause it was so filthy. . . . In fact, when I left that lady (hah hah) I said, 'I'm gonna leave it like this' [leave a paste of Comet on the sink], and *she* had to rinse it off the next day."

On reviewing this excerpt, the ethnographer decided to cut the worker's last statement—about how she maneuvered to make her employee finish cleaning up this mess herself—out of the excerpt and to use it instead in a subsequent section on house-cleaner's ways of resisting and turning the tables on their employers.

Ethnographers generally delete the reflective commentary they incorporated into the original fieldnote. Rather than retain these initial thoughts in the version of the fieldnote that appears in the finished ethnography, an ethnographer may incorporate any useful insights into the analytic discussion that follows the excerpt. Frequently, however, the researcher will have elaborated and specified analytic issues to such an extent that earlier commentary seems more simplistic or undeveloped and thus of minimal use. Furthermore, because the author writes, selects, edits, and organizes excerpts, she already has a privileged voice. Excerpts dominated by the fieldworker's explanations sound contrived and become truly redundant in a final ethnography.[13]

The ethnographic writer edits to make excerpts *readable* by using standard conventions for punctuation, spelling, and grammar. For the sake of clarity, she should take particular care to revise unclear sentences and to correct confusing tense shifts in portions of the excerpts that are not direct quotations. The author, however, should be very conservative in editing direct quotations, carefully balancing the reader's need for clarity against a commitment to providing an accurate rendering of peoples' actual use of words. Ethnographers take special care to preserve and convey speakers' dialect, idiom, and speech rhythms. Even individual speech disfluencies—false starts, pauses, and repetitions—should be treated carefully. For many purposes, producing readable dialogue (especially from tape-recorded transcripts) requires editing out many such disfluencies.[14] But in some circumstances the author may specifically want to preserve such speech in order to indicate the speaker's emotional state or mood. For example, retaining the "and- and- and-" in the following excerpt reveals the speaker's disturbed hesitancy as he talks about his "mental illness" to the researcher:

"I'm telepathic. I can actually hear thought in other people's heads. . . ." He said he wished he could tell people but . . . "they'll just increase my medication. . . . No matter how drugged I am, nothing can take away my telepathy. And- and- and- it's not because of me. It's because Jesus wills it for me."

Furthermore, editing should make excerpts *comprehensible* to readers. The author must clarify any *allusions*—such as names, places, procedures—which depend on references external to the fieldnote. She can do so when orienting the reader to the excerpt, or for briefer, less central matters by embedding a brief explanation in brackets within the text. For example, an author might identify the locally relevant status of people named in the excerpt (e.g. "the others [all students]"), or clarify the meaning of direct speech that might not be clear in context (e.g., "the only purpose we had in mind was to set it [the dynamite] off"). At this time, the ethnographer must once again verify that all details are accurate; misrepresentation of factual information or of local terms very quickly tells readers that this ethnographer is not reliable. Indeed, a few mistakes can undermine the credibility of the whole story.

Finally, an excerpt must protect the people, institutions, and communities studied by providing *anonymity*. Therefore, in completing the editing, an ethnographer changes all names and identifying markers such as personally distinctive details in descriptions. Authors provide pseudonyms, generally echoing qualities evoked (e.g., ethnic identity) by the original name.[15] We do not recommend using initials to indicate different characters, since this minimal identification makes gender difficult to remember, lacks evocative qualities, and makes it difficult for a reader to recognize that person in other excerpts.

Ordering Excerpt-Commentary Units within a Section

With the overall framework as a guideline, ethnographers usually organize their ethnographies into sections set off by titled headings. Each section generally presents one theme, perhaps divided further into several subthemes. A section is built from a series of excerpt-commentary units. For example, the section of the ethnography on the gay and lesbian high school entitled "Sexualization of Conversation" is constructed of the following units:

Unit 1

analytic point: "Sexual innuendos" are a common means by which students sexualized talk to and about teaching staff.

excerpt: On finding out that a teacher's age is twenty-seven, a student comments: "I've had sex with someone who was twenty-eight—it was gross."

Unit 2

analytic point: Students sexualize their responses specifically to staff instructions.

excerpt: A student responds to staff command to "come with me" as a sexual proposition.

Unit 3

analytic point: In some situations staff do not let the challenge implicit in student's sexualizing comments pass, but themselves respond in ways that reassert their position.

excerpt: Staff responds to a student who quipped "search my tongue" when asked to throw away his gum: "I don't want to—I'm sure many people already have."

Unit 4

analytic point: In some instances staff members themselves use sexual talk in ways that implicitly maintain their authority.

excerpt: As a student turns down the researcher's offer to help with math, staff member comments: "Go ahead, you were asking about him earlier."

Within a section, the ethnographer organizes units to develop a progression of ideas in ways that increasingly reveal the complexities of fieldnote data and analysis, so that the story progresses to a deeper understanding of the theme. In the above example, the first two units focus on students' sexualizing talk, the third introduces the added complication of how teaching staff respond to such talk, and the last looks at the more subtle issues involved when staff intiate such talk.

To aid the reader in following the progression of ideas from one unit to the next, the author should provide a clear *transition* that links the main idea of the current paragraph to those of preceding paragraphs. In some cases, constructing a transition is a relatively straightforward matter of writing an introductory sentence to the paragraph beginning a new unit. For example, the author of the "sexualization of conversation" section provides this transition sentence into his third unit:

> Although, as in the previous excerpt, the staff members sometimes don't respond to the students' sexualizing comments, this is not always the case. . . .

This transition refers back to the prior excerpt, noting one feature not commented on at the time: staff did not explicitly respond to students' sexualizing talk. This retroactively noted feature is then used to introduce, by contrast, the focus of the current unit: how staff did respond to such talk.

In other instances, when the analytic point in a subsequent unit raises a significantly different issue than that of the preceding one, the author should not rely simply on an introductory transitional sentence. Rather, the author should also revise the *preceding unit* and explicitly anticipate the idea of the later one. For example, the transition to Unit 2 of the "sexualization of conversation" section reads:

> Furthermore, the students sometimes position themselves as more powerful than the staff members by sexualizing the staff members' instructional commands. . . .

This sentence focuses on student sexualizing as a response specifically to staff "instructional commands." However, in Unit 1 the author had not considered the specific forms of staff-student interaction within which sexualizing comments occurred. To now learn that such comments are made in response to commands may leave the reader feeling slightly confused: Do students respond in sexualized ways to other sorts of staff talk, such as polite requests or general questions? Thus, the author should have revised the discussion in Unit 1 to provide more context for this upcoming distinction.

In addition to deciding on the ordering of units, the author must also write an introduction and conclusion to the section. The introduction should connect the theme of the section to the overall theme of the ethnography, and it should discuss any general features of that theme needed to understand and appreciate the ideas of the different units that follow. The author introduced the "sexualization of conversation" section, for example, with a paragraph observing that students commonly sexualized conversations in this setting and that "the sexualization is consequential to the power relations between staff member and student," thus linking this section back to the major theme of the paper. In the next paragraph, he argued that "sexual innuendos" provide one form of sexualizing, a form that is "particularly useful for students since they are ambiguous [and] indirect," allowing denial of sexual intent.

Finally, in a conclusion to the section, the author tries to draw together the implications of the excerpts and analytic commentary for the core theme of the section. He may also suggest how these issues tie in with the theme of the section to follow.

PRODUCING A COMPLETED ETHNOGRAPHIC DOCUMENT

Depending upon the time available, the ethnographer might rework units and sections a number of times, replacing initially selected excerpts with new ones, refining analytic commentary and transitions, reordering units within a section and/or rearranging sections within the overall ethnography. Although she sees still further possible changes and refinements, at some point she must stop revising and take up a series of final writing tasks required to turn the now substantial body of text into a completed ethnographic document. These projects include titling the ethnography, writing an introduction linking the topic and major theme to other research, describing the setting and methods, and providing an overall conclusion to the ethnography.

Introducing the Ethnography

The title and introduction to an ethnography provide readers with their first means of orienting to the text. The title and introduction not only tell readers what they can expect the ethnography to be about, but they also provide clues to the writer's analytic and substantive concerns.

One kind of ethnographic title communicates to the reader both the general topic and exactly what people, setting, activity, or process was studied. For example:

"Ritualized Drinking Behavior in the Fraternity System"
"Interactional Dynamics of Ethnicity at an Urban High School"
"Waiting to Die: An Ethnographic Study of a Convalescent Home"

Rather than simply stating the general topic, however, an author may attempt to convey the more abstract analytic theme of the ethnography in a title. As Atkinson (1990:76) has noted, ethnographers often do so by linking a phrase containing the abstract, "generic" issue by a colon to a phrase specifying the general topic and concrete "local" setting or activity:

"Systems of Power: Authority and Discipline in a Boys Group Home"

Finally, the ethnographer may incorporate local members' terms or phrases as key elements of a title:

"The Dynamics of Down: Being Cool with the Set"
"'These Kids Live in Their Own Little Worlds': Interpretive Framework in a Halfway House."

In the first paragraph of the introduction to the ethnography, many authors begin with an attention-getting opening. They may use an incident from their fieldnotes which focuses on the topic or briefly describes common approaches to the topic. Next the author very briefly introduces the topic and location of his own research as a bridge to presenting his thesis. In a thematic narrative, the author writes a "topical thesis" which explains the general focus of the paper and lays out the themes to be examined. In that sense, the thesis does not delineate every development in the ethnographic story, nor foreshadow the conclusions to be made at the end. Rather, the thesis gets the story going. Finally, the author generally provides an overview of the paper by presenting the thematic statement for each upcoming section.

For example, the ethnographic author of "Interactional Dynamics of Ethnicity at an Urban High School" begins by orienting the reader to his topic.

In everyday life, we commonly assume ethnicity as a given category. People belong to distinct groups with unique cultural practices. We say that the President of the United States is White, that the magic of a people in Africa is Azande witchcraft, that rap is Black music, that Cinco de Mayo is a Mexican holiday, etc. We assume that we are describing what is objectively there. We are simply stating the "natural facts" of the world. When we do become more aware of ethnicity as a category, it is often because of conflict. The newspaper reports that a "Black" girl was shot by a "Korean" storekeeper and that a "White Power" group is marching in a "Jewish" neighborhood. We ask, How did this happen? How can diverse peoples get along? But we still imply that definite aggregates of people exist and that they have distinct cultures.

In this introductory paragraph, the author points out that, in their talk about ethnicity, people commonly assume that terms that identify ethnicity refer unambiguously to naturally occurring and distinct "aggregates of people." In his next paragraph, he makes explicit the analytic stance he takes toward ethnicity:

What we ignore in this everyday discourse is that ethnicity is "social work": People identify a person, place, or thing as having a certain "character" through an implicitly interactional dynamic of inclusion or exclusion. This process creates what Barth calls "boundaries" in interaction (1969). These boundaries are not objective, but subjective borders, and they are constantly being recreated, re-affirmed, negotiated, and even discarded. Thus, in everyday life, ethnicity is a local phenomenon originating in specific situations.

He proposes to look at ethnicity not as an objectively given "fact" but rather as a product of "social work," i.e., of local, interactional negotiations of inclusion and exclusion. By citing another researcher, he suggests that this issue also interests other scholars and implies that his "new angle" contributes to a scholarly discussion.

The author next substantiates his topic, first by identifying the people and setting of his research and then by specifying the sort of data he will rely on:

> In this paper, I examine ethnicity and ethnic groups at an urban high school in Southern California. The fieldnote excerpts describe the processes by which people use ethnicity in everyday life.

Next, he presents his general thesis about ethnicity, an interpretive statement about ethnicity as situationally "recreated and modified":

> I argue that through people's interactions "ethnicity" is perpetuated by constantly being recreated and modified within a situation. This "social work" in situations and through interactions then generates the discrete units of specific groups, recognized as having particular cultures, symbols, styles, and objects. Thus, this paper is a study of how people "ascribe the ascribed" (Garfinkel 1967).

Finally, he closes this portion of the introduction with an overview of his argument, briefly describing the main idea for each upcoming section (see "Developing a Thematic Narrative," above).

In contrast to an introduction which begins by setting up an analytic idea and then subsequently identifying just what was studied, some ethnographers begin with an actual fieldnote-based description or observation. Following the presentation of the specific details, they then pinpoint a more general analytic issue or problem that this incident represents. The above ethnographer, for example, might have begun by describing an especially perspicuous instance of the "social work" that contributes to recreating and maintaining a particular ethnic identity: for example, an extreme or dramatic instance of a white student dressing, talking, or acting black. He could then have moved to identifying the general analytic problem or issue that he saw reflected in or illustrated by this incident.[16]

Linking the Study to Other Research

As part of the introduction (or in a section immediately following it) ethnographers generally link their interpretation to wider issues of scholarly interest in their disciplines. In that way, they invite their readers to consider seriously the topics to be discussed. At this point, the writer thinks again of his intended readers and selects words and ideas familiar to them.

For example, the author of the paper on ethnicity writes for sociologists and thus discusses the concept of "ethnicity" as it is used by sociologists. In each paragraph, he addresses some feature of the problem of research on ethnic issues. Although he discusses other scholars' research, he only raises those ideas about ethnicity which he addresses later in the body of the paper. In his findings, he then offers analytic ideas and fieldnote excerpts which touch on the problems he raises:

Marger (1991) notes that sociologists classify ethnic groups based on three indices: unique cultural traits, sense of community, and ascription. First, ethnic groups have some unique behavioral characteristics that set them off from other people. Second, ethnic groups display a sense of community among members. This "we" almost seems to necessitate a "they" and leads to the creation of ethnic group boundaries separating insiders and outsiders. Third, ethnic status is almost always ascribed, which usually means given by birth. In presenting these traits, Marger emphasizes a supposed objective criteria for ethnicity. Ethnicities are seen as discrete collectives that can be studied in relation to each other. This approach is typical in many studies of race and ethnic relations in the United States. And the demographic data for this paper is analyzed thus.

Unfortunately, while this approach offers information for macro studies of society, it leads to a neglect of the subjective perception and dynamic features of ethnicity in everyday life. It downplays how "ethnic identity is an acquired and used feature of human identity, available for employment by either participant in an encounter and subject to presentation, inhibition, manipulation, and exploitation" (Lyman and Douglass 1973). In this approach, ethnicity is a resource to be used in strategic creation and maintenance of self. . . .

For purposes of this study, an ethnic group is defined as "a reference group invoked by people who identify themselves and are identified by others as sharing a common historical style" (Royce 1982). An ethnic group, thus, is a subculture with symbols, style, and forms. Unlike many other subcultures though, membership in the ethnic group is held to be ascriptive.

These few paragraphs briefly raise problematic issues in ethnic studies. In this introductory section on other research, the author does not attempt to provide an overview of all possible approaches to ethnicity. He only selects those researchers' works and ideas which provide a context for his own study. Thus, this writer implicitly demonstrates the relevance of his research to the other sociologists who are his intended readers.

In sum, the ethnographer does not review "the literature" on the topic, nor does she simply cite several works others have done. Rather, she carefully selects other research which provides a context for the upcoming findings and only discusses those ideas which highlight her own analysis.

Introducing Setting and Methods

Before launching into the ethnography proper, authors introduce their setting and their methods for learning about it. Setting and methods can be discussed either in separate sections or in a single section addressing both topics.

In describing the *setting,* the ethnographer orients readers to the place, people, and situations to be examined in detail in the subsequent ethnography. This description should help the reader picture the physical and social features of the setting. It should also provide overviews of the key individuals and of procedures or processes that are central to the substance of the ethnography; the former, for example, might trace differences between core and volunteer staff in a community mental health center or between managers and canvassers in a political action committee; the latter would address how clients enter and move through the program, what basic job responsibilities entail, and perhaps the overall organization of door-to-door canvassing.

While providing an overview of the setting, its personnel, and its routines, this discussion should also anticipate and highlight specific features of the setting that are central for subsequent ethnographic analyses. For example, an ethnographer writing about the nature and consequences of staff practices for categorizing or *labeling* resident clients of a homeless shelter provides a two-pronged introduction to the setting. First, he presents the types of clients sought by the shelter:

> My field work was carried out in an emergency shelter for the homeless in the downtown area of Los Angeles. The shelter has a capacity of 54 persons, but had an average house total of 35 or so for the time I was there. The shelter's primary service is to provide food and housing for persons who are absolutely broke. While in the shelter the "clients," as they are called by the staff, are also

provided with some assistance in looking for housing and dealing with the welfare bureaucracy. That stated target group for the shelter is the "new homeless"; that is, persons who have only recently lost their homes and been thrust upon the streets. This is in contrast to those the staff refer to as the "chronic homeless" or "shelter hoppers" who have been living on the streets for some time and who are understood to move from shelter to shelter with no intention of finding a more stable residence. . . .

The shelter's other general criterion for admission is that they will take any sort of client, except for single men. They are one of the few shelters that will handle homeless families with children, a fact that they pride themselves on. In practice, the predominant client group consists of a woman with several young children.

The author then introduces the frontline staff whose routine work practices are to be examined:

The staff most relevant to the typifying tasks in the shelter are six Program Aids [PAs]. The six PAs are four black women between the ages of approximately thirty and fifty, a younger white woman recently graduated from college, and a twenty-one year old white male seminary student. None are trained social workers, perhaps due, at least in part, to the extremely low pay PAs receive. The PAs spend most of their working time in the office which overlooks the lounge on the second floor of the shelter. (The first floor contains the offices of the shelter while the third floor consists of the clients' rooms.) The schedule is such that there is only one PA on duty at a time, apart from a one hour overlap period at the boundaries of the shifts.

He continues by describing PAs' routine duties: answering the phone, screening possible clients, maintaining logs, etc.

The ethnographer may move directly from such a description of key features to an overview of her entry into the setting and of the nature of her participation in it.[17] Here, the ethnographer summarizes what she actually did to get close to and learn about the events and issues considered throughout the ethnography. In so doing, it is important to explain how and in what capacity she obtained initial access to the setting, how those in the setting understood what she was doing and/or was interested in, and how different members of the setting reacted to or treated her.

It is generally useful to consider different stages or phases in the research, distinguishing, for example, between processes of initial entry, of getting used to the setting and its participants, and of established, longer-term participation. An ethnographer working in a community mental health center, for example, traces her socialization from initial encouragement to participate in a few routine activities under staff supervision, through observation and testing of her competence in dealing with highly disturbed patients, to eventually being charged with conducting community meetings with the clients.

In presenting their *methods,* ethnographers seek to depict the varied qualities of their participation and their awareness of both the advantages and constraints of their roles in a specific setting. The ethnographer of a community mental health center, for example, analyzed these qualities of her role in the following terms:

My status is that of a "volunteer intern." When I first arrived here I was not sure what this title/status entailed. As I became associated with the staff and socialized into a staff role, I have realized that my role is that of a lower staff member. I do not have the power nor the privileges of a core staff member. For example, although I am encouraged to participate in Case Review Meetings, my "insights" are not required to be considered for staff decisions.

Such an analysis demands that the ethnographer reflect on the specific kinds of interactions and events to which she had or was denied access. For example, one student ethnographer described how her participant role in a feminist political-action committee shaped and delimited her access to and observations of key interactions in political canvassing:

I play more than a passive observer role. I am a canvasser and, as such, go out with the rest of the crew and canvass at least once a week. But I am also part of management in that they are grooming me for the position of field manager in the summer. This puts me in the ideal position to see what the canvassers are feeling and thinking and, at the same time, gives me access to information not otherwise available to canvassers. This does, however, work against me in that sometimes the canvassers will label me as management and therefore be less likely to confide in me. This becomes a particular problem when I have to act on behalf of management (such as doing retrainings) or when issues become polarized and one has to take either management's or the canvassers' perspective. . . . [Furthermore] it is hard to go to the field to observe as a researcher, because to observe means that I am there on behalf of management, and I am the authority rather than a peer.

Finally, in presenting and analyzing methods and their implications, it is helpful to include fieldnote excerpts to illustrate and support key points. The ethnographer in the study of the community mental health center, for example, presented the following fieldnotes, the first to show the character of the "testing" that she was subject to from one staff member during her first week at the center, the second to illustrate how her role differed from "regular staff":

I was playing ping-pong with a client when I saw Cathy, a caseworker, point David in my direction. David walked over to me and said: "Hi. I'm the President, and I demand that you go to the Alaskan pipeline to save the world and my sister in Kansas. You must do this—it is your duty to your Country. You must save the world." Out of the corner of my eye, I saw Cathy and a couple of other staff members giggling. I responded: "Well, David, I'm sorry but that's just too big of a responsibility for me." David: "You must save the world." He then walked away. Cathy came over to me and said: "He's really crazy, isn't he?" She laughed. "Don't worry. He's just about the craziest one we've got."

Today we were having client nominations for government. The clients were nominating other clients for President and Vice President. Norman (a client) nominated me for VP. Arlene (art therapist) stepped in and said to Norman: "Karina cannot be nominated. She is a staff member and cannot be nominated."

While discussions of the setting and of the complexities of doing field research highlight features and processes that are central to upcoming ethnographic analyses, they can also lend credibility to the final document. These descriptions may allow readers to assess whether or not the enthnographer had access to the kinds and quality of observations needed to sustain subsequent analytic claims. With this background information to draw on, the reader may be more inclined to assume that the author is credible and informed. Indeed, ethnographers may select fieldnote excerpts about their involvement exactly in order to implicitly convince the reader "that I was there and experienced this firsthand."

Writing a Conclusion

Finished ethnographic texts usually end with a section which reflects on and elaborates the thesis addressed in the introduction to the paper. Hence, while naturally among the last pieces of writing the author does, conclusions are intricately tied to introductions.[18] Often the conclusion explores the implications of the theoretical and/or substantive issues raised in the paper's introduction. In an ethnographic paper, the wording of the introductory thesis focuses the reader on the central idea, but often this idea may not be as sharply delineated as the concluding presentation of the thesis. Whereas the introduction prepares the reader to understand the upcoming analytic points and excerpts, the conclusion more precisely interconnects the ideas because, by the paper's end, the reader has read the whole ethnographic story and absorbed the details of its fieldnote excerpts. In other words, the ethnography tells a story which can be understood fully only by reading the progression of analytic ideas and fieldnote excerpts. Each section with its theme, points, and discussion of excerpts moved the reader further along toward the conclusion, with its more finely tuned thesis.

To write a conclusion, the ethnographer should review the now completed tale, paying particular attention to the framing of that story in the introduction. In most cases it is useful to write a *summary* of the major findings and themes of the paper. This summary should generally restate the thesis of the paper and then in short, concise sentences suggest how each section advances or contributes to this thesis. In some cases the ethnographer may choose to use the summary to begin the conclusion. In others, she may move directly to other issues without a summary. Yet even when one does not plan to make the summary part of the conclusion, writing a summary is beneficial to the ethnographer; it forces the author to turn from the minute problems of writing up specific ideas and segments to a review of the overall structure and flow of her paper. The result is a gestalt view of the ethnography's initial promises compared to where it has actually gone: a view which gets the writer thinking about some of its wider implications.

Whether the author summarizes or not, conclusions take up the paper's thesis. The ethnographer may do so in at least three ways: (1) by extending or modifying the thesis in light of the materials examined; (2) by relating the thesis to some more general theory or current issue in the relevant literature; and/or (3) by offering a *meta-commentary* on the thesis or on the methods or assumptions associated with it. An author might employ only one of these options, or might weave together two or even all three options in one longer, more elaborate conclusion.

As an example of the first option, consider some of the concluding portions of the ethnographic study on how family caregivers of persons with Alzheimer's disease manage the stigma associated with this condition. The introduction to this study had highlighted Goffman's (1971) concept of the "family information rule," i.e., the preference for family members to keep knowledge of the stigma (discrediting information) within the family to prevent outsiders from learning about the problem. In the conclusion, the author returns to this issue, suggesting that, as the disease worsens, there is a radical change in the family's ability to honor this information rule:

The Alzheimer's caregiver will try for as long as possible to collude with the family member, continuing to abide by the family information rule to the extent that she or he is able, and limiting initial disclosures to intimates and medical personnel. However, there may well come a point where the caregiver realizes that she or he cannot count on the person with Alzheimer's to be cognizant of what is discrediting, let alone motivated or able to collude in trying to cover it up or minimize its embarrassment. Thus, the information control within the family tends to give way to more direct caregiver interpersonal and interactional control.

The caregiver increasingly relies on a variety of management practices to control the individual, both within the private family domain as well as outside it. And, as the person with Alzheimer's can no longer play the collusive game, caregivers gradually come to align with outsiders, disclosing discrediting information.

Here the author argues that while the family caregiver initially seeks to honor the family information rule, to do so requires cooperation from the person with Alzheimer's disease. When such cooperation can no longer be counted on, the caregiver increasingly violates the rule by disclosing discrediting information to outsiders in order to enlist their help in managing the patient. In this way the author highlights in the conclusion how her findings have modified Goffman's notion to point out previously unnoted conditions underlying the operation of the family information rule and to appreciate the kinds of circumstances which may lead family members to violate it.

Another way authors might extend a thesis statement is to develop theoretical linkages between separate components of the thesis. For example, in the introduction to the study of residents in a home for ex-mental patients, the introductory thesis pointed to two conflicting tendencies within the home: resident dependence on staff members and the residents' ability to actively influence staff views of them. In the conclusion, the author uses her more specific analyses of these relations to explicitly connect these contradictory tendencies as parts of an ongoing vicious circle. Residents feel vulnerable to the power of staff and may respond by trying to build credit and good-will with them. In order to do this, they participate in therapy sessions and other staff-initiated activities. As a result they gain the staff's support and protection but thereby become more directly dependent upon the staff members who "sponsor" them. This analysis thus links two patterns which initially appear separate and indeed contradictory, pointing to an ironic outcome whereby residents' actions intended to lessen vulnerability and dependence on staff end up tightening that dependence. In this option, the writer tells an ethnographic story which progresses from an initial thesis which high-lighted conflicting tendencies, through an in-depth discussion of analytic points with appropriate excerpts, to finally come to a conclusion which intertwines these conflicting strands.

Second, a conclusion may attempt to connect the ethnography's thesis to issues raised in a relevant disciplinary literature. In the study of Alzhei-mer's family caregiving, after the paragraphs quoted above, the author relates the contrast between colluding with the person with Alzheimer's and colluding with outsiders to a more general issue in the sociology of deviance: When do family members *accept,* tolerate, and continue to look out for another family member with some kind of stigmatizing condition or behavior, and when do they turn against, exclude, and implicitly *reject* this family member? This issue had been recently addressed in a journal article entitled "Toward a Sociology of Acceptance: The Other Side of the Study of Deviance" (Bogdan and Taylor 1987) which the author cites in developing her argument:

> Recognition of these two phases of caregiver stigma management, collusion with the person with Alzheimer's, and a realignment and collusion with outsiders, allows for an integration of a sociology of acceptance with a sociology of rejection (Bogdan and Taylor 1987).

Here the author suggests the possibility of unifying sociological theories about why and how people tolerate deviants with theories about why and how people exclude and reject deviants. These reactions need not be opposed, alternative courses of action; some forms of exclusion develop exactly because of a deep and abiding commitment to caring for another, under conditions where the afflicted family member can no longer be "counted on" to aid the caregiver in tolerantly managing the situation. This unity of acceptance and rejection is frequently highlighted, the au-thor argues, in caregivers' deeply ambivalent feelings about having to take overtly rejecting actions toward the person with Alzheimer's disease:

> Many caregivers were disturbed about having to take more and more control over their family members. In monitoring the person as well as using physical coercion, they made such comments as, "I hate my nagging voice." Or as one caregiver said with regard to taking control over his wife: "I have no right."

In this way the concept of acceptance is also extended to encompass re-jecting actions that are performed reluctantly and are combined with deep regret.

A third option in writing a conclusion is to pause, step back, and reflect on the ethnography in offering some *meta-commentary* on its methods, assumptions, tone, or conclusions. In the study of resident life in the home for ex-mental patients, the author not only addressed staff-resident relations but also considered how residents related to and developed important social and supportive ties with one another. One section of the ethnography explored the ways in which residents regularly exchanged certain items with one another—cigarettes, food, small amounts of money. The author suggested that these exchanges and the continuing relations they created and sustained helped residents deal with the chronic deprivation that they faced. In one portion of her conclusion, however, she reflected on how this earlier consideration of resident exchange "strategies" presented an "overly rationalized," game-playing view of these exchanges. This view, she argued, needed to be complemented by appreciation of the caring and emotional qualities also characteristic of these exchanges as well as the role of these exchanges in fostering a sense of sharing and community among a number of residents. The prior strategies-and-tactics analysis tended to obscure and distort these critical processes.

In all these approaches to writing a conclusion, the ethnographer takes up once again the problem of identifying and writing out in explicit, elaborated form the relevance of some of her experiences, observations, and insights into others' way of life for an outside audience. But by proceeding in a way that keeps fieldnotes at the center of the analytic process, the ethnographer is often able to reach understandings and make connections that do not neatly fit existing explanations and theories in the discipline. The refined, more precise thesis to be presented in the conclusion will more likely privilege members' views and show what is interesting (and has theoretical import) about this local life in ways which convince one's scholarly readers. Thus, the more explicit thesis in the conclusion not only represents what the ethnographer saw and heard of members' experience, but also will further clarify known issues, or propose an entirely original perspective.

REFLECTIONS: BETWEEN MEMBERS AND READERS

In producing an ethnography for wider audiences, fieldworkers are constantly pulled by conflicts between representing some indigenous world and its meanings and making their own experiences with that world speak to the very different concerns of scholarly readers. In creating a finished ethnographic story, the ethnographer self-consciously orients toward the latter; in regularly returning to his fieldnote record and to the memories bound up with and evoked by this record, he is again and again reminded of the former.

While the give-and-take of relations in the field continue to shape the ethnographer's understanding, the finished ethnography is the ethnographer's version of those happenings and events. Most ethnographic conventions allow the writer to represent others (and her experience with them) as she sees best. In this sense the ethnographer openly assumes and exercises authorial privilege. Even in those instances when ethnographers ask members to read portions or to comment on certain analyses, the author has the final say about both the text itself and the extent of members' evaluations of it (see Bloor 1988; Emerson and Pollner 1988; Rochford 1992). Despite the efforts of intensive participation, the attempts to learn members' meanings, and the self-reflection in representing others' realities, the final document turns into a rather linear narrative, defined and controlled primarily by the author.[19]

Over time—beginning in the fieldwork and extending beyond writing a paper—an ethnographer develops a complex view of field experiences. Nevertheless, the ethnographic text offers one overriding perspective—his own at the time of writing. Only when the reader's interpretation differs from that of the fieldworker do the many ways to interpret a set of notes become explicit. But to keep these various possibilities in mind while writing may paralyze the writer, preventing any story from being told. Hence, an ethnography remains one author's vision of field experiences. And thus, because the author controls the text, she takes on an authoritative voice in writing.

Nonetheless, the ethnographer sometimes provides unintended glimpses into others' everyday lives. Readers may discern things which the ethnographer did not intend to reveal. In fact, reader participation in text-making can be a double-edged advantage in ethnographies built around fieldnote excerpts. On the one hand, readers more directly engage in the described social scenes and thereby convincingly follow the story line. On the other hand, they can also more readily assess the proposed analysis, at least the version presented by the author, and derive different insights from the fieldnotes.

Readers ultimately make their own sense of these fragments, even though the note-taking ethnographer created, selected, and arranged them in the text. By choosing fieldnotes for their rhetorical effects as well as for their signifying and conceptual functions, an ethnographer tries to prefigure a reader's likely range of interpretations. Still, the original fieldnotes stand there embedded within the analysis, allowing any reader to listen closely to members' voices, to vicariously experience their actions, and to imagine other interpretations. In the end, it seems, the reader has her say.

chapter eight

Conclusion

In the preceding chapters we initially examined the processes whereby field researchers transform direct experience and observation into fieldnotes. We then considered ways of using fieldnotes to develop and tell an ethnographic story, exploring a variety of procedures that can facilitate the construction of fieldnote-centered texts. In this final chapter we want to offer some further reflections on learning to write and use fieldnotes and on some broader implications of these writing processes for ethnographic research.

As we have seen, in writing fieldnotes the ethnographer makes a number of specific writing choices; through these choices she transforms experience and observations into text and data. Obviously many of these choices involve decisions about *what* to write—to note and describe the practical efforts of Alzheimer family caregivers, patterns of racial and ethnic distribution in a school playground, or audience participation in storytelling in a Zaire village. But these choices also involve intricate decisions about *how* to write about what has been observed and experienced. As we have emphasized, writing fieldnotes is not simply a matter of putting observed details on paper. Rather, the ethnographer draws on a variety of writing conventions in order to actively create characters and scenes on a page, to dramatically depict action and speech, and to effectively convey the meanings of events as perceived by those involved in them.

Ethnographers, of course, may not always make these choices consciously; because the immediate task is to get descriptions and accounts on the page, experienced writers may use skills and make choices without a conscious thought. But increased awareness of the options which make such choices possible will, we believe, improve the overall quality of ethnographic research. In the first place, heightened consciousness about writing should help ethnographers produce richer, more varied, and useful fieldnotes. In becoming aware of and adept at using effective writing conventions, the ethnographer is more likely to capture significant detail, create vivid imagery, and provide nuanced depictions of talk and events. The field researcher will have greater flexibility in making writing choices. She will know and employ to her advantage the different effects of writing in the third as opposed to the first person, of describing a scene or event from particular or from varying points of view, and of writing up others' talk as direct or indirect speech.

But in addition, increased awareness of writing choices can also inspire the ethnographer to be more attentive to details while in the field. Envisioning scenes as written can make the researcher a better observer. With knowledge of writing options, he will be attuned to features of action and talk that might be captured on paper. Furthermore, a researcher who makes choices about different points of view in his writing is less likely, when observing, to confuse his own perspective with the views of others; hence, he will be able to recognize and represent those members' voices more fully.

Furthermore, sensitivity to writing options in constructing a final fieldnote-centered text also allows field researchers to produce more compelling and detailed ethnographic stories. The writer, for example, becomes explicitly attuned to responding both to voices from the field and to the voices of envisioned scholarly readers. She realizes that she must translate and interpret members' voices into the analytic language of intended readers in order to address issues, theories, and concerns that might interest them. Thus, in creating a fieldnote-centered final text, the ethnographer includes excerpts which report members' voices but with an awareness that she controls and orchestrates their presence; she reframes and reorders members' words and doings into her ethnographic story. Sensitive to members' concerns and meanings, she can directly confront the task of re-presenting those meanings—for example, making them "interesting" or "relevant" to the concerns of anticipated readers. As a result, in a good ethnography the reader can hear these two sets of voices speaking in harmony or at least not creating dissonance. The ethnography should provide a vehicle through which the voices of the field can, in their own distinctive ways, speak; and at the same time, the ethnography should also speak the language of the readers, addressing their issues, theories, and concerns.[1]

In all these ways, increased awareness of writing choices allows for a deepening appreciation of the power and implications of writing. The ethnographer cannot help but realize that he is not simply recording witnessed events; rather, through his writing he is actively creating realities and meanings. In writing fieldnotes, he is not simply preserving those moments in textual form, for he is shaping observed moments as scenes, characters, dialogue, and recounted actions in the first place. Subsequently, in reworking fieldnotes and transposing them into a final ethnographic story, he does not simply recount the tale of something that happened; instead, he reconstructs "what happened" so as to illustrate a pattern or a make a point. Inevitably, in interpreting his fieldnotes for readers unfamiliar with that world, he constructs a version of events. Thus, while writing and analyzing fieldnotes, the ethnographer-as-author grows increasingly aware of his role and responsibility in telling the story of the people he studied; for in writing he re-presents their everyday world.[2] In so doing, he is continually reminded how the act of writing constructs meaning and knowledge.

In this sense, awareness of writing choices generates an appreciation of the *reflexivity* of ethnographic research. Reflexivity involves the recognition that an account of reality does not simply mirror reality but rather creates or constitutes as real in the first place whatever it describes. Thus "the notion of reflexivity recognizes that texts do not simply and transparently report an independent order of reality. Rather, the texts themselves are implicated in the work of reality-construction" (Atkinson 1990:7).

The growing number of critical analyses of ethnographies that focus on reflexivity (e.g., Clifford and Marcus 1986; Atkinson 1990; Van Maanen 1988) tend to address the rhetorical structure or unstated political and cultural presuppositions of completed ethnographies, examining how the ethnographer represents another culture, develops a particular line of analysis, or constructs a persuasive argument or engaging tale in a published account. However, these analyses reveal significant limitations in themselves, for they implicitly depict final ethnographies as original, unconstrained constructions produced wholly from the ethnographer's struggles to come to terms with experiences in the field. While polished ethnographies are in part culled from memories of and reflections on field experiences, they also draw heavily on the already created fieldnote record of that experienced reality. Final ethnographies are rarely new edifices built up entirely by original writings but are more commonly jerry-built projects incorporating and constrained by prior fieldnote writings. The representational processes through which fieldnote segments are selected (or ignored), linked to one another, reworked into a consistent voice, and integrated to produce a clearly recognized rhetorical style have received little or no attention. In this way most reflexive analyses neglect or marginalize fieldnotes in the construction of finished ethnographic accounts and, thereby, ignore the role of fieldnotes in the in-process work of actively constructing a polished ethnographic account.

Such critical analyses have overlooked not only the use of fieldnotes in writing final ethnographic accounts but also the prior processes whereby ethnographers actually created a fieldnote record in the first place. Yet this initial transformation of field experiences and observations into written texts involves equally profound and consequential reconstructions of social reality as does the production of polished, full ethnographies. Growing consciousness of the reflexive qualities of ethnographic texts, then, has advanced by and large without attention to day-by-day writing practices for producing what comes to be treated as ethnographic data.

To fill this gap between reflexive analysis and practice, one must look closely at exactly how ethnographers go about writing fieldnotes: how they produce, process, and finally assemble fieldnotes into texts intended for wider audiences. For, in significant ways, describing people, events, and scenes in fieldnotes gives definite shape and substance to these matters for the writer. The writer, after all, does not simply sit down and put directly on paper something already worked out in his head. Rather, he constructs his descriptions: he must decide where to start, what to put first and what later, what to include and what to ignore. While writing, he determines whose points of view to present, what is significant about a person or event, and what is incidental and can be left out. These decisions are even more salient for subsequent readers, who have no independent access to the reality often presumed to lie behind and to have shaped the written account. From a reader's perspective, then, the text about a people's way of life creates that world as a phenomenon.

In the preceding chapters we have emphasized several specific writing choices that can highlight awareness of the reflexive character of ethnographic research. First, we have advocated writing fieldnotes so that the ethnographer can be seen and heard in them, since the ethnographer's interactions in the field shape her writing. In this way the processes whereby ethnographic texts come to be produced can be preserved and made available to readers: "Being reflexive is structuring communicative products so that the audience assumes the producer, process, and product are a coherent whole" (Myerhoff and Ruby 1982:6). But in addition, in so writing the ethnographer reminds herself that what she learned and writes about occurred on a specific occasion and was shaped by her own methods and mode of participation.

Second, we have urged writing fieldnotes in ways that effectively capture and represent members' meanings—the perspectives, understandings, concerns, and voices of those studied. In order to do this effectively, the writer must clearly understand that she is in fact re-presenting member's meanings, creating, to paraphrase Geertz (1973), "meanings of meanings," or "interpretations of interpretations."

But a seeming problem arises when we recognize that members' meanings are not things in themselves, but representations of something: Why should members' meanings have priority over any other representation an ethnographer might make? Here again, we hold that fieldnotes and finished ethnographies are inevitably and unavoidably mediated by the ethnographer's person, experiences, point of view, and theoretical priorities. But the researcher's point of view and theoretical priorities are not simply pre-given; they are shaped and influenced by the relationships he forms with the people whose social worlds he is trying to understand. As a participant who has a place in the local setting and who has some degree of involvement with the people in it, the researcher is part of the world being studied and not a neutral, detached observer. The process of forming relationships with specific people subjects the ethnographer to their meaning systems, ones that must be learned and understood, if only in order to get by. The more the ethnographer involves himself in others' social worlds, the more he subjects his own presuppositions, his own ways of doing and giving meaning to events and behavior, to the challenges of members' everyday life. The ethnographer's fieldnotes, then, consist of descriptions of and reflections on the meanings acquired and jointly constructed over the course of participation in relationships with those studied. Hence, fieldnotes reflect understandings gained through subjecting oneself to the logic of others' social worlds, a logic that comes to partially constitute the lens through which the ethnographer views and understands those worlds. In the end, what he inevitably writes is his version (informed by theoretical and other concerns and priorities) of their version. But the versions an ethnographer constructs are negotiated and mediated by members' points of view, logics, and constructions of the world as well as by the researcher's. Hence, through relationships with others, the possibility exists for appreciation and understanding of the interactions the researcher observes in their, not simply his own, terms.

Reflexivity is central both to how we understand the worlds of others as well as to how we understand the research enterprise. Reflexivity, when applied to the understanding of members' worlds, helps us to see those worlds as shaped not by variables or structures that stand above or apart from people but rather as meaning systems negotiated and constructed in and through relationships. Hence, when self-consciously applied to ourselves as researchers, the reflexive lens helps us see and appreciate how our own renderings of others' worlds are not and can never be descriptions from outside those worlds. Rather, they are informed by and constructed in and through relationships with those under study. Hence, in training the reflexive lens on ourselves, we understand our own enterprise in much the same terms that we understand those we study.

Notes

Preface

1. Consider the treatment by Schatzman and Strauss of "Strategy for Recording" in their *Field Research: Strategies for a Natural Sociology* (1973:94–101). Good advice abounds on such matters as when and when not to jot notes in the field, the relative advantages of typing as opposed to taping full notes, and the utility of distinguishing between observational, methodological, and theoretical notes. Yet nothing is said about what and how one actually writes, about learning writing skills, or about the consequences of different writing styles.

2. This research was supported by the National Science Foundation grant SES-8713255, "The Pro Se Litigant: Self-Representation in Consequential Civil Cases," co-principal investigators Robert M. Emerson and Susan McCoin, 1988–89.

3. Rachel Fretz's research on storytelling among the Chokwe in Zaire in 1982 was supported by a Fulbright-Hayes award and the subsequent Zambian research in 1992 by a Fulbright grant for advanced research.

4. See, for example, Burgess 1982, 1984; Denzin and Lincoln 1994; Ellen 1984; Emerson 1988; Hammersley 1992; Hammersley and Atkinson 1983; Lofland and Lofland 1995; Schatzman and Strauss 1973; Schwartz and Jacobs 1979; Spradley 1980; Taylor and Bogdan 1984.

Chapter One: Fieldnotes in Ethnographic Research

1. The term "member" is drawn from ethnomethodology, which is concerned with ordinary persons' "mastery of natural language" and ultimately with the "commonsense knowledge of everyday activities" reflected in the use of such language (Garfinkel and Sacks 1970:339).

2. Here we are assuming that the field worker adopts an *overt* research role in the setting or scene of interest, openly taking a research identity. For a discussion

of the advantages of covert field research, see Douglas (1976) and Schwartz and Jacobs (1979); for critical considerations of covert field research, see Erikson (1967) and Cassell (1980).

3. As Mishler (1979:10) has suggested: "[any phenomenon] contains multiple truths, each of which will be revealed by a shift in perspective, method, or purpose. . . . The task is not to exhaust the singular meaning of an event but to reveal the multiplicity of meanings, and . . . it is through the observer's encounter with the event that these meanings emerge."

4. On occasion the ethnographer may feel as if he has "nonconsequential presence," i.e., is naturally and unproblematically "just an observer." But this sense is in fact a contingent and effortful achievement dependent upon the collusive cooperation of the observed (Pollner and Emerson 1988). Field researchers rely upon a variety of interactional practices to achieve and sustain the role of "observer" in the face of various pulls and seductions to participate more fully in unfolding events and hence in some sense to dissolve the very distinction between "observer" and "observed."

5. Georges and Jones (1980) describe many examples of fieldworkers whose research developed directly from the kind of relationships they formed with those encountered in the field.

6. For example, the intern is constrained by the requirements of his job, in most instances losing the ability to move around without encumbrance. On the other hand, both field researcher and intern are temporary members of the setting and are often accorded low, marginal status.

7. Geertz (1976) and Bittner (1988) explore several of the implications that flow from recognizing that an ethnographer must remain at least a partial outsider. First, having "been there" and "seen for myself" does not provide compelling authority for written accounts of another world, given that the ethnographer's experience of another world approximates rather than absolutely replicates members' experiences. See also the discussion of "ethnographic realism" in Marcus and Cushman (1982). Second, the ethnographer's limited commitment and appreciation of constraint promotes an understanding of other worlds as subjectively perceived and constructed, hence without the "traits of depth, stability, and necessity that people recognize as actually inherent in the circumstances of their existence" (Bittner 1988:155).

8. Similarly, Latour (1987:68) conceptualizes laboratory science as a distinctive form of inscription, focusing on how scientists transform a series of laboratory procedures into texts and viewing the various instruments used to do so as "inscription devices." See also Latour and Woolgar (1979).

9. All of these matters must be handled through the development of a series of writing conventions. See Psathas and Anderson (1990) for a review of the key "transcription symbols" used in making transcripts for conversation analysis.

10. In comparing fieldnotes with transcripts made from audio and visual recordings as different methods for reducing ongoing social life to texts, we do not mean to suggest a model of ethnographic research that employs only the former. Rather, most contemporary field researchers rely heavily upon *both* fieldnotes and recordings. Fieldwork manuals now regularly discuss varied methods for docu-

menting research and especially emphasize recording equipment (e.g., Goldstein 1964; Ellen 1984; Jackson 1987; Wilson 1986). Stone and Stone (1981) in particular describe the various forms of media researchers use and discuss the kinds of encoding involved, beginning with writing fieldnotes and moving to recordings. The relative emphasis placed on writing fieldnotes as opposed to recording, however, varies with the nature of the field researcher's discipline and project. Many ethnographers, for example, often tape informal interviews as well as write extensive notes—an essential practice when working in a foreign language, and often valuable when working in one's own language and culture. Similarly, other fieldworkers complement their fieldnote records by systematically tape recording significant occasions or recurrent events that are central to their theoretical concerns. In contrast, field researchers studying talk, forms of expression, and oral traditions, such as sociolinguists, folklorists, and oral historians, often give primacy to tape-recording, but nevertheless write detailed fieldnotes to supplement verbal accounts with contextual details.

11. A number of field researchers have examined the many ways that human relationships in field research influence final research findings: see particularly Clarke (1975), Ellis (1991), Emerson (1988:175–252), Georges and Jones (1980), Kleinman (1991), and Reinharz (1979).

12. As several researchers (Clifford 1983; Stoddard 1986) have shown, the seeming objectivity and "authority" of ethnographic data (and "scientific data" more widely) is achieved, in part, exactly by suppressing or ignoring its dependence upon the person of the researcher and her methods of inquiry and writing.

13. Concern with indigenous meanings, providing "accounts of other worlds from the inside" (Marcus and Fischer 1986:26), marked the rise of "interpretive anthropology" in the 1960s and 1970s.

Chapter Two: In the Field

1. Jackson (1990b:23), for example, quotes several anthropologists who emphasized the pure "doing" of ethnography as follows: "Fieldnotes get in the way. They interfere with what fieldwork is all about—the doing." And: "*This* is what I would call fieldwork. It is not taking notes in the field but is the interaction between the researcher and the so-called research subjects."

2. Jackson (1990b:25) provides an example of the former, quoting an anthropologist who gained "insight into Australian Aboriginal symbolism about the ground while on the ground": "You notice in any kind of prolonged conversation, people are squatting, or lie on the ground. I came to be quite intrigued by that, partly because I'd have to, too . . . endless dust." Pollner and Emerson (1988:244) present an instance of the latter, when a previously marginalized and detached observer is suddenly brought stage center into an in-the-home psychiatric evaluation.

3. Some ethnographers committed to experiencing immersion may put off systematic writing almost indefinitely, often until leaving the field permanently. Given our commitment to more or less contemporaneously written notes, we do not address procedures for writing fieldnotes long after the occurrence of the events of interest.

4. This term is taken from Jackson (1990b:5), who credits it to Simon Ottenberg.

5. Indeed, Everett Hughes (1971:505) emphasizes that it is less the published report than taking a detached outlook toward the personal and intimate that brings people's wrath down upon the field researcher: "The hatred occasionally visited upon the debunking historian is visited almost daily upon the person who reports on the behavior of people he has lived among; and it is not so much the writing of the report, as the very act of thinking in such objective terms that disturbs the people observed."

6. In part this lack of knowledge about what the field researcher is doing may result from the latter's evolving analytic purposes and concerns, which are not preestablished but which change with immersion in the setting (Wax 1977). As Thorne (1980:287) emphasizes, "fieldworkers usually enter the field with an open-ended sense of purpose; they tend to work inductively and may shift interests and outlooks as the research proceeds; practical exigencies may force extensive change of plans."

7. Similarly, those observed often use humor to comment on the role of the note-taking ethnographer. Again from the HUD housing office: "The workers are talking and laughing as Sam decides where to put his desk in his new office. I hear one of the workers say, 'I hope Bob didn't write that down.' I walked up. 'What?' 'Oh, I just told Sam it's good he's got space for his machete behind his desk.' They laugh."

8. Here further complications arise about whether the ethnographer will write full fieldnotes about matters that she avoided making jottings on or was asked not to make jottings on. On the one hand, a fieldworker might feel that her fieldnotes are her personal (as well as scientific) record, and that she can write anything and everything in those notes that she desires. Such a practice puts off any decision about whether or not to use these particular fieldnote writings in a paper to be seen by any outside audience. On the other hand, the ethnographer might well feel constrained by an implicit agreement not to take jottings about a particular event to also avoid writing full fieldnotes about that event, independently of whether anyone else would ever read that material. Here the fieldworker honors the personal, ethical bond with the person observed over any commitment to her fieldnotes as research record.

9. Thus, making jottings "off-phase," recommended by Goffman (1989:130) as a means of minimizing reactive effects (i.e., "don't write your notes on the act you're observing because then people will know what it is you're recording"), may risk offending others when the focus of the jotting appears to be the *current* activity or topic.

10. For example, to have made jottings during a Chokwe initiation ceremony (*mwadi*) when the older women were teaching a young woman how "to dance with a husband" by simulating the sexual act might have appeared inappropriate and might have drawn immediate criticism from participants.

11. Geer's (1964) article on her first days in the field includes detailed fieldnotes on this crucial moment of research entry into a new setting. These fieldnotes provide lively examples of events and issues that drew the attention of an

experienced field researcher; they also illustrate the range of matters that might have led to initial jottings in the field.

12. Gottlieb and Graham (1993) depict these processes of note-taking in their narrative of the course of their ethnographic research in Africa.

13. It is possible, of course, to *interview* those involved in the social world under study and to ask directly about their own inner states and motives as well as about their assessments of those of others. Such interviews, however, do not provide definitive answers to these matters, but only another set of observations which the ethnographer must still assess and evaluate. See Emerson and Pollner's (1988) consideration of the contingent, deeply problematic interpretations required to evaluate the interview statements of a mental health clinic worker asked to assess ethnographic writings describing his own work circumstances and decision-making.

14. This excerpt, as well as others in this and subsequent chapters, draw on interviews conducted by Linda Shaw in which student fieldworkers were encouraged to "talk out loud" while seated at their computers writing fieldnotes from jottings and headnotes.

15. This student ethnographer offered these reflections on this process: "Before I never could write about it. I just never could remember them [concrete events]. It seemed very small and insignificant because everything with these children is in very small steps and nothing really outstanding ever happens, but this really stood out in my mind and I wanted to remember it. At that time I told myself, 'Remember that.'"

These notes also reflect this student intern/fieldworker's distinctive *commitments* in this setting as evident in the point of view implicit in her writing. She not only identifies the incident that has just taken place as "listening to the teacher" and as a change from Nicole's prior pattern of behavior. But reflecting her real teaching responsibilities in the setting, she also *evaluates this change positively as an "accomplishment,"* as something that Nicole *should* learn. An ethnographer without job responsibilities in the setting might well characterize the incident differently (e.g., as an adult staff member's exercise of authority), and withhold immediate evaluation as to whether what Nicole did was "good" or "bad."

16. Of course, some ethnographers may eventually decide to completely abandon their commitment to research, a possibility that has long given anxiety to anthropologists concerned about the dangers of "going native." Much less recognized and discussed is the more limited, situational abandonment of research commitment that occurs when a field researcher determines not to write fieldnotes about specific incidents or persons on the grounds that such writing would involve levels of betrayal or revelation that the researcher finds personally and/or ethically intolerable.

17. Field researchers routinely use a number of interactional tactics to maintain research distance in the face of overtures to heightened involvement from those under study (Pollner and Emerson 1988). These practices include "declarations" directly declining greater involvement, "preemptive moves aimed at precluding overtures to deeper involvement," and "a variety of responses that indirectly deflect, hedge, or evade such overtures" (1988:243).

18. Jackson (1990a) uses extensive interviews with anthropologists to identify various "liminal" or "betwix-and-between" qualities of fieldnotes and the experience of writing them. Many field researchers reported feelings similar to this report of letting fieldnotes go as one begins to fit in to the rhythms of local life: "I slowed down. More concerned with the hour to hour. You forget to take notes because you feel this is your life" (Jackson 1990a:18).

19. Many ethnographers also create that same separate stance through photographing or filming events. See Jackson (1987).

Chapter Three: From Field to Desk

1. It may well be that the simple lapse of time interferes with recall less than does participating in other activities and social situations. Along these lines, Goffman (1989:127) advises against bringing spouses into the field because "it does give you a way out. You can talk to that person, and all that, and that's no way to make a world."

2. Sanjek (1990b), for example, reports a full year passed before he went from notebook to full fieldnotes; obviously he spent a great deal of time and care in writing up descriptions and events in these handwritten notebooks.

3. In addition, the field researcher with actual readers may not want to reveal very personal incidents to these others, whether instructor or co-worker. We would advise writing up these notes in a separate document. This procedure produces a written account but one seen only by the fieldworker. At a later point the latter may feel that the account is important and should be included in a final analysis; or he may decide that it is too personal and keep it private.

4. As Ong (1975) points out, writers envision audiences by imagining the kinds of readers who have read similar pieces of writing. Thus, the writer's stylistic choices are a means of addressing that imagined audience.

5. As one ethnographer commented: "That might be closer to a definition of a fieldnote: something that can't be readily comprehended by another person" (Jackson 1990b:20).

6. As Flower (1988) emphasizes, a writer's purpose is not a unitary, conscious intention but rather a set of interconnected goals; during the writing process, writers regularly revise and prioritize these goals.

7. Perl (1980) urges writers to frequently reread their work, returning to a key word or phrase that recaptures their "felt sense" of what they wanted to say about a topic. Getting in touch with this "felt sense" renews the writer's energy. Through a process of "retrospective structuring," writers refine what they want to say.

8. These jottings were originally written in a version of speed writing that is incomprehensible to most readers. We have translated them into readable form.

9. In this project, Rachel Fretz carried out many of her observations in conjunction with two other researchers working in the same village, art historians Elisabeth Cameron and Manuel Jordan. Researchers who work together in the same site can document and represent the different voices and points of view of various members.

10. Following Abrams (1988), we refer to "voice" as representing both the

unique speaking style and the distinctive perspective or "ethos" of an individual. We recognize also that an individual shifts her way of writing/speaking to accommodate different audiences and purposes. A commitment to incorporating multiple points of view into fieldnotes may lead the fieldworker to participate in the setting in ways that vary her perspective and that recognize and encourage the expression of multiple voices—another illustration of how writing fieldnotes may play back on and effect what is done in the field!

11. Many of these objections to an omniscient point of view weaken or even dissolve entirely when we turn from writing fieldnotes to writing final ethnographies. Indeed, existing discussions of omniscience in ethnographic writing all treat final ethnographies, not fieldnotes. Van Maanen's (1988:45–72) "realist tales," for example, are complete ethnographies that involve many omniscient qualities—the absence of the author from the text, minutely detailed descriptions and overviews, and "interpretive omnipotence." Similarly, Brown (1977) sees the omniscient point of view as characteristic of many classic ethnographies; the ethnographer adopts an omniscient point of view, for example, when he chooses which members' voices to present and shifts from one person's view to another's.

12. Becker (1986) emphasizes just these processes, through which writing enables any writer to clarify and develop ideas. He insists that ideas that are not put to paper are loose and fluid: "First one thing, then another, comes into your head. By the time you have thought the fourth thing, the first one is gone" (1986:55). In contrast, "a thought written down . . . is stubborn, doesn't change its shape, can be compared with other thoughts that come after it" (1986:56).

13. Although not focused specifically on fieldnote descriptions, Wolf (1992) provides a provocative illustration of the potential variation in how ethnography can portray different slices of life; she presents the "same" series of events in three different story formats—original fieldnotes, a more formal analytic account, and a fictional short story.

Chapter Four: Creating Scenes on the Page

1. Description is often referred to as one of the four chief types of composition—along with argumentation, exposition, and narration. But here we consider describing as a key strategy for picturing settings, people, objects, and actions as a part of the larger ethnographic narrative which the ethnographer tells throughout her fieldnotes, beginning the first day she enters the site and closing when she leaves and writes her last notes.

2. Lofland (1985:15) terms this "categoric knowing" in which "one knows who the other is only in the sense that one knows he can be placed into some category," particularly gender, age, and race, since these categories are readily gleaned from appearance only. In contrast "personal knowing" involves knowledge of at least some aspects of the other's actual biography.

3. In this sense, this description may be a product of, as well as advance, the ethnographer's theoretical interest in ethnic identity. That is, the observer may have come upon this scene with a pre-existing interest in how white students affiliate with African-Americans, this sensitivity leading him to appreciate the ironic symbolism and to write so vividly about the jacket. Alternatively, writing

a description of something that made an immediate impression on him may have made him begin to think about issues of cross-cultural affiliation. In either case, in subsequent fieldnotes this ethnographer continued to focus on this woman and other white students who hung out with blacks, describing other instances of ethnically distinct clothes, whites' use of black conversational styles, etc.

4. A combination of field observations and tape recordings of specific interactions marks many recent ethnographic studies of human service agencies, including schools (Mehan, Hertweck, and Meihls 1986), child protective services (Dingwall, Eekelaar, and Murray 1983), and criminal courts (Maynard 1984). See Maynard (1989) for a discussion of one approach to integrating these ways of producing textual records of key institutional encounters.

5. Often her fieldnotes were written in English, though she listened in another language; she therefore included many non-English terms to preserve local meanings.

6. For a discussion of how researchers working in second languages or explicitly focusing on verbal expression combine and integrate these methods, see Stone and Stone (1981). Some sociological field researchers advocate the use of similar sorts of "triangulation" procedures—for example, conducting later interviews with participants about what they were thinking and doing during a recorded exchange; see Cicourel (1974:124ff).

7. Shaw (1991) explores a number of other expressions of this feeling of falling short of achieving a "normal" life, and the resulting pervasive sense of stigma, that afflicts ex-mental patients in their dealings with more conventional people.

8. Grouping details not only makes writing-up easier, but the habit of marking paragraph breaks also speeds up reading and making sense of fieldnotes later on.

9. Stoller (1989) suggests that many ethnographers, reflecting their Western culture, have a bias for visual detail even though members may be attending more to other sensory impressions, such as smell or sound or movement. In this respect, the kinds of sensory details which are dominant vary from one culture to another.

10. Lederman (1990:84) emphasizes that units such as "*events*" have "an apparent 'wholeness'" that make them "good modes of entry into fieldnotes" and useful analytic units in her ethnography. One can write up an event as a brief episode or more fully describe it in a tale.

11. Johnstone (1990:18) defines a story as a "*narrative* (that is, it presents a sequence of events) with a *point* (a reason for being told that goes beyond, or is independent of, any need for the reporting of events)." However, the way storytellers structure their narratives to convey ideas varies from one storytelling tradition to another. Riessman (1987:179–88) suggests that narrative progression is culturally specific. For instance, she found that a Puerto Rican woman told her personal story of marital problems by telling about *recurring situations* within the family rather than by recounting a *sequential development* of personal stresses with her husband. Johnstone (1990) and Stahl (1989) point out that people telling their personal experiences draw on narrating conventions which are familiar to listeners in their community. What makes a good story, how to tell it, and how to interpret

it varies from one community to another. The ethnographer thus must guard against shaping events to fit her own sense of a good story.

12. Narrative conventions and patterns, however, vary from one culture to another, and the ethnographer must become conscious of these conventions in order to avoid superimposing her own sense of narrative structure and movement on that other's words and actions; she should not imagine connections where there are none and infer a sequential development of actions toward an outcome when no such movement was intended. For example, in Western hero tales, the protagonist sets forth on a quest, moves through difficulties, and conquers the monster or finds the holy grail. The story is one of personal success and conquest. In contrast, in many cultures the focus is less on an individual's success and personal development and more on the way relationships between people unfold and have consequences for their community or extended family. In such narrative traditions, the listeners pay attention more to how the characters negotiate their relationships and to whether or not they act appropriately toward their relatives and friends. Thus, the teller of a story about an authority figure and a young person in an educational situation might be concerned with the effects of the student's actions on his family, about the student's respect for authority, and about the disciplinarian's opinion of the students' relatives. If an ethnographer infers a personal conquest plot when writing fieldnotes about a non-Western tradition, he probably will misinterpret the storytelling and substantially distort what the people themselves intended. Thus, when writing up stories which a community member tells about local events, the ethnographer should stick closely to the teller's sequencing and report carefully the connections the teller makes between actions. Often researchers tape record historical accounts and myths, folktales, and legends to document them explicitly.

13. Of course, even in initially writing a tale, the ethnographer's understanding of its structure tends to change: what in jotting notes she sensed as a series of unrelated actions, she may come to understand in writing as interconnected. Or, in the midst of writing her tale, she might suddenly have a flash of insight and see an alternate way of perceiving events and might change how she composes her tale accordingly.

14. The current ending of the police tale results from our editing decisions and reflects our search for a loosely structured tale which was relatively short. Had we begun the cut at an earlier point or ended at a later one, the reader's sense of the story line might differ. Or, if we had shortened it further, to begin with the stop at the 7–11 store and to end with the second car stopping, the tale might have seemed more cohesive and more clearly the story of mundane police work broken by moments of excitement.

15. See chapter 6 for discussion of memos connected with coding and analysis when attention has turned from fieldwork to writing a finished ethnographic text.

16. Schatzman and Strauss (1973:99–101) recommend tagging each fieldnote segment with an initial label, either "Observational Notes" (ON), "Theoretical Notes" (TN), or "Methodological Notes" (MN). Many field researchers find this procedure helpful in marking transitions in writing focus and intent. We generally

avoid using these tags because we think that the distinctions are not only theoretically problematic but also practically difficult to apply in many instances.

17. Some ethnographers come to view their own fieldnotes as poor substi-
tutes for their actual experiences and observations in the field. Jackson (1990a:19),
for example, quotes one person's comment: "I was disappointed that they weren't
as magical as my memory. . . . there are a lot of visual features to my memory,
whereas fieldnotes were much more sort of mere rendering." While fieldnotes
may never completely capture the lived experience in the field, improving writing
skills will suffuse notes with at least some of this "magic." We see wide gaps
between memory and fieldnote as evidence of insufficient attention to writing.

Chapter Five: Pursuing Members' Meanings

1. Many studies do not directly claim that a group's beliefs and ideas are fallacious, but indirectly diminish these beliefs and ideas by depicting them as self-
serving. Berger (1981) proposes the concept of "ideological work" as an alternative way of handling these issues. Many sociological analyses, he argues, "take as
their task 'exposing' the 'real' interests served by ideas or 'unmasking' or debunking ideas by revealing the contradictions between what ideas apparently profess and the day-to-day behavior of those who profess them" (1981:19–20). The
ethnographer has a different task—"not to expose discrepancies or contradictions
between practice and preachment" (1981:114) but to look closely at and document the ways in which people resolve and reconcile any such discrepancies. For
example, rather than "unmasking" rural hippies' use of chain saws as a contradic-
tion of their professed distrust of modern "technology," Berger carefully and non-
cynically examines how these hippies come to view the chain saw as a "tool"
distinct from "technology" (116). These sorts of interpretive acts, "aimed at
bridging gaps, sweetening dissonances, and restoring (perhaps only temporarily)
a measure of harmony and consistency" between practice and belief, represent
"remedial ideological work" (1981:114).

2. Jordan's (1993:41–61) discussion of masking traditions in the circumcision
(mukanda) rituals of Northwest Province, Zambia, explains variation as characteristic of these rituals; he found that innovation in mask decorations can be a means
through which people cope with political realities in the region.

3. Hunt's (1985) analysis of the use of force by police illustrates an alternative,
more naturalistic approach that seeks to identify what sorts of force the police
themselves recognize as excessive or "brutal" and what sorts as legitimate or "normal." Hunt refrains from passing her own judgments in order to learn how and
where particular officers apply these distinctions to specific instances of the use
of force.

4. Ben-Amos (1982) in particular has argued that the examination of indigenous classifications has been hindered by the "discrepancy" between ethnic and
analytic systems and advocates that researchers document and explain the terms
and categories which the people studied use. However, scholars studying oral
traditions continue to insist on the comparative value of analytic categories. Okpewho (1992) urges continued use of analytic categories to further comparative
discussion even while he commends the practice of using indigenous terms for

narrative categories. In an introduction to "folk narratives," Oring (1986) identifies analytic features generally associated with "myth," "legend," and "folktale."

5. Ethnographers may also receive "non-answers" when they appear woefully ignorant of the matters they ask about. Diamond (1989) recounts the story told by an eminent ethnobiologist who has spent years with the Kalam people of the New Guinea Highlands working with native informants to identify folk terms for 1,400 species of animals and plants. Yet when at one point he asked about rocks, his Kalam informants insisted they had just one word covering all rocks. A year later he returned with a geologist friend who within an hour came back with a long list of Kalam terms for rocks. The ethnobiologist angrily confronted his Kalam informants, demanding to know why they had lied to him about not classifying rocks. They answered: "When you asked us about birds and plants, we saw that you knew a lot about them, and that you could understand what we told you. When you began asking us about rocks, it was obvious you didn't know anything about them. Why should we waste our time telling you something you couldn't possibly understand? But your friend's questions showed that he does know about rocks" (Diamond 1989:30). Diamond concludes that the ethnoscientist has "to know almost as much" as those questioned in order to elicit their native terms and classificatory principles.

6. Cognitive anthropologists in particular (e.g., Frake 1964; Spradley 1979; Agar 1982) have sought to provide techniques to avoid imposing outside categories by "discovering" appropriate and meaningful questions from within another culture.

7. Frake's classic ethnography, "How to Enter a Yakan House" (1975), includes a detailed analysis of local ways of passing by and greeting others in Yakan society.

8. Of course, paying close attention to ordinary questions and appropriate answers also helps the field researcher learn how to participate in conversations in a natural way, and hence is a key part of the resocialization process involved in fieldwork.

9. In a similar vein, see Sudnow's (1967:36–42) subtle observations of the patterned differences in how new medical personnel talk about deaths as "countable" occurrences.

10. Many other fieldworkers also recount socialization through teasing and laughter (cf. Yocom 1990).

11. In these circumstances "what happened" is necessarily summarized or "glossed"; moreover, "what happened" will be presented as having particular import for or significance to the specific persons to whom it is recounted. In these respects this member's account involves a distinctive "formulation" (Garfinkel and Sacks 1970) of the event. And any event can be formulated in a variety of different ways, depending upon the nature of the person's concerns and interests.

12. In his classic field study, Cicourel (1968) examines how police and probation officers dealing with youth read and interpret the various written records generated in delinquency cases, including arrest reports, probation investigations, and school reports. He also emphasizes the distinctive practical and strategic considerations which shape how police and probation officers turn their conversations

with youth into written reports in the first place (see particularly the case of Audrey, 130–66).

13. The kinds of answers people give in response to a researcher's inquiries are shaped by the kinds of questions asked as well as the circumstances of an interview. Spradley (1979:85–91) explains how to ask "descriptive questions" which produce meaningful answers. Briggs (1986) discusses the ways the social situation and the language the researcher uses determine the kinds of responses the interviewee offers.

14. Johnstone (1990) discusses the way people structure and give meaning to experience through storytelling, both drawing on the group's conventions for storytelling and expressing themselves in their own unique style. Stahl (1989) points out that storytellers often pattern their experiences to fit community values and notions of a story. In interpreting stories, the researcher must infer the implicit values of the teller.

15. Of course, this story is also told to the researcher, and presumably has been adapted to his concerns and interests and to his relationship with the teller. Consequently, the ethnographer should not only tell "the story" in his fieldnotes but also describe the context of the storytelling: what conversational questions or comments triggered the story, where the storytelling happened (in private or as a part of other activities), and who else was listening.

16. Mills (1990) notes that folklorists, with their emphasis on face-to-face interactions in oral expression, have for some time studied and documented in detailed transcriptions the multiple voices and differing perspectives expressed during performances. Viewing oral performances as emergent and unique, many scholars of oral narrative (for example, Bauman 1992a, 1992b; Briggs 1988; Georges 1981) analyze in detail the dynamics of each performance. They examine the way narrators shape their style and themes to accommodate the audience, situation, and specific circumstances. By documenting several versions of the "same" oral story, they demonstrate that narrators often create their stories to express their views about a topic. For example, Cosentino (1982) in his study of Mende storytelling in Sierra Leone, documents three women who argue with each other through their contrasting versions of a folktale: each story has distinctly different details and clearly differing outcomes.

17. This discussion is based on Rachel Fretz's research among the Chokwe of Bandundu Province, Zaire, in 1982 and 1983, and of Northwest Province, Zambia, in 1992–93. It elaborates and extends the earlier discussion in Fretz (1987).

18. Ben-Amos (1982) suggests that in studying indigenous categories of expression the researcher should describe the cognitive, expressive, and behavioral levels. He points out that sometimes a people's system of expression includes distinctions made behaviorally, but which are not marked by distinct terms and therefore must be discerned through observation of actions in differing social situations.

19. Here we draw directly from Moerman's (1969:464) idea of "intracultural contrast." Moerman notes that the seemingly innocuous descriptive claim, "the Thai are noisy in temple," implicitly involves an *inter*cultural comparison on the order of, "The Thai I saw in temple were noisier than Methodists are supposed

to be in church." Intracultural contrast of Thai religious behavior would require the ethnographer to compare behaviors in different settings within the society, contrasting organizational and interactional patterns found within them. Thus, one might compare the noise (and other aspects of social behavior) in temples with the noise in other locally comparable situations (among the Thai, for example, dispute hearings, village meetings, and casual conversations).

20. In this instance, what counts as a satisfactory, "official" explanation shifts as speakers change language, but neither explanation fully describes what people do about AIDS/sorcery illnesses. The ethnographer needs to recognize that explanations often are no more than pointers to how the people momentarily see events or how they wish them to be. Explanations do not constitute experience/reality. Jackson (1982:30–31) in his study of the Kuranko people in West Africa suggests that people invoke verbal, official explanations in times of crisis to validate some claim, but that people's everyday experience rarely conforms to such explanations. Verbal explanations and actions are two different types of experience.

21. Classifications, then, should be seen not as determined by particular attributes of the objects being categorized (that is, as "trait driven") but rather as driven by actors' "practical purposes at hand" (Schutz 1964). This stance directs attention from cognitive categories inside actors' heads to actual interactions and the practical "purposes at hand" actors pursue in them; attributes take on actual salience or relevance vis-à-vis these shifting, emergent purposes. Such purposes at hand will vary widely from moment to moment, situation to situation, as actors' purposes emerge, develop, and change.

22. Researchers working within the interdisciplinary field of "the ethnography of speaking" have as their aim a detailed record and description of the differing kinds of expression within a community. Sherzer (1983 and 1992) notes that such studies examine not only the range of expression but also their functions within the community.

23. The fieldnote account leaves opaque Ellen's perspective on these events, indicating only "I heard her out" but without reporting what she said specifically in her own defense. Her reported claim that she did not realize that the author was helping the wife would suggest that she recognized that she had "mistakenly" made the sale to the husband, a stance which might suggest it was not "snaking" because she had not taken the sale "deliberately." It is also possible that she maintained that she had made the sale legitimately, that the customer in fact "belonged" to her because he was making a purchase independently of his wife, or because of the practical contingencies of managing the purchase of a surprise present.

24. In this instance, it is likely that a female ethnographer's presence at the chief's pavilion initially encouraged a woman to narrate; she may well have been reprimanded later for having done so; in any case, no women narrated in that location again. The researcher's gendered presence is frequently consequential in field settings, although often in subtle ways that can only be identified with close, long-term observation. For examinations of the influence of gender in field research, see Camitta (1990), DeVault (1990), Golde (1970), Lawless (1993), Mills (1990), Reinharz (1992), Thorne (1993), and Warren (1988).

25. Wiseman's (1970) study of how alcoholics "make the rehab route" on skid row in the 1960s uses just such a procedure to examine how a category of people similar to the homeless made contact with and moved through various "supporting institutions."

26. However, field researchers would be well advised to interview people specifically about interactions and occasions that they have observed; such interviews provide not only sometimes critical background but also a series of individual perspectives on these events.

Chapter Six: Coding and Memoing

1. Glaser and Strauss (1967) provided the initial statement of the grounded theory approach. Schatzman and Strauss (1973), Glaser (1978), Charmaz (1988), and Strauss (1987) have subsequently elaborated this approach, taking somewhat different tacks toward the use of the core grounded theory procedures of coding and memoing to develop analytic categories from qualitative data. Substantively, much of the field research using grounded theory methods has examined the treatment and experience of illness; see particularly Glaser and Strauss (1965), Biernacki (1986), Corbin and Strauss (1988), and Charmaz (1991).

2. Of course, quantitative research involves similar sorts of category creation and refinement, typically at the pre-test stage, but it does not term this "coding."

3. Computer software programs designed specifically for qualitative data analysis offer fieldworkers a variety of approaches to coding and analysis (Pfaffenberger 1988; Tesch 1990; Richards and Richards 1994). At the present time, such programs are most effective in managing massive amounts of field data through a "code and retrieve process"; here the fieldworker labels "passages of the data according to what they are about or other content of interest in them (coding or indexing)," and then relies on the program to collect passages labeled in the same way (retrieving) (Richards and Richards 1994:446). Richards and Richards (1994:447–49) argue that existing software programs using such code-and-retrieve procedures can advance theory construction, but at the present time only through various "textual-level operations." These programs currently lack the substantial "conceptual-level operations" needed to develop, elaborate, and test theories. Whether or not an ethnographer decides to use a computer program to code and sort her data, she nonetheless is the one who conceptualizes, interprets, and reconfigures the fieldnotes. The quality and usefulness of the resulting coding categories always depends on the ethnographer's thinking. In any case, she must engage in the processes of reading, interpreting and coding fieldnote data that we describe.

4. Qualitative data analysis reverses the sequence of procedures employed in quantitative analysis: rather than using preestablished categories to sort and then analyze the data, the researcher first analyses the data by means of initial coding and only subsequently sorts it. Thus, in qualitative data analysis, sorting is subordinated to developing and refining analyses; it is more a byproduct of the coding process than the end of that process.

5. Richards and Richards (1994) provide an excellent overview of a number of

current "code-and-retrieve" software programs. However, students with smaller amounts of data may find it easier to simply create new files using the standard block and copy functions of their word processing program.

6. See Blum (1991) for the completed analysis of these and other issues.

7. That is, that you have only one instance or case in your data does not affect many of the analytic claims that you can develop from it. What is important is the theoretical relevance or import of the instance. A single unusual incident may reveal critical but rarely observed processes within a particular setting (Harper 1992), or reflect issues that rarely surface in everyday life but that are of deep concern to members. Similarly, advocates of the sociological procedure of "analytic induction" insist that finding a *single* negative case that contradicts the theoretical explanation that the researcher has developed requires modifying either that explanation or the phenomenon to be explained (Katz 1988). In this way theory grows more dense and sophisticated when the researcher looks for and incorporates such negative cases into her analysis.

Chapter Seven: Writing an Ethnography

1. Richardson (1990), however, does discuss ethnographic writing for general audiences in high-circulation trade books and for mass-circulation magazines.

2. Our concept of thematic narrative in ethnography draws heavily upon Atkinson's (1990:126–28) discussion of "fragmented narratives" as the most common form of "conventional ethnography." Fragmented narratives are nonlinear, rearranging and presenting everyday events in "atemporal, paradigmatic relationships" (1990:126). Atkinson contrasts such fragmented narratives with the more classic "chronological narratives" which provide a linear "extended chronicle of events" (1990:126).

3. Many of our recommendations for writing final ethnographies resonate with and often draw upon the ideas and advice Becker (1986) has developed for social science writing in general. Indeed, we strongly recommend that all field researchers who are turning to the process of writing final ethnographies consult Becker's book directly for themselves early on in their project.

4. Thus, in a logical argument, the thesis is explicitly stated at the outset, the subsequent points develop that thesis, and the evidence illustrates and confirms the points. Richardson (1990:13) notes how such arguments draw on "logico-scientific codes" of reasoning and representation that stand in sharp contrast to the narrative forms employed in most ethnographies. In practice, the local, concrete commitments of ethnography preclude the highly formal forms of analytic argumentation that may be found in other areas of social science. See also Richardson's (1994:520) discussion of a range of "writing formats" appropriate for ethnographies.

5. Each of these topics suggests a theoretical concern related to a specific scholarly literature; indeed, each might well have been formulated because of familiarity with such a literature. "Ethnicity as social construction in high school," for example, expresses an interest in examining ethnic differences as recognized and acted upon by high school students. Similarly, "parental involvement in juve-

nile court hearings" implicitly addresses raises issues of the factors that influence outcomes in juvenile court proceedings. But neither theory nor literature need be explicitly addressed at this point.

6. This is exactly what is involved in the process of analytic induction, where one can modify either the conceptual category or what is being explained, or both, in order to "form a perfect relation between data and explanation" (Katz 1988:130). Note, however, that modifying themes or conceptual categories to fit fieldnote data may make prior coding irrelevant; indeed, initial code categories often do not hold up throughout the writing.

7. For contemporary examples of ethnographies relying on integrative strategies, see Berger (1981), Diamond (1992), and Thorne (1993). Anderson (1990), DeVault (1991), and Emerson (1989) make heavy use of excerpt strategies.

8. Long incidents or episodes are difficult to handle in the excerpt style, requiring either intimidatingly long excerpts or arbitrary separation into a choppy series of shorter units.

9. Some critics argue that writing analytic ideas in the "ethnographic present" creates a false sense of continuous actions which are ahistorical. Fabian (1983) explores these issues in examining the conceptions of time and history underlying anthropological research. We contend that the included fieldnote excerpts and commentary clearly ground any discussion in specific times, places, and social conditions.

10. However, this exerpt might be used effectively to depict the probation officer's routine practices and concerns, a more appropriate focus given this ethnographer's strong identification with staff.

11. This issue was suggested by Okpewho's (1992:183–203) analysis of "historic legends." Okpewho argues that when telling about events that occurred within the recent past, the narrator produces an account which listeners, some of whom may have been witnesses, can accept as factual. Nevertheless, the teller uses well-known stylistic devices and narrating conventions to recount the event; as a result, "historic legends" sound very similar to "mythic legends" whose events no one witnessed.

12. This idea was in part triggered by Young's (1988:121–58) discussion of the links between landscape and narration. She points out that certain rock paintings among the Zuni people have narratives associated with them which people tell when they pass by them. In a similar kind of association, the Chokwe historical narrative incites listeners to see the landscape as linked to the story; in the moment described here, they collapsed the past of the story and the present moment and reenacted tracking reversed footprints.

13. Under some circumstances, however, a researcher can effectively incorporate analytic or other commentary made in the original fieldnotes into a final text. One might well include such a commentary as a self-contained excerpt in order to dramatize how an initial theoretical insight gave way to later, more comprehensive understanding. Or a field researcher might use an initial fieldnote commentary to set up or introduce the theme of a section of the final ethnography. For example, a student researcher studying how street people use a public library

began a section entitled "Library Materials as Masks" in this fashion: "This is an observation I made early on in my setting: 'There is something that I have always wondered about the "street people" who sit all day at our library. I wonder, as they stare at the pages with that typically blank expression, whether they are actually reading, or simply looking down with their thoughts focused on a completely different place in an entirely different time.'"

14. Consider the original brief transcribed quotation characterized by the journal editor as "incomprehensible," and the edited version which ultimately appeared in print (Emerson and Pollner 1988:193) (material in parentheses is either completely or partially inaudible).

Original: "How does that jibe with your feelings here about what (   ) other formulations seem to. Were there any parts that you thought were um, um (   ) say just way, way, way y' know (we were) stretching it, off the—off the mark? ohh"

Edited: "How does that jibe with your feelings? . . . Were there any parts that you thought were, say just way, way, way y' know, we were stretching it, off the mark?"

15. Folklorists often offer the original names of storytellers, wishing to credit their creativity. In collaborative research, fieldworkers also list their assistants' and coauthors' names. However, when people describe sensitive issues—such as in telling some religious, political, or historical accounts—most ethnographers change the names, as did Rachel Fretz in the Mushala fieldnote.

16. This strategy can also be used to introduce the theme of one section in the ethnography.

17. Indeed, Altheide and Johnson (1994:485) insist that "assessing and communicating the interactive process through which the investigator acquired the research experience and information" provide core components of the underlying "logic" or "ethic" of ethnographic research.

18. Indeed, Becker (1986:50) quotes the following advice from Everett Hughes to write introductions last: "Introductions are supposed to introduce. How can you introduce something you haven't written yet? You don't know what it is. Get it written and then you can introduce it." Becker (1986:55) himself recommends the following specific practice in this regard: "You usually find out, by the time you get to the end of your draft, what you have in mind. Your last paragraph reveals to you what the introduction ought to contain, and you can go back and put it in and then make the minor changes in other paragraphs your new-found focus requires."

19. Efforts to develop alternatives to these conventional forms of ethnography, such as those represented by Krieger (1979a, 1979b, 1983) and Crapanzano (1980), as well as feminist alternatives such as those proposed by Reinharz (1992), encounter a number of problems and limitations. Krieger's (1979a) stylistically innovative *Hip Capitalism,* for example, has been characterized as lacking both "a sense of shape and purpose" and a narrative with well-ordered episodes; these qualities "leave the reader searching for an interpretative framework" (Atkinson 1990:125–26).

Chapter Eight: Conclusion

1. One problem with conventional ethnography is the one-sidedness of this arrangement: Since ethnographies are written for and circulated almost exclusively among scholarly audiences, those whose lives and voices are depicted rarely get an opportunity to read and respond publicly to how they have been represented. A number of field researchers (e.g., Tedlock 1979; Handler 1985; Bloor 1988; Emerson and Pollner 1988, 1992) now urge taking ethnographic accounts back to those whose lives they represent, not primarily to "validate" those accounts, but rather to open up active dialogue between members and researchers about the meaning and import of such accounts. Such "dialogue" aims not to produce agreement or consensus but rather to highlight the inevitable differences that will mark the concerns of ethnographers and those whom they have represented (cf. Emerson and Pollner 1992:95–96).

2. Johnson and Altheide (1993:105) summarize these many conflicting demands by insisting that the ethnographer/writer must seek "to locate oneself vis-à-vis the subjects, to accept authority with its responsibility, fallibility, and limitations, and to tell 'your' story about the subject matter, making it clear that you have 'biased' the account with specific focus, selection, description, and interpretation of the materials."

References

Abrams, M. H. 1988. *A Glossary of Literary Terms.* 5th ed. New York: Holt, Rine-hart and Winston.

Adler, Patricia A., Peter Adler, and E. Burke Rochford, Jr. 1986. "The Politics of Participation in Field Research." *Urban Life* 14:363–76.

Agar, Michael H. 1982. "Whatever Happened to Cognitive Anthropology: A Partial Review." *Human Organization* 41:82–86.

Altheide, David L., and John M. Johnson. 1994. "Criteria for Assessing Interpretive Validity in Qualitative Research." In Norman K. Denzin and Yvonna S. Lincoln, eds., *Handbook of Qualitative Research,* 485–99. Thousand Oaks, Calif.: Sage Publications.

Anderson, Elijah. 1990. *Streetwise: Race, Class, and Change in an Urban Community.* Chicago: University of Chicago Press.

Atkinson, Paul. 1990. *The Ethnographic Imagination: Textual Constructions of Reality.* New York: Routledge.

Barth, Fredrik, ed. 1969. *Ethnic Groups and Boundaries.* Boston: Little, Brown.

Batchelder, D., and E. Warner. 1977. *Beyond Experience.* Brattleboro, Vt.: The Experiment Press.

Bauman, Richard. 1992a. *Story, Performance, and Event: Contextual Studies of Oral Narrative.* Cambridge: Cambridge University Press.

———, ed. 1992b. *Folklore, Cultural Performances, and Popular Entertainments: A Communications Centered Handbook.* Oxford: Oxford University Press.

Becker, Howard S. 1986. *Writing for Social Scientists: How to Start and Finish Your Thesis, Book, or Article.* Chicago: University of Chicago Press.

Ben-Amos, Dan. 1982. "Analytical Categories and Ethnic Genres." In Dan Ben-Amos, *Folklore in Context: Essays,* 38–64. New Dehli: South Asian Publishers.

Berger, Bennett M. 1981. *The Survival of a Counterculture: Ideological Work and Everyday Life among Rural Communards.* Berkeley: University of California Press.

Biernacki, Patrick. 1986. *Pathways from Heroin Addiction: Recovery with Treatment*. Philadelphia: Temple University Press.

Bittner, Egon. 1988. "Realism in Field Research." In Robert M. Emerson, ed., *Contemporary Field Research: A Collection of Readings*, 149–55. Prospect Heights, Ill.: Waveland.

Bleich, David. 1993. "Ethnography and the Study of Literacy: Prospects for Socially Generous Research." In Anne Ruggles Gere, ed., *Into the Field: Sites of Composition Studies*, 176–92. New York: The Modern Language Association of America.

Bloor, Michael J. 1988. "Notes on Member Validation." In Robert M. Emerson, ed., *Contemporary Field Research: A Collection of Readings*, 156–72. Prospect Heights, Ill.: Waveland.

Blum, Nancy S. 1991. "The Management of Stigma by Alzheimer Family Caregivers." *Journal of Contemporary Ethnography* 20:263–84.

Blumer, Herbert. 1969. *Symbolic Interactionism: Perspective and Method*. Englewood Cliffs, N.J.: Prentice Hall.

Bogdan, Robert, and Steven J. Taylor. 1987. "Toward a Sociology of Acceptance: The Other Side of the Study of Deviance." *Social Policy* 18:34–39.

Briggs, Charles L. 1986. *Learning How to Ask: A Sociolinguistic Appraisal of the Role of the Interview in Social Science Research*. Cambridge: Cambridge University Press.

———. 1988. *Competence in Performance: The Creativity of Tradition in Mexicano Verbal Art*. Philadelphia: University of Pennsylvania Press.

Brown, Richard H. 1977. *A Poetic for Sociology: Toward a Logic of Discovery in the Human Sciences*. Cambridge: Cambridge University Press.

Burgess, Robert G. 1982. *Field Research: A Sourcebook and Field Manual*. London: George Allen & Unwin.

———. 1984. *In the Field: An Introduction to Field Research*. London: George Allen & Unwin.

Cahill, Spencer E. 1985. "Meanwhile Backstage: Public Bathrooms and the Interaction Order." *Urban Life* 14:33–58.

Camitta, Miriam. 1990. "Gender and Method in Folklore Fieldwork." *Southern Folklore* 47:21–31.

Cassell, Joan. 1980. "Ethical Principles for Conducting Fieldwork." *American Anthropologist* 82:28–41.

Charmaz, Kathy. 1988. "The Grounded Theory Method: An Explication and Interpretation." In Robert M. Emerson, ed., *Contemporary Field Research: A Collection of Readings*, 109–26. Prospect Heights, Ill.: Waveland.

———. 1991. *Good Days, Bad Days: The Self in Chronic Illness and Time*. New Brunswick, N.J.: Rutgers University Press.

Cicourel, Aaron V. 1968. *The Social Organization of Juvenile Justice*. New York: John Wiley.

———. 1974. *Cognitive Sociology: Language and Meaning in Social Interaction*. New York: Free Press.

Cicourel, Aaron V., and John I. Kitsuse. 1963. *The Educational Decision-Makers*. Indianapolis: Bobbs Merrill.

Clarke, Michael. 1975. "Survival in the Field: Implications of Personal Experience in Field Work." *Theory and Society* 2:95–123.

Clifford, James. 1983. "On Ethnographic Authority." *Representations* 1:118–46.

———. 1986. "On Ethnographic Allegory." In James Clifford and George E. Marcus, eds., *Writing Culture: The Poetics and Politics of Ethnography*, 98–121. Berkeley: University of California Press.

———. 1990. "Notes on (Field)notes." In Roger Sanjek, ed., *Fieldnotes: The Making of Anthropology*, 47–70. Ithaca, N.Y.: Cornell University Press.

Clifford, James, and George E. Marcus, eds.. 1986. *Writing Culture: The Poetics and Politics of Ethnography*. Berkeley: University of California Press.

Corbin, Juliet M., and Anselm Strauss. 1988. *Unending Work and Care: Managing Chronic Illness at Home*. San Francisco: Jossey-Bass.

Cosentino, Donald. 1982. *Defiant Maids and Stubborn Farmers: Tradition and Invention in Mende Story Performances*. Cambridge: Cambridge University Press.

Crapanzano, Vincent. 1980. *Tuhami: Portrait of a Moroccan*. Chicago: University of Chicago Press.

Denzin, Norman K., and Yvonna C. Lincoln, eds. 1994. *Handbook of Qualitative Research*. Thousand Oaks, Calif.: Sage Publications.

DeVault, Marjorie L. 1990. "Talking and Listening from Women's Standpoint: Feminist Strategies for Interviewing and Analysis." *Social Problems* 37:96–116.

———. 1991. *Feeding the Family: The Social Organization of Caring as Gendered Work*. Chicago: University of Chicago Press.

Diamond, Jared. 1989. "The Ethnobiologist's Dilemma." *Natural History*, no. 6 (June): 26–30.

Diamond, Timothy. 1993. *Making Gray Gold: Narratives of Nursing Home Care*. Chicago: University of Chicago Press.

Dingwall, Robert, J. Eekelaar, and T. Murray. 1983. *The Protection of Children: State Intervention and Family Life*. Oxford: Basil Blackwell.

Douglas, Jack D. 1976. *Investigative Social Research: Individual and Team Field Research*. Beverly Hills, Calif.: Sage Publications.

Ellis, Carolyn. 1991. "Sociological Introspection and Emotional Experience." *Symbolic Interaction* 14:23–50.

Ellen, R. F., ed. 1984. *Ethnographic Research: A Guide to General Conduct*. London: Academic Press.

Emerson, Robert M. 1987. "Four Ways to Improve the Craft of Fieldwork." *Journal of Contemporary Ethnography* 16:69–89.

———. 1989. "Tenability and Troubles: The Construction of Accommodative Relations by Psychiatric Emergency Teams." In Gale Miller and James A. Holstein, eds., *Perspectives on Social Problems: A Research Annual*, vol. 1, pp. 215–37. Greenwich, Conn.: JAI Press.

———, ed. 1988. *Contemporary Field Research: A Collection of Readings*. Prospect Heights, Ill.: Waveland.

Emerson, Robert M., and Sheldon L. Messinger. 1977. "The Micro-Politics of Trouble." *Social Problems* 25:121–34.

Emerson, Robert M., and Melvin Pollner. 1976. "Dirty Work Designations:

Their Features and Consequences in a Psychiatric Setting." *Social Problems* 23:243–255.

———. 1988. "On the Uses of Members' Responses to Researchers' Accounts." *Human Organization* 47:189–98.

———. 1992. "Difference and Dialogue: Members' Readings of Ethnographic Texts." In Gale Miller and James A. Holstein, eds., *Perspectives on Social Problems: A Research Annual,* vol. 3, pp. 79–98. Greenwich, Conn.: JAI Press.

Erikson, Kai T. 1967. "A Comment on Disguised Observation in Sociology." *Social Problems* 12:366–73.

Fabian, Johannes. 1983. *Time and the Other: How Anthropology Makes Its Object.* New York: Columbia University Press.

Fetterman, David M. 1989. *Ethnography: Step by Step.* Newbury Park, Calif.: Sage Publications.

Fine, Elizabeth C. 1984. *The Folklore Text: From Performance to Print.* Bloomington: University of Indiana Press.

Flower, Linda S. 1988. "The Construction of Purpose in Writing and Reading." *College English* 50:528–50.

Forester, John. N. d. "Notes on Writing in and after Graduate School." Unpublished paper.

Frake, Charles O. 1964. "Notes on Queries in Ethnography." *American Anthropologist* 66, no. 3, pt. 2: 132–45.

———. 1975. "How to Enter a Yakan House." In Mary Sanchez and Ben Blount, eds., *Sociocultural Dimensions of Language Use,* 25–40. New York: Academic Press.

Fretz, Rachel I. 1987. Storytelling among the Chokwe of Zaire: Narrating Skill and Listener Responses. Ph.D. diss., Folklore and Mythology Program, University of California, Los Angeles.

———. 1994. "Through Ambiguous Tales: Women's Voices in Chokwe Storytelling." *Oral Tradition* 9:230–50.

———. forthcoming. "Answering-in-Song: Listener Responses in *Yishima* Performances." *Western Folklore.*

———. N. d. "Storytelling as Doing: Constructing Each Other in Ethnographic Research."

Garfinkel, Harold. 1967. *Studies in Ethnomethodology.* Englewood Cliffs, N.J.: Prentice Hall.

Garfinkel, Harold, and Harvey Sacks. 1970. "On Formal Structures of Practical Actions." In J. C. McKinney and E. A. Tiryakian, eds., *Theoretical Sociology,* 338–66. New York: Appleton Century Crofts.

Gearing, Frederick O. 1970. *The Face of the Fox.* Chicago: Aldine.

Geer, Blanche. 1964. "First Days in the Field." In Phillip Hammond, ed., *Sociologists at Work,* 322–44. New York: Basic Books.

Geertz, Clifford. 1973. "Thick Description: Toward an Interpretive Theory of Culture." In *The Interpretation of Culture,* 3–30. New York: Basic Books.

———. 1976. "From the Native's Point of View: On the Nature of Anthropological Understanding." In K. H. Basso and H. A. Selby, eds., *Meaning in Anthropology,* 221–37. Albuquerque: University of New Mexico Press.

————. 1983. *Local Knowledge: Further Essays in Interpretive Anthropology.* New York: Basic Books.

Georges, Robert A. 1981. "Do Narrators Really Digress? A Reconsideration of 'Audience Asides' in Narrating." *Western Folklore* 40:245–52.

Georges, Robert A., and Michael O. Jones. 1980. *People Studying People: The Human Element in Fieldwork.* Berkeley: University of California Press.

Glaser, Barney G. 1978. *Theoretical Sensitivity.* Mill Valley, Calif.: Sociology Press.

Glaser, Barney G., and Anselm L. Strauss. 1965. *Awareness of Dying.* Chicago: Aldine.

————. 1967. *The Discovery of Grounded Theory: Strategies for Qualitative Research.* Chicago: Aldine.

Goffman, Erving. 1961. *Asylums.* Garden City, N.J.: Doubleday.

————. 1971. *Stigma: Notes on the Management of Spoiled Identity.* Englewood Cliffs, N.J.: Prentice Hall.

————. 1989. "On Fieldwork." *Journal of Contemporary Ethnography* 18:123–32.

Golde, Peggy, ed. 1970. *Women in the Field: Anthropological Experiences.* Chicago: Aldine.

Goldstein, Kenneth S. 1964. *A Guide for Field Workers in Folklore.* Hatboro, Penn.: Folklore Associates.

Gottlieb, Alma, and Philip Graham. 1993. *Parallel Worlds: An Anthropologist and a Writer Encounter Africa.* New York: Crown Publishers.

Gusfield, Joseph. 1976. "The Literary Rhetoric of Science: Comedy and Pathos in Drinking Driver Research." *American Sociological Review* 41:16–34.

Hammersley, Martyn. 1992. *What's Wrong with Ethnography?* London: Routledge.

Hammersley, Martyn, and Paul Atkinson. 1983. *Ethnography: Principles in Practice.* London: Tavistock.

Handler, Richard. 1985. "On Dialogue and Destructive Analysis: Problems in Narrating Nationalism and Ethnicity." *Journal of Anthropological Research* 41:171–82.

Harper, Douglas. 1992. "Small N's and Community Case Studies." In Charles C. Ragain and Howard S. Becker, eds., *What Is a Case? Exploring the Foundations of Social Inquiry,* 139–58. Cambridge: Cambridge University Press.

Heritage, John. 1984. *Garfinkel and Ethnomethodology.* Cambridge: Polity Press.

Hughes, Everett C. 1960. "The Place of Field Work in Social Science." In Buford H. Junker, *Field Work: An Introduction to the Social Sciences,* v–xv. Chicago: University of Chicago Press.

————. 1971. *The Sociological Eye: Selected Papers.* Chicago: Aldine.

Hunt, Jennifer. 1985. "Police Accounts of Normal Force." *Urban Life* 13:315–41.

Hymes, Dell. 1991. *"In Vain I Tried to Tell You." Essays in Native American Ethnopoetics.* Philadelphia: University of Pennsylvania Press.

Jackson, Bruce. 1987. *Fieldwork.* Chicago: University of Illinois Press.

Jackson, Jean E. 1990a. "'Deja Entendu': The Liminal Qualities of Anthropological Fieldnotes." *Journal of Contemporary Ethnography* 19:8–43.

————. 1990b. "'I Am a Fieldnote': Fieldnotes as a Symbol of Professional Identity." In Roger Sanjek, ed., *Fieldnotes: The Making of Anthropology,* 3–33. Ithaca, N.Y.: Cornell University Press.

Jackson, Michael. 1982. *Allegories of the Wilderness: Ethics and Ambiguity in Kuranko Narratives*. Bloomington: Indiana University Press.

Johnson, John M., and David L. Altheide. 1993. "The Ethnographic Ethic." In Norman K. Denzin, ed., *Studies in Symbolic Interaction*, vol. 14, pp. 95–107. Greenwich, Conn.: JAI Press.

Johnstone, Barbara. 1990. *Stories, Community, and Place: Narratives from Middle America*. Bloomington: Indiana University Press.

Jordan, Manuel. 1993. "Le Masque comme processus ironiques: Les *Makishi* du Nord-Ouest de la Zambie." *Anthropologie et Société* 17:41–61.

Jules-Rosette, Bennetta. 1975. *Vision and Realities: Aspects of Ritual and Conversion in an African Church*. Ithaca, N.Y.: Cornell University Press.

Junker, Buford H. 1960. *Field Work: An Introduction to the Social Sciences*. Chicago: University of Chicago Press.

Karp, Ivan, and Martha B. Kendall. 1982. "Reflexivity in Field Work." In Paul F. Secord, ed., *Explaining Human Behavior: Consciousness, Human Action, and Social Structure*, 249–73. Beverly Hills, Calif.: Sage.

Katz, Jack. 1988. "A Theory of Qualitative Methodology: The System of Analytic Fieldwork." In Robert M. Emerson, ed., *Contemporary Field Research: A Collection of Readings*, 127–48. Prospect Heights, Ill.: Waveland.

Kleinman, Sherryl. 1991. "Field-Workers' Feelings: What We Feel, Who We Are, How We Analyze." In William B. Shaffir and Robert A. Stebbins, eds., *Experiencing Fieldwork: An Inside View of Qualitative Research*, 184–95. Newbury Park, Calif.: Sage Publications.

Krieger, Susan. 1979a. *Hip Capitalism*. Beverly Hills: Sage Publications.

———. 1979b. "Research and the Construction of a Text." In Norman K. Denzin, ed., *Studies in Symbolic Interaction*, vol. 2, pp. 167–87. Greenwich, Conn.: JAI Press.

———. 1983. *The Mirror Dance: Identity in a Women's Community*. Philadelphia: Temple University Press.

Latour, Bruno. 1987. *Science in Action: How to Follow Scientists and Engineers through Society*. Cambridge, Mass.: Harvard University Press.

Latour, Bruno, and Steve Woolgar. 1979. *Laboratory Life: The Social Construction of Scientific Facts*. Beverly Hills: Sage Publications.

Lawless, Elaine. 1993. *Holy Women, Wholly Women: Sharing Ministries through Life Stories and Reciprocal Ethnography*. Philadelphia: University of Pennsylvania Press.

Lederman, Rena. 1990. "Pretexts for Ethnography: On Reading Fieldnotes." In Roger E. Sanjek, ed., *Fieldnotes: The Making of Anthropology*, 71–91. Ithaca, N.Y.: Cornell University Press.

Lofland, John, and Lyn H. Lofland. 1995. *Analyzing Social Settings: A Guide to Qualitative Observation and Analysis*. 3rd ed. Belmont, Calif.: Wadsworth.

Lofland, Lyn H. 1985. *A World of Strangers: Order and Action in Urban Public Space*. Prospect Heights, Ill.: Waveland Press.

Lutkehaus, Nancy. 1990. "Refractions of Reality: On the Use of Other Ethnographers' Fieldnotes." In Roger E. Sanjek, ed., *Fieldnotes: The Making of Anthropology*, 303–23. Ithaca, N.Y.: Cornell University Press.

Lyman, Stanford M., and William A. Douglass. 1973. "Ethnicity: Strategies of Collective and Individual Impression Management." *Social Research* 40:344–65.

Lynch, Michael. 1985. *Art and Artifact in Laboratory Science: A Study of Shop Work and Shop Talk in a Research Laboratory.* London: Routledge and Kegan Paul.

Marcus, George E. 1986. "Afterword: Ethnographic Writing and Anthropological Careers." In James Clifford and George E. Marcus, eds., *Writing Culture: The Poetics and Politics of Ethnography,* 262–66. Berkeley and Los Angeles: University of California Press.

Marcus, George E., and Richard Cushman. 1982. "Ethnographies as Texts." *Annual Review of Anthropology* 11:25–69.

Marcus, George E., and Michael M. Fisher. 1986. *Anthropology as Cultural Critique.* Chicago: University of Chicago Press.

Marger, Martin. 1991. *Race and Ethnic Relations.* Belmont, Calif.: Wadsworth.

Matza, David. 1969. *Becoming Deviant.* Englewood Cliffs, N.J.: Prentice Hall.

Maynard, Douglas W. 1984. *Inside Plea Bargaining: The Language of Negotiation.* New York: Plenum.

———. 1989. "On the Ethnography and Analysis of Discourse in Institutional Settings." In James A. Holstein and Gale Miller, eds., *Perspectives on Social Problems,* 1:127–46. Greenwich, Conn.: JAI Press.

Mehan, Hugh, Alma Hertweck, and J. Lee Meihls. 1986. *Handicapping the Handicapped: Decision Making in Students' Educational Careers.* Stanford: Stanford University Press.

Mills, Margaret A. 1990. "Critical Theory and the Folklorists: Performance, Interpretive Authority, and Gender." *Southern Folklore* 47:5–15.

Mishler, Elliot G. 1979. "Meaning in Context: Is There Any Other Kind?" *Harvard Education Review* 49:1–19.

Moerman, Michael. 1969. "A Little Knowledge." In Stephen A. Tyler, ed., *Cognitive Anthropology,* 449–69. New York: Holt, Rinehart and Winston.

Myerhoff, Barbara, and Jay Ruby. 1982. "Introduction." In Jay Ruby, ed., *A Crack in the Mirror: Reflexive Perspectives in Anthropology,* 1–35. Philadelphia: University of Pennsylvania Press.

Okpewho, Isidore. 1992. *African Oral Literature: Backgrounds, Character, and Community.* Bloomington: Indiana University Press.

Ong, Walter J. 1975. "The Writer's Audience is Always a Fiction." *PMLA* 90:9–21.

Oring, Elliott. 1986. "Folk Narratives." In Elliott Oring, ed., *Folk Groups and Folklore Genres: An Introduction,* 121–45. Logan: Utah State University Press.

Ottenberg, Simon. 1990. "Thirty Years of Fieldnotes: Changing Relationships to the Text." In Roger E. Sanjek, ed., *Fieldnotes: The Making of Anthropology,* 139–60. Ithaca: Cornell University Press.

Perl, Sondra. 1980. "Understanding Composing." *College Composition and Communication* 31:363–69.

Pfaffenberger, Bryan. 1988. *Microcomputer Applications in Qualitative Research.* Newbury Park, Calif.: Sage.

Pollner, Melvin, and Robert M. Emerson. 1988. "The Dynamics of Inclusion and Distance in Fieldwork Relations." In Robert M. Emerson, ed., *Contemporary Field Research: A Collection of Readings*, 235–52. Prospect Heights, Ill.: Waveland.

Pollner, Melvin, and Lynn McDonald-Wikler. 1985. "The Social Construction of Unreality: A Case Study of a Family's Attribution of Competence to a Severely Retarded Child." *Family Process* 24:241–54.

Psathas, George, and Timothy Anderson. 1990. "The 'Practices' of Transcription in Conversation Analysis." *Semiotica* 78:75–99.

Reinharz, Shulamit. 1979. *On Becoming a Social Scientist: From Survey Research and Participant Observation to Experiential Analysis*. San Francisco: Jossey-Bass.

———. 1992. *Feminist Methods in Social Research*. New York: Oxford University Press.

Richards, T. J., and Lyn Richards. 1994. "Using Computers in Qualitative Research." In Norman K. Denzin and Yvonna S. Lincoln, eds., *The Handbook of Qualitative Research*, 445–62. Thousand Oaks, Calif.: Sage.

Richardson, Laurel. 1990. *Writing Strategies: Reaching Diverse Audiences*. Newberry Park, Calif.: Sage Publications.

———. 1994. "Writing: A Method of Inquiry." In Norman K. Denzin and Yvonna S. Lincoln, eds., *Handbook of Qualitative Research*, 516–29. Thousand Oaks, Calif.: Sage.

Riessman, Catherine Kohler. 1987. "When Gender is Not Enough: Women Interviewing Women." *Gender and Society* 1:172–207.

Rochford, E. Burke, Jr. 1985. *Hare Krishna in America*. New Brunswick, N.J.: Rutgers University Press.

———. 1992. "On the Politics of Member Validation: Taking Findings Back to Hare Krishna." In Gale Miller and James A. Holstein, eds., *Perspectives on Social Problems: A Research Annual*, vol. 3, pp. 99–116. Greenwich, Conn.: JAI Press.

Royce, Anya P. 1982. *Ethnic Identity: Strategies of Diversity*. Bloomington: Indiana University Press.

Sanjek, Roger, ed. 1990a. *Fieldnotes: The Making of Anthropology*. Ithaca, N.Y.: Cornell University Press.

———. 1990b. "Preface." In Roger Sanjek, ed., *Fieldnotes: The Making of Anthropology*, xi–viii. Ithaca, N.Y.: Cornell University Press.

———. 1990c. "A Vocabulary for Fieldnotes." In Roger Sanjek, ed., *Fieldnotes: The Making of Anthropology*, 92–121. Ithaca, N.Y.: Cornell University Press.

———. 1990d. "The Secret Life of Fieldnotes." In Roger Sanjek, ed., *Fieldnotes: The Making of Anthropology*, 187–270. Ithaca, N.Y.: Cornell University Press.

Schatzman, Leonard, and Anselm Strauss. 1973. *Field Research: Strategies for a Natural Sociology*. Englewood Cliffs, N.J.: Prentice Hall.

Schutz, Alfred. 1964. *Collected Papers*, vol. 2: *Studies in Social Theory*. The Hague: Martinus Nijhoff.

Schwartz, Barry. 1975. *Queuing and Waiting: Studies in the Social Organization of Access and Delay*. Chicago: University of Chicago Press.

Schwartz, Howard, and Jerry Jacobs. 1979. *Qualitative Sociology: A Method to the Madness*. New York: The Free Press.

Shaw, Linda L. 1988. Board and Care: The Everyday Lives of Ex-Mental Patients in the Community. Ph.D. diss., University of California, Los Angeles.

———. 1991. "Stigma and the Moral Careers of Ex-Mental Patients Living in Board and Care." *Journal of Contemporary Ethnography* 20:285–305.

Sherzer, Joel. 1983. *Kuna Ways of Speaking: An Ethnographic Perspective*. Austin: University of Texas Press.

———. 1992. "Ethnography of Speaking." In Richard Bauman, ed., *Folklore, Cultural Performances, and Popular Entertainments: A Communications Centered Handbook*, 76–80. Oxford: Oxford University Press.

Snow, David A., and Leon Anderson. 1993. *Down on Their Luck: A Study of Homeless Street People*. Berkeley and Los Angeles: University of California Press.

Spradley, James P. 1979. *The Ethnographic Interview*. New York: Holt, Rinehart and Winston.

———. 1980. *Participant Observation*. New York: Holt, Rinehart and Winston.

Stacey, Judith. 1991. "Can There Be a Feminist Ethnography?" In Sherma B. Gluck and Daphne Patai, eds., *Women's Words*, 111–19. New York: Routledge.

Stahl, Sandra Dolby. 1989. *Literary Folkloristics and the Personal Narrative*. Bloomington: Indiana University Press.

Stoddard, Kenneth. 1986. "The Presentation of Everyday Life: Some Textual Strategies for 'Adequate Ethnography'." *Urban Life* 15:103–21.

Stoller, Paul. 1989. *The Taste of Ethnographic Things: The Senses in Anthropology*. Philadelphia: University of Pennsylvania Press.

Stone, Ruth M., and Verlon L. Stone. 1981. "Event, Feedback, and Analysis: Research Media in the Study of Music Events." *Ethnomusicology* 25:215–25.

Strauss, Anselm L. 1987. *Qualitative Analysis for Social Scientists*. Cambridge: Cambridge University Press.

Strauss, Anselm L., and Juliet Corbin. 1990. *Basics of Qualitative Research: Grounded Theory Procedures and Techniques*. Newbury Park, Calif.: Sage Publications.

Sudnow, David. 1967. *Passing On: The Social Organization of Dying*. Englewood Cliffs, N.J.: Prentice Hall.

Taylor, Steven J., and Robert Bogdan. 1984. *Introduction to Qualitative Research Methods: The Search for Meanings*. 2d ed. New York: John Wiley.

Tedlock, Dennis. 1979. "The Analogical Tradition and the Emergence of Dialogical Anthropology." *Journal of Anthropological Research* 35:387–400.

———. 1983. *The Spoken Word and the Work of Interpretation*. Philadelphia: University of Pennsylvania Press.

Tesch, Renata. 1990. *Qualitative Research: Analysis Types and Software Tools*. London: Falmer Press.

Thorne, Barrie. 1980. "'You Still Takin' Notes?' Fieldwork and Problems of Informed Consent." *Social Problems* 27:284–97.

———. 1993. *Gender Play: Girls and Boys in School*. New Brunswick, N.J.: Rutgers University Press.

Van Maanen, John. 1978. "The Asshole." In Peter K. Manning and John Van Maanen, eds., *Policing: A View From the Street*, 221–38. Santa Monica, Calif.: Goodyear.

———. 1988. *Tales of the Field: On Writing Ethnography.* Chicago: University of Chicago Press.

Walker, Anne Graffam. 1986. "The Verbatim Record: The Myth and the Reality." In Sue Fisher and Alexandra Dundas Todd, eds., *Discourse and Institutional Authority: Medicine, Education, and Law,* 205–22. Norwood, N.J.: Ablex Publishing.

Warren, Carol A. B. 1980. "Data Presentation and the Audience: Responses, Ethics, and Effects." *Urban Life* 9:282–308.

———. 1988. *Gender Issues in Field Research.* Newbury Park, Calif.: Sage Publications.

Wax, Murray L. 1977. "On Fieldworkers and Those Exposed to Fieldwork: Federal Regulations and Moral Issues." *Human Organization* 36:321–28.

———. 1980. "Paradoxes of 'Consent' to the Practice of Fieldwork," *Social Problems* 27:272–83.

Willis, Paul. 1977. *Learning to Labor: How Working Class Kids Get Working Class Jobs.* New York: Columbia Unversity Press.

Wilson, William A. 1986. "Documenting Folklore." In Elliott Oring, ed., *Folk Groups and Folklore Genres: An Introduction,* 225–54. Logan: Utah State University Press.

Wiseman, Jacqueline P. 1970. *Stations of the Lost: The Treatment of Skid Row Alcoholics.* Englewood Cliffs, N.J.: Prentice-Hall.

Wolcott, Harry F. 1990. *Writing Up Qualitative Research.* Newbury Park, Calif.: Sage Publications.

Wolf, Margery. 1992. *A Thrice-Told Tale: Feminism, Postmodernism, and Ethnographic Responsibility.* Stanford: Stanford University Press.

Yocom, Margaret R. 1990. "Fieldwork, Gender, and Transformation: The Second Way of Knowing." *Southern Folklore* 47:33–44.

Yoder, P. Stanley, ed. 1982. *African Health and Healing Systems: Proceedings of a Symposium.* Los Angeles: Crossroads Press.

Young, Jane M. 1988. *Signs from the Ancestors: Zuni Cultural Symbolism and Perceptions of Rock Art.* Albuquerque: University of New Mexico Press.

Index

Lofland, John, 217
Lofland, Lyn H., 217, 223
Lutkehaus, Nancy, ix
Lyman, Stanford M., 200
Lynch, Michael, 2

McCoin, Susan, 217
McDonald-Wickler, Lynn, 163
Marcus, George E., vii, 13, 15, 218,
219, 234
Marger, Martin, 200
Matza, David, 109
Maynard, Douglas W., 224
Mehan, Hugh, 224
Meihls, J. Lee, 224
member (defined), 217
members' meanings, 2, 12–13, 28,
75, 103, 108–41
and analytic memos, 109
and analyzing fieldnotes, 147
and asking questions, 114
and close participation, 4
in coding, 147
as constructions, 140
and contradictory explanations,
126
and eliciting description, 116, 228
as everyday questions and answers,
113–14, 227
imposing exogenous meanings,
109–12, 122, 126–28, 226–27,
228–29
and indigenous contrasts, 122–24
as interpretive constructions, 108,
118, 220
and interviews, 140, 230
as jointly constructed, 215–16
linking local events and social
forces, 138–39, 230
and member explanations and
theories, 124–26, 139, 229
and members' categories in use,
126–28, 139–40, 227, 228, 229
and members' differing versions,
117–19

and members' everyday terms in
interaction, 131–33, 140, 227
and members' stories, 116–17, 228
and members' terms, 28–29,
112–13, 119–22, 131–33,
139–40
and members' types, 119–24, 127,
139–40, 148, 150
and multiple voices and points of
view, 117–19, 124–26
and naturally occurring
description, 114–16, 140,
227–28
and naturally occurring
interaction, 28–29, 108, 139,
140
and ordinary work practices and
concerns, 117, 227
and privileging insider
descriptions, 28, 30, 109–12,
226
race, gender and class, 133–38,
229
as reflections of members'
"purposes at hand," 117, 127,
140
and socialization of fieldworker,
115, 227
and storytelling as doing, 128–30,
229
and tensions between concerns of
scholarly readers, 208–9,
226–27, 213–14, 234
and transposing fieldnotes into
ethnographic text, 174
as what members say and do,
112–13, 139
members' terms, 76
and members' meanings, 28–29,
76, 103, 108
and members' types, 119–22, 148,
150
member types, 119–22, 148, 150
and member meanings, 122–24,
127, 139–40